P9-CFK-314

RE-ENGAGEMENT IN LATER LIFE: Re-Employment and Remarriage

WITHDRAWN

Ruth Harriet Jacobs
Barbara H. Vinick

How to save the old that's worth saving, whether in landscape, houses, manners, institutions, or human types, is one of our greatest problems, and the one that we bother least about.
— John Galsworthy, *Over the River*, ch. 39

The prosperity of a country is in accordance with its treatment of the aged.
— Chasidic saying

HV
1461
.J33

To our children, David and Edith Jacobs
and Jeffrey and Anne Vinick

Copyright© 1979 By Greylock, Inc.

No part of this book may be reproduced by any mechanical, photographic, or electronic process, or in the form of a phonographic recording, nor may it be stored in a retrieval system, transmitted, or otherwise copied for public or private use without written permission of the publisher.

Printed in the United States of America.
Library of Congress Catalog Card Number: 79-89073
ISBN: 0-89223-038-X (cloth cover)
ISBN: 0-89223-037-1 (paper)

GREYLOCK PUBLISHERS
Stamford, Connecticut

MAR 16 1981

Contents

IV

Preface

In *Re-Engagement in Later Life: Re-Employment and Remarriage,* we are pleased to bring to public awareness two subjects that are overdue as both topics of academic research and areas of practical information: re-employment and remarriage of older people. Until now, these topics have barely been explored.

To fill this gap, each of us planned a study and conducted it more or less independently, using methods that we felt were appropriate, given the demands of the study, as well as our own goals, backgrounds, training, and interests.

Part I, the study of re-employment in later life, was conceived and carried out by Ruth Harriet Jacobs with support from NIMH (National Institute of Mental Health) grant number 22278-01. Part II, the study of remarriage, was conceived and conducted by Barbara Vinick and supervised by Ruth Harriet Jacobs with funding from NIMH grant number 26932. We thank NIMH, which made these two studies possible.

Because of the obvious linkages, both theoretical and substantive, in the issues concerning re-employment and remarriage in later life, we felt it was useful to present the report of these studies in one volume. Although retirement issues recently have become a political issue of national interest, there has been little concern with employment possibilities for people considered beyond traditional working age. Remarriage among older people, with the exception of one previous study by Walter C. McKain, has been glossed over, possibly as being trivial or not worthy of serious attention.

We cannot thank our respondents enough for sharing with us their insights, experiences, and information. Even though almost all of the people we met were cooperative, we were not without certain qualms and conflicts. Were we prying too much, and giving too little in return? We were able to overcome occasional feelings of reticence and discomfort because of hospitality, openness, and friendliness of the people we interviewed.

We owe a great debt of gratitude to our editor, Grace Sheldrick of Wordsworth Associates, Wellesley, Massachusetts for her efficiency, perspicacity, and fortitude.

Our sincere thanks also to our able typists Anne Hazelton, Jonnie Scott, Anita Prensky Gordon, and Sharon Bjork, and to Ellen Friedman who did interviewing for the re-employment study. We also thank Kay Satow and Yo Satow, of the Boston University Computing Center, and John Mogey and Arnold Vinick for advice and aid in various stages of the remarriage study.

Two older people, by their late life work, have served as inspiration to us — Margaret E. Gordon of Mountain View, California, and Everett C. Hughes of Cambridge, Massachusetts.

Ruth Harriet Jacobs
Barbara H. Vinick

Introduction

Re-Engagement in Later Life: Re-Employment and Remarriage recounts the responses of nearly eighty people over age sixty who faced the loss of a job or a spouse.

Part I concerns finding new jobs in the later years. People from sixty-five years old through the eighties talk about their desire to become re-employed, how they found their jobs, and how they now feel about their work. Each chapter deals with a different type of employment. For contrast, chapter six concerns unemployed people who could not re-engage.

Part II examines remarriage and uses a process model, starting with accounts of remarried older people about their time alone and progressing to their current marital situation.

Situations of loss such as these present the most serious challenges for older people in our society. As people age, experiencing some loss is almost unavoidable. Loss of employment, loss of the spouse and of friends through death very often are a part of aging with which people must cope. The people we have included in this book did not accept their losses as permanent. Most were able to re-involve themselves, to substitute for their loss of work or spouse.

Not everyone can "re-engage" as these people did; nor, indeed, does every older person want to. Cumming and Henry's influential fifteen-year-old book on aging[1] posited a mutually satisfying withdrawal of the aged from society: well adjusted "disengaged" elders accepted losses that were precursors of death and made room for other people in the society. This theory of disengagement started a controversy that raged for years and only recently has been laid to rest. Most experts on aging, including Cumming and Henry, now believe that there are a variety of responses to aging that are satisfying for different people, depending on personal "style." In general, people who were active and involved in their younger years are happier to be active when they are older. Some people are happy to regain lost roles, as did the people in our studies; other people are satisfied to substitute one role for another. For example, some retired men can find satisfaction in hobbies or activities with their families; some widowed women can find satisfaction in group life with friends or in work. There is no one solution for all older people. In fact, some studies have shown that older people, as a group, are more diverse than any other segment of the population.

Although there are many valid responses to loss in later life, we are focusing on this group of re-engaged people in order to counter some of the negative stereotypes of old age that are prevalent among both younger people and older people themselves. By concentrating our attention on a group of older people who were able to start over again in an important aspect of life, who did not give up and settle into the rocking chair, we hope to add to the growing awareness of old age as a positive, potentially pleasurable segment of the life span.

Most older people are independent, mobile, in good spirits, and mentally vigorous. Unfortunately, the image of old age persists as a time of mental and physical decay, dependence, and misery. Researchers should study the problems associated with institutionalization, ill health, and financial need among the elderly. These pressing problems of old age desperately need the attention of policy makers. But we also need to focus on the average independent older people who make up the majority of our elderly population.

It is especially important for older people themselves to shed the straitjacket of negative thinking about old age. Undoubtedly, thousands of people dread reaching age sixty-five or seventy when they become "old" and think they have to act "old." By presenting older people who do not fit the stereotypes in important ways, we hope to broaden the perspectives of readers, both young and old.

In many ways, being old is to play a role without a script. As sociologist Irving Rosow and others have observed, there are few guidelines about "proper" behavior in old age. This book can aid older people by giving them some role models — some illustrations of the behavior of others — and can aid younger people by presenting a rather rare view of competent, active older people. In these pages, many readers will see parts of themselves or people whom they know; identifying with a person they read about may make their own situation a little more clear.

Re-Engagement in Later Life was written to appeal to a wide audience — people who are studying aging in an academic setting and who work with older people, as well as older people themselves and their families. To this end, we have tried to avoid terms that have meaning only to gerontologists and have tried to simplify and clarify while retaining the significance of our findings. This was a rather difficult undertaking. Articles by the authors and about their work have appeared and will appear in magazines and journals that address more specialized audiences.[2]

For the most part, we have allowed the people in our studies to speak for themselves. The words of the older people involved say more about problems in aging and their solutions than any number of tables, graphs, or columns of figures. We have tried in each chapter to summarize the main points made by our informants and in the concluding chapter of each part to offer some practical considerations.

We hope that the words of the people we interviewed will give a sense of relevance and veracity to the questions of re-employment and remarriage in later life, and that different audiences will be able to gain information according to special needs and concerns.

Notes

1. *Growing Old: The Process of Disengagement,* New York: Basic Books, 1961.
2. For example Ruth H. Jacobs, "Adjustments in Later Life," Dynamic Years, Nov./Dec., 1977; Janet Sherbin, "Why Older Marriages Work," *Modern Maturity,* Feb./March, 1977; Barbara H. Vinick, "Remarriage in Old Age," *Family Coordinator,* Vol. 27, 4 (October, 1978).

Part I
RE-EMPLOYMENT

Chapter One
Introduction

"If someone had said seventeen years ago that [my father] couldn't practice medicine, he wouldn't be here today."

Part I of this book is both for and about older people who want to remain part of America's work force. It describes how some older persons were able to get new jobs after age sixty-five. Today, most American adults arrange their lives around their work. Individuals and families often uproot themselves and move where jobs are or promotions lead them. Many summer vacations are only a brief two- or three-week respite from the busy weeks of work. Some jobs are so demanding that their holders have little time or energy to develop hobbies or build friendships outside of work. While involved in careers, many people do not even have enough time for family life. We are a society that generally describes and rewards people in terms of their occupations; self-esteem and work frequently are twins.

What happens, then, to a work-oriented person, man or woman, when one day he or she celebrates a sixty-fifth or seventieth birthday and must retire? Or when such a person retires in order to collect Social Security and/or a pension? What becomes of the older worker who loses a job, without ever reaching the formal retirement age and then cannot find another job?[1]

The statistics here tell the story: Only about one person in ten over age sixty-five holds a full-time job. In a total population of twenty-two million men and women over age sixty-five (as of 1976), only 2.7 million worked full time and of this number only one million working people were older than seventy.

We are an aging society. More people are living longer. Some increase in longevity plus adoption of Social Security in 1935 have in large part been responsible for statistical changes in older people's work patterns. In 1900, only 3.1 million people were sixty-five or older; this figure was about 4.1 percent of the total United States population. Of these 3.1 million elders, two out of three men and one out of twelve women worked. Today, 22 million people over age sixty-five represent 10 percent of the total population, but only one man out of five and one woman out of twelve work.[2] By the year 2030, it is estimated that about 17 percent of the population will be over age sixty-five.

As these figures show, retirement on a large scale is a fairly new phenomenon in our society, which, since Colonial times, has always stressed the value of hard work. Retirement is the great leveler that often razes carefully built careers and removes the gratification inherent in working from a person's self-image.

Retirement can have many meanings since people are as varied in old age as they are in youth.

"Retirement in old age is a significant event which is managed and coped with in different ways. Some retirees are content and live out a pleasant retirement existence, while others die the day before or after; [they get] get depressed. . . ."[3]

Some people who retire leave the labor market gratefully and with sufficient funds; they find new activities to fill their lives. People who may have hated or at best tolerated their jobs may in their retirement enjoy a variety of recreational, educational, and social activities — they play golf and bridge, travel, garden, do volunteer work, enjoy their friends, families, and senior centers, for example. These people are to be admired for their flexibility in finding new roles in a society that links identity and work.

Other people, however, want to continue working in order to keep busy, earn some needed income, maintain both their identity and some contact with other people, and give some meaning and structure to their lives. These men and women often desire less strenuous jobs or part-time work, but they cannot imagine enjoying life without being employed in some way. Some may want to try out a new type of job.

Some people who initially accept retirement grow to resent it as their time alone or with spouses expands and their income contracts. These people often seek to re-engage in work. They experience the "post-fixing-up-the-house" syndrome when boredom replaces zest and causes personal deterioration, both physical and psychological.[4]

In fact, an American Medical Association publication ("Position on the Employment of Older Persons") states that some aged who actually are in reasonably good health adopt the sick role and fill doctors' offices because they prefer to consider themselves sick rather than useless. Such a role often is the only one allowed them by circumstances. In this book, we show the possibility of other roles.

Sadly, just when some people finally have time for personal relationships at retirement, they often experience the loss of a beloved spouse, or friends and family by death or geographic moves. When faced with such devastating losses, they may seek to fill their lives with work. But for men and women over sixty-five, traditional jobs located through traditional channels are not easy to come by, as we shall see. When they are rejected, many older people feel victimized and angry. This brief item from the National Council on Aging bulletin illustrates the ambivalent feelings that many people, young and old, have toward retirement.

"Most Americans regard retirement with mixed feelings, according to a recent survey by the Institute of Life Insurance. Ninety-five percent of the respondents, from all age groups, felt that lack of money was a problem for retirees, while seventy-eight percent believed that retirement 'often makes a person feel useless.' When asked if 'it's better to keep working than to retire at a fixed age,' forty-six percent said yes, with an additional thirty percent agreeing somewhat." The findings generally correspond to the Louis Harris/NCOA 1975 survey.

The seniors we interviewed also were concerned about having enough money. At retirement, income usually halves, just when one has more time to spend money. More than 3 million people, or about one-fourth of the people over age sixty-five live in poverty; older women living alone are an especially desperate group, more so if they are black. One-third to one-half of all older Americans (about 3 million men and women) live solely on benefits from Social Security or Supplemental Security Income (SSI) in their old age.[5] There are thirty-one Social Security beneficiaries for every one hundred workers.

Consequently, the recent 1978 federal legislation extending official mandatory retirement for most people to age seventy was not passed entirely out of sympathy with older people who want to work. This legislation was a recognition of the financial burden of retirement on today's society. The sheer number of older persons has social planners worried. Their concern, plus pressure by older constituents, influenced legislators at the federal level who voted overwhelmingly to extend the mandatory retirement to age seventy for workers in private industry and to eliminate all mandatory retirement for most federal employees.[6]

It is predicted, however, that this legal change will not significantly influence the number of people who continue to work after sixty-five at their regular jobs, partly because mandatory retirement affected only 10 percent of all workers.

In some cases, industry also is looking for ways *not* to have to retain older workers, including making voluntary retirement more attractive. Many corporations are concerned about the new law, as is reflected in a *Fortune* magazine article (May 8, 1978) entitled "Retirement at Seventy: A New Trauma for Management." The National Association of Manufacturers and the Institute for Advanced Professional Studies sponsored a large meeting on May 31-June 1, 1978, in New York City in order to discuss the problems raised by the 1978 legislation extending mandatory retirement.

Because of resistance by employers, the attractions of retirement, and the fact that Social Security payments now are indexed to rise with inflation, post-sixty-five employment figures are not expected to increase dramatically.

Massachusetts Congressman Robert Drinan of the House Committee on Aging estimates that perhaps only 200,000 extra persons will stay on at their jobs as a result of the new law. This figure is only one-tenth of 1 percent of the total labor force! The rest of the working people will join those who are already retired and not protected retroactively by the law. Many people probably will continue to take Social Security at sixty-five, or even younger, perhaps working part time. Indeed, as of 1977, 72 percent of the people who had left the labor force to receive Social Security immediately or later were sixty-two when they stopped working.

In addition, some private pension plans that still specify retirement at age sixty-five will not be affected immediately by the new legislation. (See Note 6.) In 1974, the Department of Labor's Bureau of Labor Statistics estimated that more than 40 percent of workers enrolled in private pension plans were covered by age sixty-five retirement provisions. Certain employees receiving more than $27,000 per year in pensions at age sixty-five are exempt. Until July, 1982, faculty members in private colleges also may be retired at age sixty-five.

Many people lose their jobs long before retirement becomes an issue. Companies often find it cheaper to hire younger people than to keep experienced workers who have had salary increases over the years. Prejudice against older workers still exists, too, and young people push from below for promotions. Many displaced people will want or need to work part-time while collecting Social Security. If receiving Social Security had no earnings limit attached to it, probably even more people would seek new work or stay on at old jobs.[7]

The strong pressures on aging people to move out of the labor force undoubtedly will continue since our society does not have full employment. The official 6 to 7 percent unemployment rate in this country actually is believed to be lower than the real unemployment figures. Many of the unemployed, especially older workers, exhaust both their patience and their benefits and drop out of the official unemployment tallies.

Paradoxically, the aged are criticized both for working and so taking jobs younger persons could have and also for not working. We are experiencing a counter trend that condemns aged people because they do retire and thus cost the taxpayers money. This backlash sentiment considers other people as parasites and faults them for taking Social Security or SSI. Even though middle-aged people are strained by the dependent old and young, this narrow view ignores two important points:

- Many older people either cannot for health reasons or do not want to work. If they are receiving Social Security and/or pension fund money, it is only because they have worked hard for many years and contributed their share. If they receive SSI, it often is because they could not accumulate Social Security quarters for many good reasons, such as raising a family or lack of jobs covered by Social Security. Their savings have been eroded by inflation and by medical needs not covered by insurance.
- Many older people who do want to work cannot because they are unable to find jobs, or lack transportation, marketable skills, or information on how to get work.

Late in life, people have a right to dignity and choice; they should not be forced to go to work at the marginal jobs generally available to older persons. These older people should be able to work only if they so desire and are capable of working. For some older people who cannot find jobs, enforced idleness leads to poverty, and also to illness, severe depression, and even suicide.[8] These people should be helped to find work since such illnesses have a high cost for both the individual and society.

Actually many elderly persons are unnecessarily sick with treatable conditions that go untreated, according to Robert N. Butler, director of the National Institute of Aging. In his book, *Why Survive? Being Old In America,* and in articles and speeches, he points out that many physical and emotional conditions considered by older persons and some relatives and physicians to be "just old age" are really neglected illnesses.

Sick, unhappy old people are more than a tragedy in themselves. The young and middle-aged fear old age because too often they know of only sick old people. They need to see healthy older people out in active positions so that they themselves will not fear growing old. Older people at jobs provide marvelous models and wisdom for the young, as we shall see.

In an attempt to improve the image of the aged, the National Council of Older Americans in 1977 launched an extensive media campaign with the theme "Get out of your rocker." Unfortunately, many elders do not have information on how to "get out of the rocker," and, as we will see, often are discouraged by well-meaning others. Retirees seeking new post-retirement jobs often feel as if they are re-inventing the wheel. We hope this book will make their task a little earier.

Despite the scarcity of jobs and information about how to get them, people can and do succeed as later-life workers. In recent years, however, most of those who have been able to continue working have tended to be professionals, the self-employed, agricultural workers, and the more skilled. For example, physicians often find it hard to empathize with their older patients who mourn the loss of work because older physicians themselves can continue working.

Recently, ex-Governor Michael Dukakis of Massachusetts said of his eighty-two-year-old father, a physician, "If someone had said seventeen years ago that he couldn't practice medicine, he wouldn't be here today."

Elders without professional status have more trouble remaining in the workforce. Not enough is known about competent average elders who can perform well when given the chance. Perhaps when more is known, more opportunities will be opened. The National Institute of Mental Health funded our research on re-employment in order to learn more. The people in the chapters constituting Part I of this book all wanted to work, some for financial reasons, others just to see people, to keep busy, and to feel useful or important. Many of them experienced a great deal of difficulty getting work because of the prejudice against older persons, their lack of information about jobs, and a basic lack of jobs. Most of them were able to re-engage in work that for them was new; you will learn in chapters two through five what these new jobs were and how they got them. Other people were less fortunate; you will see why they were not able to obtain work from some examples presented in chapter six.

Many of the older men and women we studied were able to re-engage in new occupations because they had adaptable rather than specific skills. They were average persons from all walks of life who exhibited a capacity for growth and new activities as they got older. We believe such capacities, given opportunities, are more widespread in old age than has been recognized. Too many people, including older persons themselves, falsely assume that one cannot learn in old age. Actually, one can learn a great deal, as shown by the people in this book who welcomed the chance to do new kinds of work and did it well.

It is important to examine the circumstances under which some older persons who want to work were able to do so. Thus, these older people shared their stories to show how others have managed the often difficult transitions into and out of retirement. After we present their stories in detail, we will summarize their experiences in the last chapter of Part I and offer some further suggestions for many different ways of re-engaging.

The stories in these chapters are typical of those we heard in the many interviews conducted with over age sixty-five re-employeds, would-be re-employeds, and people not seeking employment.

Notes

1. From 1947 to 1973, for example, the participation of men ages fifty-five to sixty-four in the labor force declined from 90 to 78 percent.
2. It is interesting to note that the percentage of women over sixty-five working today is the same as in 1900 (one out of twelve); but the statistics also tell us that there are many more older women today than there were in 1900.
3. Martin Berezin, "The Fate of Narcissism in Old Age." *Journal of Gerjatric Psychiatry* X: Volume 1 (1977) pp. 9-26. This quotation appears on p. 21. Dr. Berezin is a noted geriatric psychiatrist.
4. The following chapter, "Older Workers in Business and Industry," describes this phenomenon and its impact in terms of the entire retirement cycle.

5. In 1978, monthly Social Security payments ranged from $121 to $459 ($1,452 to $5,508 yearly). A 1977 report by the Bureau of Labor Statistics of the U.S. Department of Labor (USDL Release 77-690 August 4, 1977) reports that in 1976, the average annual cost of the lower-level budget for an urban retired couple amounted to $4,695 and at intermediate and higher levels the budget was $6,738 and $10,048.
6. The text and an explanation of the 1978 changes in mandatory retirement can be obtained from B.N.A. Books, 1231 25th Street, N.W., Washington, D.C. 20037, for $2.50. This April 1, 1978, publication, "Labor Relations Reporter: Fair Employment Practices Manual, Supplement 341," includes an explanation of the 1978 Age Discrimination Acts Amendments and reports of the House-Senate Conference Committee on the bill originally introduced by Representative Claude Pepper.

   Briefly, the Acts prohibit involuntary retirement of most employees under age seventy. However, employees who are covered by a collective bargaining agreement providing for earlier retirement that was in effect on September 1, 1977, are not protected until either the contract expires or until January 1, 1980, whichever comes first. The Acts allow compulsory retirement at age sixty-five of employees working in a *bona fide* executive or high policy-making position and entitled to a pension of at least $27,000 per year. An annual adjustment in this amount will be based on the cost of living. Colleges and universities may continue to retire tenured employees at age sixty-five until July 1, 1982; thereafter, they must be retained until age seventy. Most federal jobs, except for those requiring extreme physical exertion, now have no retirement age. The Acts also contain provisions for legal procedures by persons who feel they have been unjustly retired in violation of the 1978 regulations.
7. Pressure is being exerted by some people to be allowed to collect Social Security even if a person's yearly earnings exceeds the $3,240 limit in 1978 for people under sixty-five and the $4,000 limit for people over sixty-five. In 1978, people between ages sixty-five and seventy-two may earn $4,500 without losing any Social Security benefits. In 1980, the amount of yearly earnings increases to $5,000 and in 1982, to $6,000. For every two dollars earned above the allowed amount, one dollar must be returned to the government. There is no limit on earnings for people over age seventy-two. Starting in 1982, there will be no limit for people over seventy.
8. Persons over sixty-five account for more than 25 percent of all the suicides in this country, even though this age group represents only 10 percent of the population.

9. Robert N. Butler, *Why Survive? Being Old in America.* New York: Harper and Row, 1975. Also see his articles, including "Psychiatry and the Elderly: An Overview," *American Journal of Psychiatry* 132:9, September 1975, pp. 893-900. In this article, he scolds psychiatrists for not providing the elderly with the treatment, research, and services commensurate with their needs. Also see the article, "Geriatrics" by Knight Steel, M.D., and T. Franklin Williams, M.D., in which these physicians point out that "geriatrics is a large and largely neglected area. . . ." *Archives of Internal Medicine* Vol. 134 (Dec. 1974) pp. 1125-1126.

Chapter Two

Older Workers in Business and Industry

"You go bananas doing nothing."

After retiring, many people need jobs for extra income or for diversion. What opportunities are there for retired people to work in stores, offices, and other businesses in your community? Does any business make a concerted effort to hire retired people and give them jobs in which they are both useful and visible to the entire community? Six men we will meet learned that one chain of supermarkets does, and all found part-time jobs there that they enjoyed.

Or, do many businesses openly discourage retired people from applying for jobs? Many senior citizens who look for work in their communities think and say so. In the second part of this chapter, we will meet five men and women of various work experience and ethnic and educational backgrounds who, either by luck or after a lot of diligent searching, eventually found jobs. First, let us meet the six men who found work as "bundle boys."

Bundle Boys

The large sign in the window of King Brothers Supermarket said:

HELP WANTED: BUNDLE BOYS
To Pack Groceries and
Wheel Bags to Customers' Cars
Work Part Time

Harry Lewis

Harry Lewis was out of bed before the alarm rang at 7 A.M. After showering and shaving, he trimmed his thin gray mustache and combed his sparse hair. At age sixty-seven, Harry was looking forward to his first day of work as a bundle boy at King Brothers Market.

Harry's story follows the same cycle as the stories of many other retired people: retirement from a long-held job, initial enjoyment of leisure time, and catching up with the tasks at home, boredom (accompanied by depression or imagined illness), and then, for the lucky ones, re-engagement—finding a new occupation—sometimes a hobby, and sometimes a different type of job.

Harry was sixty-five when he retired. He had been employed in the electronics industry for forty years and had earned more than $30,000 per year for many years. Since retirement represented no money problems to Harry and his wife, Dora, they were expecting to enjoy a leisurely time together.

"I have a summer home and a winter one," explained Harry. "I left my job in May and did some fishing and some clamming. I spent a lot of time at the beach house and got that in good shape. Then, since I like to work and I'm reasonably handy, I fixed things in my winter home. Dora and I made a few trips, not extensive ones, but we were away four or five times. I don't particularly have any hobbies outside of doing things and working around the houses."

After about 15 months, Harry began to feel restless and anxious. "The newness of not working at all finally wears off and you want something to do." Harry's experience is not uncommon. Many persons eagerly look forward to retirement as a time to relax and catch up on tasks around the house and pleasures. Yet, after some time, they get bored and become nostalgic for the social contacts and for the structure and routine that work provided.

As Harry's leisure became a burden, he withdrew into himself and worried about his health.

"After you retire, you think about yourself. That's what I began to do. I figured I had this sickness, or that sickness. I spent a lot of time at the doctor's. My doctor said I would put one of his kids through Harvard with the fees I paid him!"

Harry's sense of humor and his long commitment to the value of working saved him from further hypochondria.

"There's no question about it," Harry said emphatically. "Everyone should work. Do something, because if you have been active for many years, the worst thing in the world is not to do anything."

Another important factor in Harry's ability to overcome his depression and think of working again was his wife's attitude. "Dora did not object when I said that I wanted to work. In fact," he added proudly, "she does volunteer work at the hospital."

Harry also received further support from his doctor. "I kept pestering him about my symptoms," Harry recalled. "He told me I was all right and should find something to do with myself."

But for Harry, deciding to re-engage by working again was just the first step; he now had to find something useful to do.

"I could probably have gone back to my former trade," Harry says, "but I made up my mind to stay away from it. Being retired, your selection of jobs is pretty darn small. If you don't have to have the money, it makes it a lot easier." Harry found out what many older people are learning every day — for retired people, both job information and jobs themselves are scarce.

But luckily Harry happened to be in the right place at the right time and thus found a job by accident.

"One afternoon I went food shopping at King Brothers, the big supermarket in town. I saw a sign on the door — Bundle Boys Wanted. I came in and talked to the manager. They had a job for me and that's the way I started. That was the first job I tried for. I was lucky."

Harry is pleased with his work schedule, which allows him enough time to relax, go fishing, and keep up with the news.

"I work Mondays and Tuesdays. Wednesday is my day off. I work Thursdays and Fridays. I work ten 'til three and I have one-half hour for lunch. Sometimes they call me in when someone can't make it," he added.

Harry also finds his new job relaxing; he no longer has to take his worries home from the office. "In my former job, I did a great deal of buying that ran into a lot of money, like ten to thirty thousand dollars I spent at a time. And sometimes when I'd be in bed, I'd wonder whether or not I had made the right move. I don't have that any longer. Now I enjoy life. I'm quite happy."

Dora did not object that Harry's job was of lower prestige than his previous electronics work. Her attitude helped him adjust to being a bundle boy."When I first started working here, I put on my red bundler's coat. My friends came in and they are people who have done fairly well in business, but that didn't seem to bother me so much. It sort of wears off after a while. They are glad to see me and I'm glad to see them." More important than prestige to Harry was meeting new people and old acquaintances every day and having a daily routine.

Working again and seeing old friends have made such a great difference in Harry Lewis's life that his doctor now has to remind Harry to come in for his check-ups!

Some Other Bundle Boys

Some of the other bundle boys at King Brothers Market also are retired men of different ages and from various walks of life. As we meet some of these bundle boys we will see that despite their differences, they, like Harry Lewis, feel happier working.

Pat Sullivan

Pat Sullivan is seventy-three. He is a short, spry man with lively green eyes surrounded by laugh lines. His hair is snow white. Only his freckles give away that at one time his hair must have been bright as a carrot.

He retired at age sixty-seven, after working for more than forty-five years as an assembler.

"They closed my department," he said. "They tried to shift us but I didn't care for the other two jobs. The work was too heavy and it was too cold in those departments. I loafed for three years. I took trips around and then other times stayed home. But you go bananas doing nothing," he admitted, "so I figured I'd better get a little part-time job.

"So I said to my wife one day, 'I think I'll take a look and go to King Brothers.' She encouraged me. She said, 'Sure, honey, get a little job for yourself.'"

Pat knew about other older men working at King Brothers because his brother used to live near the market.

"I came down on a Monday morning and met the manager. I introduced myself and said, 'I'm looking for a job as a bundle boy here.' He told me to come back the next morning, which I did, and he gave me the red jacket. I work Tuesday through Friday, ten to three. My daughter was tickled pink when I got the job," he said.

Pat likes his job because it keeps him in touch with people. "It's a nice company. They are all nice here, even the girls," he added with a smile. "You meet a lot of nice people, customers also. You get to know who they are. I met a lot of people I never knew before, some of them lived in my town and didn't know who I was."

People are important to Pat Sullivan, who still keeps in touch with many old friends. Every Monday, his day off from the market, he goes down to the old plant where he walks around and talks to the men he worked with for so many years.

Pat's only complaint about being a bundle boy are his legs. "You get tired because you do a lot of walking to the cars. I go to bed early. I'll stay here, though, as long as the old legs hold up."

On the whole, Pat is content. After retiring, he gave his house to his married daughter and he and his wife moved to a senior citizens' apartment just two blocks from King Brothers. They could manage financially without Pat's work, although Pat enjoys spending his extra earnings on going out to dinner and on gifts for his family.

Tom Davis

Tom Davis, at age sixty-nine, is a tall, distinguished-looking gentleman. For thirty years he was a top salesman in the prestigious men's wear section of a large department store, but he was required to retire as soon as he reached sixty-five.

After retiring, he kept himself busy for several months by repapering and repainting his home.

But Tom's house was empty. His wife had died several years before and his daughter and grandchildren lived out of state.

Tom made an effort to avoid feeling lonely by going fishing and attending church and Bible school regularly. "Really, I haven't felt very lonely because of the various activities I engage in. Any time I get a little sorry for myself, I get busy and see somebody that's sorrier than me. Still, you wonder what you are going to do to keep you occupied," he muses. "You wonder if you'll start talking to yourself."

Happily, he found a job before too much wondering led to depression.

He recalls, "One day, as I was just sitting on the back porch, my neighbor came over and asked me to take her shopping because her car had conked out. I said, 'Of course, I'll take you over.' I was glad to have something to do. At the store, there was a sign that bundle boys were wanted. On an impulse, I went to talk to the boss. He said, 'Go right upstairs and put on a red jacket and go to work.' So I thought maybe I would do it for two or three weeks, and I'm still doing it."

Tom likes his job because it gets him out of his empty house.

"I work four days a week, eighteen hours a week. I enjoy it. It's simple and it keeps me occupied. I prefer something like this to sitting around."

He also finds it relaxing. "You can't really call this work. You don't have to take any work home at night and plan. You just put the food in the bags and walk out to the cars. The people are friendly and like to pass the time of day."

Tom thinks it is inspiring to work with other retired men. "I'll be seventy next month. I think I'm old until I look at Alec Hardy down there. Alec is already seventy-three or -four."

Tom Davis and Harry Lewis realize that they were lucky. Just when each man knew that he needed some work to keep on going, each one happened to find a job. Many, if not most, senior citizens, however, do not encounter such a fortuitous circumstance. Good information about jobs for retired people is lacking in many communities and jobs themselves often are not available for older people. Pride, too, often prevents some older people from seeking or even expressing interest in such jobs.

Three Other Bundle Boys

King Brothers is a large, busy supermarket. In all, the market employs six older bundle boys, including the three we have just met. The other three are Alec Hardy, George Rogers and Cal Pickett.

Alec Hardy is a seventy-three-year-old retired telephone lineman and mental-hospital aide. He does not need the money from his job since he has a good pension and Social Security. He faithfully deposits all his earnings from King's into a savings account for his grandchildren's education. "I adore my son's two beautiful little girls. I'm glad I can do something for them."

George Rogers also is seventy-three years old. "I retired at sixty-two," he explains, "because I was away from home too much as a traveling shoe salesman. I just couldn't keep up the hectic pace any more. Here, I now work part time; I get along all right." Financially, George does not need the job. He does need it, however, as a diversion and change of scene. His wife is bedridden and his daughter lives with them and takes care of her. George and his family recently moved to an apartment more than 12 miles from King's. Ironically, Goerge now is traveling again; he gladly drives the 24 miles round trip to King's every day because his job is important to him.

Cal Pickett, at age sixty-three, is the youngest old bundler. He retired from a large investment company because the firm was making personnel cutbacks. The company enticed him into retiring early by making his pension available before he reached sixty-five. After he retired, Cal fixed up his house and garden, took a vacation, and played a lot of golf. By the end of six months, however, he was bored and actively looking for work. "My wife thought it would be better if I had something to take up my mind. I tried three or four supermarkets. One wouldn't hire me because I was retired. The others were filled up. But I came here to King's and they told me there was an opening." Cal likes keeping busy during the cold winter months when he can't work in his yard and he also is enthusiastic about his job as a bundle boy.

"This job is relaxing. There's not too much pressure. I like it here. I think I made a good decision."

Cal's decision, and the decisions of the other five bundle boys, were good for the men, the market, and the community. All six men benefitted from their decision to work part time and most of them from their luck or relative ease in finding a job. The job as bundle boys got them out of the house and out of themselves and once again into the world of people, without tying them down with too much unwanted responsibility and worry.

By re-engaging, these men had come full circle; their individual stories indicate that the six men went through the same retirement cycle. Each man retired and had enough money to live (although many elderly who work *do* need the money). Each man enjoyed some leisure time just after retiring, usually fixing up the house, traveling, playing golf, going fishing, and just sitting around and reading and relaxing.

But for some people, relaxing at home leads to loneliness, to becoming withdrawn and often depressed, and even to hypochondria. The men felt useless and isolated when they were not working.

This feeling of not being needed anymore was not always expressed in so many words. It is manifest, however, in many of their statements that "a person needs to be doing something." The need to feel useful can be inferred in the poignant words of Harry Lewis.

"Everyone should work, should do something, because if you have been active for many years, I think it is the worst thing in the world not to do anything. Because you do find that many people don't live long after they retire if they don't do anything. You think about yourself. That's what I began to do."

These men were fortunate for two reasons.

First, their need or drive to work was in most instances supported by their wives and families, and also in Harry's case by his doctor. Family support is a crucial factor in a retired person's ability to end his depression and think about re-engaging, especially when re-engagement is in a low-prestige job.

Secondly, for all men, the opportunity to work at King's leapt out at them: "Help Wanted: Bundle Boys" read the large sign.

Three of the men, Harry, Tom, and Alec, first saw the sign on routine trips to the market. They had not been looking for work. The other three men, Pat, George, and Cal, went looking for work. For Pat and George, King's was the first place they looked, and they were hired. It is difficult to know whether each man would have continued to look further had he not been accepted at King's. George Rogers did say, however, that he was "feeling way down" when he applied for the job. "I don't know what I would have done if I hadn't gotten the job here. This friend of mine who lives 40 miles away has been refused work by several markets. Now he doesn't look any more. He just sits and stares at the TV."

The impact of the market on the bundlers is easier to assess. The men all like the relaxing atmosphere and the absence of tension and worries to take home at night. They like the people they work with, especially the mothers who work behind the cash registers in the mornings while their children are in school.

Alec Hardy, whose only daughter lives out of state, was especially outspoken about what he considers the fringe benefits of his job.

"The young mothers and their little children," he states emphatically. "The little kids are so cute and open and ask such wonderful questions. I always keep a supply of lollipops in my jacket, but I make sure to ask their mother first." For Alec, seeing children eases his feeling of separation from his daughter's family.

The bundlers have had an impact on the customers, too. Many people today live near and usually associate only with people of their own age. At first, some of the customers felt uneasy about having older men lifting their heavy grocery bags; they did not know the capabilities, pride and willingness of these men. Tom Davis recalled one incident that occurred during his first week as a bundler:

"While I was bagging this lady's groceries, she kept staring at me and saying, 'Be careful, don't drop that.' I kept quiet. As I wheeled her bags out to her car, she kept a tight hold of her little girl's hand. When we got to the car, she opened the door and started to put her bags in. She wouldn't let me touch them. I finally had to say something. I told her that it was my job to do that, that the store owners hired me because they knew I could lift grocery bags, even if my hair was white and I was almost seventy, I wasn't senile or dead yet.

"We are now good friends," Tom continued. "Her parents are in Florida and her little Jody has adopted me as her local Grandpa."

For customers like this young suburban mother, the bundle boys have been an eye-opening experience. Just by being present and visible in an unexpected environent, a supermarket, these six bundle boys have expanded the horizons of many younger suburbanites. Shoppers at King Brothers are now aware of the existence of their elderly neighbors and their wisdom and humor. They also have been made aware of the lack of job opportunities and information for elderly people since the men often talk about acquaintances who cannot find jobs and don't know where to look.

All six bundle boys did not mind that the pay was mininal. For some, the low pay was an advantage, since it did not interfere with their Social Security benefits. If they earned more at the market, their Social Security would be reduced. To keep his salary under the maximum, Cal Pickett takes July and August off. This summer vacation gives him the opportunity to play a lot of golf and to go fishing. During Cal's absence, the market hires an extra high school student.

All in all, this arrangement works out very well for the bundle boys, for the high school students, and for the whole community.

The bundle boys get a chance to work in the mornings when they are fresh. And they know that they are not taking jobs away from younger people who need the money since the high school students do the same job after school, on Saturdays, and during the summer vacation.

The market benefits in several ways. Most obviously, it

gets the services of six willing and good workers for not much money. By hiring the elderly men, King Brothers can provide a service that other markets do not have until high school gets out for the day and their own baggers report for work.

King Brothers is an unusual employer. The market in which our six bundle boys work is one of several markets in a small, family-owned-and-operated chain. The two King Brothers, and their extended family, have their roots in the several communities served by their markets. They show their special interest in the communitities' elder residents by hiring retired men and also by sponsoring a senior citizens' bus in each town. Each bus stops at various shops in the town, not just at the King Brothers Market.

The six bundle boys were able to find jobs for two reasons. First, the job was in a visible place—everyone has to buy food. Second, King Brothers is an unusual employer because it takes an active interest in elderly people.

Elderly people who want to work need to be able to find out about jobs in less visible places in every community. Many businesses and stores need to take a more active interest in hiring retired people and helping them re-engage. Civic associations, such as the Chamber of Commerce, also could be a tremendous help by undertaking community-wide campaigns to develop job information and find jobs.

Job Openings: People Over Sixty-Five Need Not Apply

Unlike King Brothers Market, many stores, factories, and businesses throughout the country operate as if they had put this big sign in the window and pencilled it on their application forms. Many seniors are not as lucky as the six men who found work as bundle boys. Many spent long, tiring hours and months and even years looking for work, and when they eventually found a job it often had one or more disadvantageous features.

With the exception of Anna Armanian, who like the bundle boys, found a job in a market by luck, and Joan Tucker, who obtained office work, the three other people we will meet next all experienced age discrimination and rejections before finding work. Anna Armanian experienced no rejection because she did not look for a job, assuming that she would not be hired. Teacher Joan Tucker, who had to retire from a job she loved at age sixty-five had only recently left that job when this study was made.

Samuel Solomon

Sam Solomon is always in motion. At eighty years old, his slim, short frame moves quickly and with the same grace with which he plays the violin and sings. His lively dancing rhythms, even as he walks, and his cheerful humming are signs of his continuing celebration of life.

But life has not been easy for Samuel Solomon. He has experienced tragedy and frustration and yet always survives with his faith in God and his good-natured smile intact. Sam has owned and operated several variety and grocery stores. He had owned his most recent variety store for twenty years, until past his sixty-ninth birthday. But urban renewal's bulldozers demolished Sam's store and with it his livelihood. Sam has many warm memories of his years as a variety store proprietor:

"When I had the store, I made a nice living. I was always happy. I liked to make the customers feel right. I enjoyed our store; it was closed on Saturdays [the Jewish Sabbath] and on Jewish holidays. People warned me that I would never make a living. But I made a very nice living, thank you, we had a lot of friends. On Saturday evening when we reopened after the Sabbath, people would be waiting to come into the store. I was very sorry to give up the store, but at nearly seventy I felt too old to start up my own business again, so I started to look for work with someone else." And so, eleven years ago, at age sixty-nine, Samuel Solomon began job hunting; he never thought about retiring. He spent a whole year looking for a job.

"I got a few odd jobs now and then at the Jewish community center," he explains, with his slight accent, "but these didn't last very long. Every day I looked at the newspapers for jobs nearby."

Like many older people, Sam does not drive anymore and thus must look for work near home or depend on the vagaries of public transportation.

"I saw an ad for one company near my home," he continues. "When I went to see them, they looked at me with cold faces. I said, 'I know, you don't want an old man, even though I can do more than the young men.' But I realized the truth is the truth: they don't want to start out an old man."

But Sam persisted. "I went to a lot of places and had a lot of people tell me no. Then one day I saw an ad for a factory where one of my son's friends is a boss now. So I went to see my son's old friend from our neighborhood and this fellow got me the job and I liked it. I'm a janitor now," he says with a slight smile on his face. "I come into the factory twice a week and keep the work tables neat and generally help keep the place clean. My sister, who was just eighty-three, was upset when I told her I took a job as a janitor. But my wife and children and I feel honest work is dignified whatever it is. My son, who is a chemist, and my daughter, who is a sociologist, were both delighted when I told them about my job, especially when I told them that their friend from high school helped me get it."

His family's support of his job obviously is important to Sam, as it is to many retired people. This support reinforces Sam's own commitment to the job. Sam chuckled as he added, "I do so much in the place and move around so happy that the boss introduces me as 'the employee with the oldest years but the youngest spirit.' "

Spirit is indeed what has charaterized Sam Solomon all his long life, which has been one of struggle and change. He came to the United States from Russia in 1921, after enduring two harsh years as a political prisoner in a Russian jail. When his children were young, his wife died. After several difficult years alone in his new country, he married Sadie, a warm woman who has been a wonderful stepmother to his two children and a loving companion to Sam.

Many residents in the small, tightly knit neighborhood also know Sam and Sadie through all of their volunteer and charitable work. At age eighty, Sam is not content with his paid job two days a week. Sam and Sadie are both very active in the religious life and social service activities of their community. Sam loves to sing in the synagogue choir and he frequently travels to the cemetary to chant Hebrew prayers for mourners who do not know the language. All the money Sam receives for these jobs he donates to his favorite charitable causes.

In the comfortable kitchen of their four-room apartment, Sam diligently rehearses the prayers he leads every evening at his neighborhood synagogue. Several years ago, Sam gave a violin concert to a full house in the synagogue. He also plays his violin in a musical group that entertains at nursing homes.

Sam's bitter experiences in prison camp left him dedicated to helping struggling Jewish people, especially in Israel. For many years, he and Sadie have been known as the 'couple who send bundles to Israel.' They painstakingly wash old clothes that people donate and then use the cloth to sew lightweight but sturdy pouches that can be mailed inexpensively to Israel, filled with any merchandise they can persuade people to donate. To transport their bundles to the local post office, the Solomons rely on what they playfully call "our Cadillac." The 'Cadillac' is a small, two-wheeled squeaky shopping cart that they take turns pulling down the street.

Age has been responsible for Sam's having to curtail one of his favorite projects. Until a few years ago, he and Sadie sold Israel bonds door-to-door, but they can no longer climb all of the stairs in their three-story-tenement neighborhood.

Despite his age, Sam is a do-er, not a quitter. "In my dictionary," he declares, "there is no such word as 'no.'" He does not dwell on the difficulties of his own life, either past or present. He sees his own harsh losses of his young wife and later of his business in the perspective of the tragedies of the world, and by his continuing efforts tries to right them. He loves life and is grateful to have seen so much of it. Sam's strength comes in part from his basic good nature.

He jokingly says, "I always hum at work, and when I don't people are asking me, 'What's wrong, don't you feel well?' "

It also is important to Sam that he is recognized as a positive, continuing force in his community.

"I am respected," he says with dignity; "I'm very much

liked. That's good."

The wages from Sam's part-time job go to his charities, enabling the Solomons to know that they are helping people. Their attitude contrasts with many older people who are depressed because they can only take, not give. The Solomons' life illustrates the point that Gray Panther Maggie Kuhn makes in her many speeches: that older people lose the purpose of living if they work only for themselves and are only passive recipients.

Sam sums up his total commitment to life when he says:

"In my work, I appreciate the work. In my home, I try to keep up the life. I read; I play the violin; I go out; I go out for walks. I'm always busy. I like to keep the day interesting."

Frank Brown

Frank Brown is a clean-shaven, serious-looking man of seventy whose thin gray hair is carefully combed. He is always immaculately dressed in a jacket and tie with a matching handkerchief in his breast pocket and newly shined shoes. His well-groomed appearance indicates that Frank Brown cares about himself and his place in the world.

Frank graduated from business college and was very successful in the insurance business for many years. In his late fifties, he left the insurance company and opened his own brokerage firm, also a profitable venture. When he sold the firm and retired at seventy his income was more than $20,000 per year, with enough set aside for a comfortable retirement in which he did not plan to work.

But the unforeseen happened. Both his wife and his best friend died, leaving him grieving and deprived of companionship. His two daughters were married and living out of state. Frank needed something to do and some people to be with, as he himself realized.

"I didn't want to think of myself all the time like many elderly people who sit around and brood and have nothing to do with their time. I wanted to get away from myself," he says with some insight. "Many elderly people seem to bring illness upon themselves; they become hypochondriacs or they sit and complain about this and that. I wanted to keep myself busy; I couldn't think of any particular hobbies. Some of my friends in my apartment building didn't want to work. They have hobbies and are content, and that's good if you can do it, but I have always enjoyed working. I think that it is important to be active mentally as well as physically. I walk five miles a day. I walk to work. I walk a mile before breakfast and dinner."

Frank discovered that finding a job was difficult. However, with his experienced business mind, he made the task easier on himself.

"I started to look every week in the paper and make phone calls. I always asked if there was an age factor involved in hiring because why should I bother to go all the way down to these jobs just to learn that they do not hire people over sixty-five? It would be a waste of time. So, most places I called said yes, they did have an age limit."

His reaction to the age limits set by many employers was philosophical and business-like rather than personal and hurt.

"I did not give up or get disgusted. I understood. It's not discrimination — it's just that many companies can hire people who are younger who will stay longer."

Frank found several clerical jobs, which he soon left because the work bored him. He eventually took a job in a credit department, where he has the responsibility and authority to approve or disapprove credit. His attitude toward his job is ambivalent; he enjoys the responsibility and busy hours, but misses the personal contact.

"I am very happy here. Sometimes, though, I get frustrated at this job because I don't see people all day. I used to deal with customers in person, but this job is all handled over the phone. That is the only reason my present job is disappointing at times," he explains.

His long business experience has taught him how to handle the job and satisfy the customers when the pace gets too hectic.

"Where I work, there are nineteen telephone lines; sometimes they all ring at once. But I learned that you can only handle one thing at a time. Something suffers if you do too many things at once. I handle the calls quickly, but I give each enough time. I'm happy with the work and they are happy with the work I do." Like Sam Solomon, Frank is pleased and proud that his work is appreciated.

Frank also is quite conscious of his limitations at the age of seventy. Despite his loneliness and need for companionship, he realizes that he could not handle working full time. "I used to work full time," he says, "but it was just too much for me."

After a busy four hours working, he relaxes and enjoys the rest of his day. "When I come home from work at three, the day is almost over. I come home, read the paper or watch TV for a few hours and walk before I prepare dinner. I very rarely go out to eat. On Thursdays I'm with my sister. We get along famously. I used to go to the senior citizens' group on Tuesday nights, but now that I work on Tuesday, I find it's too much for me. Besides, the meetings are usually made up of all women."

Attending the senior citizens' group sparked Frank's interest in working with other elderly people. On his walks or during his trips for groceries he would ask elderly men he encountered why they did not participate in the senior citizens' meeting. "I talked some of them into going. I make friend easily and I often will strike up a conversation with a stranger,"he added.

After his initial success in talking with some elderly men, Frank tried to get a paid job working with the elderly. His reception when he inquired and his reaction unfortunately are all too typical of problems that many elderly people face.

"They hire young people to work with the elderly. I spoke to the man in charge of the elderly and he said, 'I'm sorry, but we don't hire people over fifty-five.' Can you imagine that? I was angry. These younger people can't possibly know what it is like to be elderly. How can they relate to the problems and obstacles facing elderly people? If someone complains to a young person, they will listen and not tell them to get up and help themselves. I've had experience and I experience many of the same feelings. I can tell them to get off their behinds and do something with their lives."

He was willing to work for very little money at this job with the elderly, but not to volunteer his services. His pride in his ability to work for pay was paramount in this situation.

"I said, 'I'll even take five dollars a month.' I think I should get paid a little, no matter how little, and I think that they should have at least one elderly person hired to work with the elderly. Why shouldn't I make money this way?"

But Frank continued his interest in and work with other older men in another direction, a direction of his own choosing. Every so often, Frank would stop at the bar down the street from his apartment for a drink and a little companionship. What he saw both surprised and upset him.

"The men in there," he says, "literally were drinking themselves to death."

He began talking with them and befriending them, trying to discover why they drank so heavily.

"These men," he recalls, "were lonely and felt useless. They felt as if society had put them aside and that the only thing that would make them forget was to drink. The little money they had was spent on drinks. They were losing their health because they did not have enough money to purchase food."

Frank felt gratified that he did have a measure of success with a few of these men. He then thought about becoming involved in a hospital program to help alcoholics but did not. His interests pulled him in other directions.

"I'd like to work around young people. It keeps me young. I like to associate with younger people because I like to bridge the generation gap. I enjoy listening to their thoughts and ideas. When I'm with a group of older people, I feel older. They seem to dwell on the past instead of the present and future."

Frank also is considering taking a second part-time job, one in which he can combine his need to be with people with his sartorial good taste.

"I might take another job. I went to a men's shop a few days ago; I liked the store and the merchandise. I even bought something. I introduced myself to the manager and asked him if he had any openings a few nights or Saturdays. He is supposed to call me."

Frank Brown, at age seventy, probably will continue to be successful. His abilities and his faith in himself, plus his determination to be with other people and to help them, make Frank Brown, and the many seniors like him, a rich resource for any community.

Anna Armanian

Anna Armanian is one of many Americans who need to work after retirement in order to supplement the income received from Social Security.

Anna is sixty-eight and a widow with four children, eight grandchildren, and is about to become a great-grandmother. She is short, with an ample figure that testifies to her prowess in the kitchen. Anna had worked full time in a supermarket as a cashier until she was sixty-five and had to stop working. Like Frank Brown, she did not plan on returning to work after retiring. But, like Frank, she, too, lost her spouse. Her husband died, leaving her lonely and with very little money to live on.

"I have to pay a two-hundred-dollar-a-month mortgage on my house," she explains, "and I could not afford it if I were not working, and I did not want to depend on my children. I like to give, not take." Despite her predicament, Anna, unlike Frank, did not actively look for work.

"I felt it would be hopeless to go look for a job," she explains. "It's so hard after they've made you retire to find another job anywhere."

But like some of the bundle boys, Anna was lucky; her previous experience in a market helped her immensely, as did her outgoing personality.

"One day," she explains, "I was out shopping in a different market and I got started talking to the manager, a nice young man. Well, one thing led to another, and I told him how high the prices are when you are on Social Security. I also told him that I'd worked at the other market and before you know it, he offered me a job wrapping produce. I told him I could only earn so much a year because of my Social Security. He said that was okay and still wanted me to come to work here."

Anna paused a minute and expressed her delight at having been offered a job. "You know, that's very unusual, I want you to know. It's so hard to get a job today, to have someone offer you a job is wonderful." This offer obviously added in large measure to her self-esteem. She went on to explain her Social

Security problem.

"I only work four hours a day, which isn't much. I'd like to work more, but the manager explained that I can't because if I do, I'll make too much money and lose my Social Security benefits. It doesn't seem fair," she concluded in an exasperated tone.

"And besides that," she continued, "I have to take a long vacation. The manager figured it all out and says I'll reach my maximum on Social Secuirty so I'll have to take off and not work during November and December. What's he going to do during that busy season, with all the holidays coming? He says they'll probably have to hire someone to replace me, but that means they might not be able to hire me back in January. It's just not fair!" she emphasized for the second time.

Despite this frustration about money, Anna is glad to be working again. She says that she was surprised at how she felt after she first retired.

"I was really miserable," she explains. "You can only bake so many cookies. Oh, I knitted and crocheted and did some church work. That volunteer work was good," she adds, "because you help people and you also meet people. God forbid, someone dies, we give the mourners a dinner when they come from the cemetary. We hold meetings. We help sick people. To help people is a wonderful thing. But I can still do this while I am working."

Money, companionship, and helping others — these are Anna's three reasons that her job means so much to her. Put another way, these reasons can be stated as: having enough money to live independently; having people around to talk with to avoid feeling depressed, gloomy, and lonely; and having a job that contributes to the well-being of other people and thus helps society to function while making the worker an important, integral part of that society — that is what re-engagement after retirement is really all about.

Despite this simplistic statement, the problems of re-engagement, as we have seen, are many and varied. Many people, like Anna, feel that job hunting late in life is a hopeless endeavor. Without a bit of luck, she would not be working. But in a sense, Anna helped make her own luck. She talked to someone about her problems and it so happened that the someone was in a position to help her. This gives us a clue that many people are needed who can talk to retired people, who can discover their needs, talents, and experience, and coordinate that with available jobs.

Before such counseling can be effective, people in all communities must be made aware of the need for such jobs at all levels, and these jobs must be made available through the cooperation of merchants, factories, businesses, and other employers.

Joan Tucker

On the last day of school in June, Miss Tucker stood in the middle of all the elementary school children. They sang and gave her drawings, flowers, and small gifts. At this, her retirement party, Joan Tucker's blue eyes filled with tears. She became sixty-five a month ago and so had to retire as an elementary school teacher and leave the red brick school that had been her second home for more than forty years. As she hugged the children and sang with them, an unwanted thought crept into her mind: "What will I do in September when school starts again and I'm not here?" She thrust the small voice aside for now and concentrated on the shining young faces giggling all around her.

Joan felt touched and very pleased that the school had given her such a lovely party. She especially appreciated the substantial retirement gifts of money and luggage from both the teachers and the parents. And yet, she thought, "this is the saddest day of my life." Tears welled up in her eyes as she left school, now allowing herself to think, "I don't know what I'll do with myself."

Up until this June, she had always looked forward to summer as a time to travel, catch up on work around her small house, prepare for the fall, and just relax. But not this year. Now she was consumed by worry about the future. She wanted to continue working because, as she explained, "I need to build up Social Security quarters; I can receive my teacher's pension, but teachers in this state are not eligible for Social Security."

She also needed to feel that she could still be an active, contributing member of society, albeit in a different capacity.

"I want to get a job where I can be useful and do interesting things and I don't want to stay home alone all day," she says emphatically, repeating with a note of disdain in her voice, "I don't want to stay home all day. I never did like to play cards or watch TV."

Like Maria Sanchez, whom we will meet next, Joan was a career woman for whom retirement, as for many men, was very painful. But beyond her commitment for working, she had no specific ideas.

"I don't think I should sign up with the temporary agencies," she reasoned, "because I don't really have any office skills."

A seemingly natural job for Joan would be working with children in some capacity. Two friends of hers, also former elementary teachers, had opened a nursery school in their home. But Joan, after some reflection, realized that she had changed and would like to do something different.

"I know I don't have the patience any more for children and I couldn't bear to be cross with them; besides I really am tired of working with children. It's such exhausting work."

In September, three months after her retirement party Joan admitted that she felt a little sad about not starting school once again. But fortunately, during the summer, friends had convinced her to sign up with a temporary agency, telling her she had more skills than she realized. Such support is crucial to retirees who feel inadequate and are wary of trying new types of work. So she filled out all the forms and had been given several office jobs that kept her fairly busy.

"I am enjoying being a temporary and getting sent to different places and meeting lots of *adults*." She emphazied that last word — adults! "I'm filing and doing routine clerical chores and it doesn't matter that I don't type very fast, but I'm out of the house and building up those Social Security quarters."

Like Frank Brown and Anna Armanian, Joan also suffered a personal loss soon after retiring. That first winter her sister died. She had shared a small house with her only sister, and now, never having married, Joan was without family.

Being able to go out to work in an office almost every day, through a temporary agency, helped Joan handle this loss and feel less isolated.

Joan has survived her retirement and bereavement fairly well because she does not now feel that she lost her only identity when she relinquished her former professional role. Like Sam Solomon, she readily and indeed eagerly accepted a lower prestige job rather than retire completely from life.

Many professional people, however, cannot bring themselves to accept such lower prestige work (or downward mobility) after retiring from positions to which our society attaches a lot of prestige. Other professional people, including teachers and other nurturers, look forward to relaxing when they retire. They feel that they have made a significant contribution to society, as indeed they have, and now they want to enjoy the leisure of retirement living, especially if they have the means. Some retirees have a wonderful time and are constantly busy without jobs. Others, however, soon discover that leisure bores and, like Harry Lewis, the bundle boy, they soon seek new jobs as outlets for their energies.

Another single woman teacher who retired a year before Joan Tucker is a good example of this last point. Lucretia Hicks drove to Florida and bought a retirement home in one of the state's many leisure communities. She hated the life, and so she sold her home, drove north again, and enrolled in Boston University's summer Gerontology Institute. She now wants to start an agency that would cater only to elderly job seekers. Such agencies for elderly people of all backgrounds are needed all over this country. The American Association of Retired Persons sponsors branches of such Mature-Temps agencies in some communities, but many more are needed.

Maria Sanchez

Maria Sanchez is a youthful-looking seventy-year-old business woman whose appearance belies her age. Her deepset eyes are handsomely set off by a skillful use of cosmetics and by her rich, black hair that shows only a touch of gray at the roots. Maria takes pride in how she looks and likes to appear tastefully dressed, even if her suits and polished stiletto heels are no longer in vogue because she cannot afford new clothes very often.

Maria had been married once. "Briefly," she says; "it was a disaster." She has no children. She has always worked and for many years held a responsible position as a bank teller. But when she reached sixty-five, she was forced to retire. Retirement, especially mandatory retirement, can be just as traumatic and upsetting for women as for men. Maria is a good example of this. Like many men, her major identity for most of her adult life has been with her job; in addition, most of her friendships and social contacts had been made at work. Going out to lunch with other workers was an important part of each day.

But Maria was not the retiring type of person. "I was tired of staying home because I wasn't used to it," she says. After a lot of canvassing in her neighborhood, she found several jobs, each of which lasted only for a short time; then, as she says, "I was put on a limb."

Unlike many people, men and women alike, Maria did not sink back into her easy chair and become depressed. Nor, like Anna Armanian, did she wait until an opportune encounter found her a job.

Maria made her own opportunity and found herself a job. She enjoys relating this story.

"One day I got a brainstorm. I used to pass this electrician's company time and time again and I often wondered what it was and I never saw anyone around there very much. A couple of times I did see an ad for a bookkeeper. I thought, well, if he has a bookkeeper, maybe he'll need someone when she goes on vacation. I called him and he called me several times. He was busy checking on me. So one day he called me and asked if I would come in and talk to his auditor. So I went in and talked to him and so he said, 'Well, I'll call the boss and tell him that you're going to work.' The boss there never asked my age. I don't think it would have made a difference. If his auditor thought I could do the work, which he did, that's all the boss would be interested in. So, I went to work. When I first went there, they hadn't had a bookkeeper for a while, since

February, and I went in July. That's why the auditor was interested to see who was coming in because there was a lot of work to be done and it had to be done fast because it was soon tax time. I worked steady then for about a month or more. I worked every day and after that I worked three days for a while. Then it was only one day a week."

Maria had worked so efficiently and so well that the job no longer provided enough work to keep her busy for more than one day each week. Now, except for this one day, she again had nothing to do.

She continued looking for a job. Unlike Frank, who questioned each company over the telephone about whether it hired workers over age sixty-five, Maria never mentioned her age at interviews unless forced to. And because of her well-groomed and young-looking appearance she very nearly got a job at the local gas company.

"One place I did have trouble," she admits. "At the gas company, which is just a few streets from my apartment, I went in one morning and filled out the application. I lied about my age. What else can you do?" she asked defensively. "I had hardly walked back into my house when I got a call from the personnel manager. He wanted me to come in. He said, 'I did see you through the glass window and I looked your credentials over and it looks like you would be the one who would be perfect for the particular job.' He said, 'You'll have to go for a physical.' I thought, 'Oh, here it comes now,' so I said to him, 'Well, just how deep do they go into this thing?' He said, 'First, you'll have to bring your birth certificate.' I said, 'I'm sorry but that leaves me out then.' He asked what I meant. I said, 'I'm pretty close to the retiring age and if that matters, it lets me out.' I did not tell him my real age," Maria said coyly. "He said, 'I'm sorry I called you. I wouldn't have called if I had realized that. I saw you, but I never realized you were that age. It wouldn't do me any good to hire you because I would just have to fire you right afterwards. There's no point in that.' He said, 'I'm sorry that I called you to make you feel bad, but I never dreamed you were that age,'" Maria repeated. "That made me feel good," she added. "But it also made me feel bad because I thought, 'Well, here I am able to work but then nobody wants me."

Maria also is able to view her predicament from another angle — the financial one. Working full time is what Maria wants to do and feels that she can do, but paradoxically she could lose her Social Security money by working.

"I'd like to find a steady job," she states, "but then I'll have to freeze my Social Security check. I think that's how it works. I ran into a problem last summer," she continues. "I had a chance to take a full-time temporary job for four months at a good salary. But when I went to inquire about it, I learned that you have to pay back the Social Security, dollar-for-dollar, over the allowed. When you reach a certain amount each month, you lose your check. Then if you go over that you have to pay back what you've already drawn, from the first year. So, I couldn't take the job. It wouldn't pay me to work.[1]

"If you do get Social Security, even if they do take your check from you, they shouldn't expect you to pay them back," Maria said. "The same thing happened to me with unemployment. I didn't realize it until afterward. By taking this job, I lost out on unemployment benefits. They figure the difference between what you earn and what you have coming to you, each week. That stretched over until more than the year in my case. At the end of the year, they asked me to resign and I asked why and they said, 'You haven't run out of money but you have run out of time.' That was the answer I got. I wasn't satisfied, but after all, you can't argue with the federal government." She is right. She could not collect unemployment while working part time.

Maria sounds very bitter when she thinks and talks about mandatory retirement.[2]

"The person who set the age at which you have to stop working must have been someone who hated life," she says, almost passionately.

Work was the only focal point in Maria Sanchez's life. Unlike Sam Solomon and Anna Armanian, religion was not a sustaining part of her life that offered either comfort or an outlet for some of her energy to do volunteer work. About ten years ago, Maria did volunteer work at a local hospital.

"I enjoyed that," she says. "I was there a few years in the evenings. I used to wash glasses," she recalls. "And I'd go around to the patients' rooms and pick up water pitchers. I used to bring the patients paper, pens, and stamps. It was interesting. I found that stamps were one thing that people really missed having the most. They leave home in a hurry if it's an emergency and they never think of paper and stamps. They are glad to have someone furnish them with something like that."

She recently has thought about returning to volunteer some of her time, but she now has a back problem.

"I'm really afraid to take a job or volunteer where I would be on my feet a lot. If I do very much standing, I get into trouble. That's the only reason I haven't gone back. Otherwise, I would try one of the hospitals."

At this point in Maria's life, she needs some direction. She could greatly benefit from good counseling to give her some ideas for volunteer work, such as school volunteering, that would not require her to be on her feet all day.

To keep going, Maria needs to be with people; she enjoys helping them and feeling useful, as her volunteer activity indicates. Maria also needs to get away from her apartment and into a cheerier environment.

"My neighborhood is not the best," she reports. "The biggest complaint I have is vandalism and damage to cars and so on." Like many senior citizens, she lives in a dilapidated area where rents are lower.

So far, however, Maria has been able to maintain a sense of discipline about her life.

"I go up the street every day. I make it a practice whether I feel like going or I don't feel like going. I have a dog and I take her out." But she can feel herself losing her tenuous hold on that disciplined existence and it obviously bothers her.

"I don't know any more how I spend my time when I'm not working. I get lazy. Somehow or other the time gets away from me. I'm just plain lazy now," she repeats, "I like to read. Lately, I've been more on the television bug. I never was much for television, but it's a form of entertainment. And of course I have telephonitis. So the time flies and the telephone bills go up. Every time the bill comes in I say, 'You're going to have to stop.' And then someone gets sick, and I call, feeling that the money is well spent."

Maria's new interest in television and her dependence on the telephone are her ways of reaching out of her narrowing world for contact with other people. She is too proud to admit to loneliness, but it shows; it shows in her dark eyes and in how she now is living her life. Without work or some other regular activity outside of her apartment with other people, Maria might easily become depressed and even withdrawn.

She could become one of the many older Americans who wait to find work but are not able to. We will meet five such people in chapter six.

Summary

The people we have met in this section all have experienced some measure of success in re-engaging after retiring from long-held, responsible positions. How successful each person has been is best determined by each person's own satisfaction with life and his or her view of success in coping with job hunting, age discrimination, financial worries, lower prestige jobs, and loneliness.

Except for the bundle boys and for Sam Solomon, who celebrates life with every step he takes and basks in the praise he gets for being an enthusiastic factory janitor, all of the people in this section are dissatisfied with at least one aspect of their jobs. But this dissatisfaction did not make them quit.

Frank Brown likes his job giving credit references over the telephone, but this extroverted man would like more face-to-face contact with people. Anna Armanian thoroughly enjoys her job as a produce wrapper in a local supermarket and enjoys the social contacts but is upset that she has to quit work for two months a year in order not to earn too much money. She does not really understand how the system can allow this to happen and is worried that she might not get her job back in two month's time. Anna also feels insecure at her job — perhaps because of her age. She cut short her interview for this book, afraid of displeasing her boss, even though he had approved the interview.

Joan Tucker, after initial worries about how she would adjust to the world outside of elementary teaching, now seems happy doing temporary office chores at various places of business. But she knows that these jobs are of a temporary nature and thus that she could soon be out of work and not building up her needed Social Security quarters. In addition, she had only been retired for a few months when this study was made. It therefore is difficult to say how she will be doing or what her attitudes and emotional state will be like in a few years time.

Maria Sanchez, the resourceful retired bank teller who found a job as a bookkeeper, would like to work more than just one day a week and feels discriminated against because of her age as she looks for other jobs.

Despite the widespread age discrimination that these retired people found as they tried to re-engage, they were successful, in large measure because of their contacts, their persistance, their personalities, and their good luck. These capable people were determined to find work (except, of course, for Anna Armanian) and several had to go outside society's regular channels, or had to create their own jobs, or had fortunate encounters. Most seniors face the same age discrimination as these five people and are defeated by rejection. Why this happens we shall see in the last chapter on retired people who tried unsuccessfully to re-engage through the traditional employment route rather than the route of hobbies and volunteering.

Suggestions

If you would like to re-engage and find a job in a business firm, here are a few suggestions. Reading them probably will give you other ideas of your own.

1. Check with your local office of the U.S. Employment Service.
2. Check with Mature Temps, the AARP's temporary office agency, if there is one in your area.

3. In your public library, look up the magazine *Perspective on Aging,* published by the National Council of the Aging, Washington, D.C. The July/August 1977 issue contains the excellent article "Okay, I'm Retired — Now What?" by Dr. Dayton Benjamin, executive director, Washten County Council on Aging, Ann Arbor, Michigan.

   In this article, Dr. Benjamin, a retired educator, suggests the following ways that retirees can earn some money: board cats, edit a newsletter, sell novelties, drive a small van or bus part time, get a real estate or insurance license, do odd jobs and repair work, make and sell handicrafts for money, be a parking lot attendant or a watchman, get a job as a store clerk, be Santa Claus for pay, serve on a jury, fix up old furniture, start your own business, teach an adult education course, work part time for your former employer, raise bees. Of course, these are just a few interesting suggestions.
4. Action for Independent Maturity (AIM) Workshops, sponsored by the American Association of Retired Persons, use a workbook that suggests these and many other business possibilities for bridging the income gap: auto repair; babysitting; house sitting; housecleaning; bookkeeping service; bread baking; dog grooming and walking; fruit, vegetable, and herb growing; party planning; mail order business; writing; tutoring; typing.
5. Once you decide on a service you can offer, post ads in laundromats and supermarkets, take out an ad in the local paper, and tell everybody you know.
6. In its AIM seminar, the AARP recommends these publications as good sources:

   The book *Not Quite Ready to Retire* published by MacMillan, Inc., Riverside, N.J., contains 351 jobs and businesses for older workers. It is described as a comprehensive guide to full- and part-time jobs. This and other similar books may be in your local library.

   Small Business Bibliographies are available from the local office of the Small Business Administration of the United States, or write Small Business Administration,

Publications Division, 1030 First Street, N.W., Washington, D.C. 20416.

The booklet "Starting and Managing A Small Business of Your Own" is available from the Superintendent of Documents, Goverment Printing Office, Washington, D.C. 20402. $1.35 order S.B.A., 1.15. 113.

"Your Retirement Job Guide," single copies are available from the American Association of Retired Persons, 1909 "K" Street, N.W., Washington, D.C. 20049.

Notes

1. Maria is only partly correct. In 1978, a person over sixty-five could earn up to $4,000 yearly without losing his or her Social Security. The basic rule is that for any earnings above $4,000, $1 is withheld for every $2 made. (See note 7 in chapter one for more details.)

   The monthly test to which Maria refers was eliminated in 1978, except for the first year of retirement. After that, the yearly rate governs. Maria was interviewed before this change.
2. When Maria related her story, mandatory retirement was at age sixty-five. Now it is age seventy.

Chapter Three

Municipal and Community Service Employees

"I like to be busy and active."

American society tends to be age-segregated. Children and adolescents rarely have any sustained contact with people much older than their parents. Teachers, admittedly influential to children, generally retire by age sixty-five; many active teachers are indeed much younger.

In our mobile society, grandparents often live hundreds of miles away. Some children may see them once a year, perhaps only on special occasions like Christmas. Children also are presented with a distorted picture of elderly people in the television programs they watch and even in the books they read.[1]

Many newer suburban communities are populated by couples under age forty and elders tend to be disproportionately housed in inner-city areas.

Where are the senior citizens who can serve as examples of active older people who love working and living with people of all ages? Some of them are the bundle boys. Others are working for the community itself in various volunteer projects such as RSVP and Foster Grandparents. Some also hold paid jobs in organizations that are community oriented, such as the YMCA and community recreational centers. We will meet four such people in this chapter, plus a man who created a job for himself that serves people in his community.

Charles MacDaniel

It is easy to see that Charles MacDaniel, "Dan," once was a large, husky man. Now, at age seventy-eight, he is tall and spare, his broad shoulders somewhat stooped, but not his spirit.

Dan, who just celebrated his seventy-eighth birthday and his eleventh year as a paid employee at his community's YMCA, retired as a milk truck driver at age sixty-five. His favorite quip is, "Even though I'm Scotch, my favorite drink is milk."

Dan came to this country from Scotland when he was twenty-four and still has a heavy Scottish accent that rolls off his tongue. Always an active man, he drove the milk truck during the day and held down a second job nights and weekends.

"I had five boys growin' up at home," he says. "Besides, I love to work."

After he retired, Dan had little to keep him busy. He had been so busy working that he had never developed hobbies.

"Oh, I fixed up the house a wee bit, and planted some bulbs, but I wanted to do more. I joined the local retired man's club. We had a good time talkin' and playin' cards. But I really joined in the hopes of finding a bit o' work to keep me busy."

His strategy paid off. Through a friend at the club, Dan got his job at the local YMCA.

"I work in the swimming pool office. It's a full-time job. I check the swimming cards and collect swimming fees. I also hand out towels and look after pocketbooks and watches."

For Dan, the best part of the job is the children.

"I love seeing all those youngsters and getting to watch them grow. It's just as if my own boys were young again."

The children at the "Y" have come to love Dan, too.

"Sometimes they ask how old I am. I always tell them. I think it's important they know that I am a senior citizen and can still work and love to be with people."

Dan's job has another benefit — he doesn't have to work during the summer.

"During the school vacation, the "Y" likes to give these jobs to high school kids who need the money. I think it's great. It gives me and the wife a chance to take a little vacation. Our children come to visit summers. Besides, I don't like to work when it's really hot; I'm no spring chicken, you know," he quipped.

Rose Bresnick

Rose Bresnick, who teaches art in her town's community center, looks more like sixty-one than eighty-one. Silver hair surrounds her lively face, and her small slim hands are well-manicured and adorned with colorful rings.

For many years, Rose and her husband ran a small antique shop. When he became very ill, she sold the shop so she could devote all her time to caring for him.

"After he died, I was all alone," she recalled; "My two daughters, Paula and Amy, were both married and living in the same town about 200 miles away. They insisted that I move there so I wouldn't be alone. I did, but I got my own apartment, of course. I've always been very independent.

"Paula knew that I couldn't just sit at home and look at the walls. She called the community center and found out that they had an afternoon drop-in lounge, so she drove me over. I don't have a car. Well, she left me off and went to do her shopping. And that's how it started," Rose said brightly. "I started talking to this one woman about antiques, and also about art, which I've always loved. It turned out that she was the center's supervisor and they needed volunteers. So, I started helping as a hostess, greeting people, you know. After several months, she asked me to volunteer to teach a painting class. I was delighted and loved it. The class, in still life, meets every Tuesday. Most of my students are young mothers. They want to learn to paint while their children are in school. They are usually surprised to find out how old I am. They say I was like a second mother or grandmother to them, especially the ones who live far from where their own people are.

"One young woman, about thirty, was like a little lost soul. Like an orphan. She was lost. She had just moved here when her husband changed jobs. Someone told her to join the class. She said she didn't know anything about art but joined anyway. She is now so happy. She can't wait till the next lesson comes.

"Well, my class soon lasted from eleven in the morning until three in the afternoon. That was too much. I didn't have any time for myself." Rose said she needed some help because her painting class was so popular and well attended. She told the director, "You have to get another volunteer to help me out. I'll train the volunteer. I'll do all I can. I always come and give every bit of energy I can, but I can't feel like I'm tied up so that I can't skip a Tuesday if I want to go someplace."

To her surprise, the director offered to pay Rose if she would stay. Delighted to be earning some money again, Rose said yes, on the condition that she could take some time off occasionally for her other activities.

In her often hectic schedule of teaching and painting, Rose makes the time to serve on her town's Council of Aging. "It's important to me," she emphasizes, "and it is important to this town. The people here should know that creativity is still alive even after the hair turns white."

Rose has always been a hard-working, independent spirit. She was born in Russia and came to this country as a young girl with her parents and older brothers and sisters.

"My father was very old," she remembers. "He was a carpenter, with two fingernails missing. He always worked hard. He felt that for a girl, high school was enough. But I didn't, so I went to night school and took up as many English courses as I could. I also took up bookkeeping. It helped a lot when my husband and I had the antique shop."

When her daughters were growing up, Rose joined a woman's philanthropic club.

"When I became active in organization work, I decided I would have to take up public speaking."

She has always been conscious of speaking with an accent, althouth it is barely noticeable.

"I went to a man who trained some of the biggest men in politics today. He was terrific. You can tell that I have had speech training. I was very quiet and shy before." Now, it is hard to imagine that anyone as outgoing and friendly as Rose ever could have been shy!

Rose loves learning and is proud of the efforts she had made.

"I took up vocabulary building. I could have gone and used all my credits towards a degree, but I didn't bother. I didn't need it. It proves that no matter how old your children are you can go to school."

Her main interest now is art.

"I've always liked painting, but never did any myself until my girls were grown up. Like Grandma Moses, I guess," she adds with a laugh. "But I made up for lost time. I met someone who recommended a painting teacher to me. That was how I started. Then I started to go to college at nights, adult education it's called. I went year after year. I went there because they had live models there and I'd never done live models."

Rose is a good teacher because she is still such an active learner. In addition to teaching her own class, she also is a student in another class at the community center.

"The instructor has a very good art background. We do outdoor sketching. I have never done that before. She takes us out in her car and we get out at different places and we sketch, which I love. It's beautiful around here. I always wanted to do outdoor art work but I never could because I was in the antique store all day long. My art lessons were at night after a day's work."

Rose Bresnick is an exceptional example of a person who has re-engaged by turning a hobby into a paid job. And more important, she has become an active, contributing member of a community that was new to her just two years ago.

The support she has gotten from her daughters has been important to Rose after the death of her husband.

"They convinced me to move here. Paula first told me about the community center. My girls love my work. They have my paintings all over their houses! They are very glad that I'm busy doing something that I like. They know that I'm happy. They know that I'm here and near them."

Paula and Amy consider their mother's personality and needs and react to her as a strong, independent woman. They do not just think of her as a person of advanced age — eighty-one — as some families do when they tell older parents to relax, to disengage.

"I like to keep busy and active," Rose repeats again and again; "It's wonderful for me."

Jack Miller

Retirement at age sixty-five does not automatically change a person's abilities. A man who was a leader in business still has leadership abilities when he retires, as Jack Miller proved. At age seventy-four, he is very active in several retired men's organizations and also is paid by his town to program voting machines.

"I am an electrical engineer," Jack says in his precise manner. "I like to work with my brain and my hands and I'm good with people. At one time, I directed a large project and had almost five thousand men reporting to me.

"I worked for one of the large public utilities in this state. I had a very responsible job and I did it well. But," he says, "at sixty-five I had to retire. It didn't seem right then and it still doesn't.

"I was willing to continue to work and so I went looking for a job. But nobody wants any one over sixty-five."

When he tried the usual routes to find employment, Jack experienced the same rude awakening that so many other retired people experience.

"My health was good so I just went down to the employment bureau. They tried to get me an electrical engineering job, but nothing came up. Then I went to various places myself. But by this time I knew that they probably wouldn't hire me. I went to numerous places in my field. But these companies all have a cut-off age of sixty-five. I think it's tied in with some of the insurance they have. Sixty-five it is and then they don't want you longer."[2]

The next few months were crucial in Jack's life. He had reached the part of the retirement cycle at which many once active men become depressed and withdrawn. But Jack refused to vegetate and turned his enormous energy in other directions.

"I wanted to see how other retired men felt, so I started to get involved in all these retired social activities. There are several retired men's clubs around here. Men are different than women," he stressed. "Men have been active all their lives; they have not had housework to do and they wouldn't do it anyway. They are not used to staying in the house. I think the women have a much easier time adjusting than the men.

"It's amazing the number of things that are going on in these retired centers," Jack continues.

As he begins to talk about his present activities, the tight tension lines around his hazel eyes seem to relax.

"I do a little choral singing and each one of these groups has a men's glee club. The one here has about forty men who get up and sing. We're out up until the bad weather starts about three times a month. We sing for church groups and senior citizens and all around the various suburbs in the schools and so on. But because I've done some choral singing and I've done some directing, it was a natural outlet for me to get into it."

Jack's attitude towards his volunteer activities reflects that of the bundle boys toward their new jobs. They liked the lack of any real pressure and the relaxing atmosphere.

Jack says, "In many ways, I'm a busier man than when I was working, but its a nice kind of busy. And I know I don't have to do these things if I don't want to."

Jack does want to because he likes to keep active. "I think it's important for a man to keep going," he says. He was a leader when he was working and he is a leader in retirement activities, too. He is vice-president of a fraternal club for men of all ages.

"This club is important," says Jack; "It lets the younger men see that being retired from work does not have to mean being retired from life."

Jack maintains his ties with his old job by serving as president of all the retired employees at the utility company for which he worked. He was offered his paid job as voting machine programmer because he had been president of the retired men's club.

"The executive director of the election commission got ahold of me one day and said, 'I've been having firemen do this on their days off, but its hard to schedule them; could you get half a dozen men from the retired men's club to put the programs on the voting machines?' So I did, and I never give anybody anything that I'm not willing to do myself, so I became one of the programmers."

Jack's job is seasonal; he programs the voting machines two weeks before every election — national, state, or town.

"These machines have to be set up and all of the slips put in," Jack explains. "There is a programming panel in the back of each machine with little pins and wedges you have to put in." He likes explaining exactly how the machines work and even more, he likes the challenges of working on a technical project and of directing men to help accomplish an important task.

At this stage in his life, Jack feels very thankful that he is involved in both his volunteer and paid activities. When his wife of forty-five years recently died, he realized with certainty that his activities and many friends helped sustain him. Although his two sons, also engineers, now live out of state, their attitude helps their father. "They think my activities and my job are great for me. They know I'm doing the things I enjoy doing."

Jack's attitude reflects his whole outlook on life and explains his involvement with living and working. Reaching sixty-five or seventy, the so-called retirement ages, does not mean that a person suddenly changes his involvement with and commitment to life. Commitments to working hard and the need to contribute to society do not go up in smoke when the candles on the birthday cake are blown out.

Arthur Donato

Arthur "Chief" Donato had been a fireman for forty years when, at age sixty-five, he retired as the town's fire chief.

"I didn't want to retire," he says, "but that's the way it is. I had to retire, so I did."

'Chief,' as he is still affectionately called, is a short, stocky man with large, rough looking hands and large features. His black wavy hair at age seventy-one is thick and peppered with grey.

"I also figured I would find something else to do. I didn't want to hang around the fire house, much as it had been my whole life. I felt that my successor needed to have me out of the way so he would have a free hand without me looking over his shoulder. I respected him and I had had my years as chief."

After so many years of working with people and helping them in adverse circumstances, the chief was good at sizing up a situation involving other people. Of course, he knew his beloved community and its citizens very well. So just one year after he hung up his red fire chief's hat, he threw his political hat into the ring and again became a chief — chief of select-men.

"I like the people in this town and I thought I could still help them."

Evidently they thought so, too, for when he ran for the post of chief of selectman he was elected by a large majority.

"Arthur was thrilled when he heard how many people in town voted for him," says his wife Bea, a short, outgoing woman with large brown eyes and unruly graying hair. Though busy with their own healthy children and grandchildren, she and the Chief also were known and respected in their town for their efforts to help children with emotional and behavioral problems. They had raised money for a facility for these children and for training them. They also gave of themselves to these children by serving as volunteer teachers.

"Every summer we had cookouts at our place for these kids. They all love it."

Chief has been the chief of selectmen for five years. He is paid $1,000 for the job and works long and hard.

"The money isn't that important to me. It's helping the people in the town that I love to do."

Chief has his office at the town hall.

"I go there every day when I'm not busy around town. A lot of people come to sit and talk. I have a lot of other retired men who come in. They are lonely and bored."

Chief also likes the visible aspects of his new job.

"It's important to me that the people in town see that I'm retired and still working. Bea and I love to ride in the Fourth of July parade and then meet the kids at the field afterwards."

Chief summed up his feelings toward working in his town in this way:

"I like to be busy. I love this country and this town. Both

have been good to me. I want to continue serving as long as I can."

Hal Crane

Even though Hal Crane's job is not quite like the other jobs we have seen in this chapter, it is of interest here for two reasons. First, because he created a job for himself after retiring at age sixty-five, and secondly, through his new job, he is known in his community by people of all ages. Hal Crane calls himself the "Little Shaver." Daily, no matter what the weather, he walks one mile to the local hospital and shaves the men, young and old, who are too ill to shave themselves.

At seventy-nine years old, Hal is short, wiry, and still energetic. He has a mellow voice and a grave face that turns into a smile as he walks into each patient's room. "In a way I was lucky to wind up in the hospital four years ago, although, of course, an appendectomy was no fun."

As he was recovering in his room with three other men, he noticed that none of them had shaved for quite some time.

"These men were all very sick. Not being shaved made them look worse. And the nurses didn't have the time to shave each man every day. So I said to myself, 'Why can't I do it?' So I did. Every day while I was recovering, I shaved each man in my room. One day one of the nurses asked if I could shave some of the other men in different parts of the hospital. I was glad to."

At the end of his two-week stay, Hal had quite a clientele.

"The men really looked better after being shaved. And, you know, they seemed to feel better. Maybe its because they knew they looked better."

Hal is too modest to say outright that it was his interest in the other patients that helped them recover.

"As I shaved, slowly, we talked. Some of these men had led colorful lives. Mostly, I think, they enjoyed having someone to talk to, especially another man. The nurses are pretty, but you can't talk to them about men's problems. Besides, they are always too busy to chat. And the doctors are always very rushed, too.

"I was sorry in a way to leave the hospital," Hal admits. "For the first time in years I had something interesting to do.

And worthwhile, too." Hal had retired at age sixty-five. As a young man, he ran his family's general store.

"Then my father passed away, so I sold the store. For years after that I was a representative for a manufacturer of electrical appliances. I used to travel around, but never too far. When I retired, I never thought about working. My wife and I, we had enough saved to live on. But I did try to keep busy. I helped at the church a lot."

Hal was also active in his local veteran's group. But his life seemed to him without purpose.

"I hadn't thought much about what I'd do after I left the hospital. Then one of the men asked if I could come shave him once in a while. Then it hit me — I knew I had another job that I really wanted to do. After I got home, I started walking to the hospital maybe three or four days a week to shave the men and cheer them up. That was nine years ago! Now I go seven days a week, rain or shine. I get a great deal of satisfaction out of shaving the men; after all, it sure is necessary. And it's an every day thing. Whiskers do not wait a few days for someone to come in and shave them. They grow every day and therefore, someone must come in every day. I'm there on Sunday's, too," Hal adds. "I wouldn't miss a day. It keeps me busy and I feel as though I am doing something worthwhile."

An added fringe benefit to Hal from his job are the number of men he now knows all over town.

"Just about every time I go to the market, someone will look up and say, 'There's Hal; he's the man who shaved me when I was in the hospital.' I meet a lot of their families, their children and grandchildren, too."

The daily occupation also saw Hal through some tragic personal losses. When his wife and then his daughter died, he was able to survive because he knew he had to go to the hospital each day with a smile on his face to cheer the sick men.

It is obvious to see that Hal is proud of both his accomplishment and his ability to keep going.

"I sat down one day to figure out just how many shaves I give. I do twenty, sometimes twenty-five, a day. That comes to more than seven thousand shaves each year. That's a lot of whiskers!"

Hal could get paid for his job. "But I don't need the money. I do this because I like it. I don't really consider it a job."

Hal's statement reveals our American concept that a volunteer activity is not really a job because no pay is involved. But for Hal that distinction didn't matter; the activity itself is important to him, not what it is called. Hal is a good example of a man who re-engaged by creating a job to fit his own needs.

Conclusion

The people described here are all employed helping others in their communities. They meet and know people of all ages and thus are in marked contrast to older persons who live in secluded retirement villages.

Even in good financial circumstances, well-to-do retired people are not always happy, despite their plush environments, if their surroundings lack stimulation and contact with people of all ages. Many wealthier retired men spend a lot of their time on the golf course, in the pool, or relaxing in the opulent lounge, reminiscing to each other about all of their successes, as if their identity rested on who they once were.

Even though these men appear to be enjoying their life of ease, many actually are living in the past, when they worked and were productive, contributing members of society.[3] Poorer older people whose housing is bad often are doubly deprived — they lack a good living standard and worthwhile activity.

Dan, Rose, Jack, Chief Donato, and Hal have all tried hard to maintain that vital link with society, to remain an integral, contributing part of their communities. It has not been easy for many of them. Often business and industry, with their compulsory retirement policies and their unwillingness to hire workers over age sixty-five, or even over age fifty, have made it difficult, as has the lack of good job information for retired people. These two areas are undergoing change so that more retired people who want to work, can, and can continue to be an active part of community life.

Retirement is the great leveler. As in the case of Jack Miller, retirement changes people from persons of importance to people who must work hard to maintain an identity in their community and a sense of self worth. Such opportunities that allow seniors to serve and not just be served should be available to more people.

Suggestions

ACTION, a federal program, provides stipends for community service jobs under various rubrics such as RSVP and Foster Grandparents. For fuller information on volunteer and stipended work in the community, see the concluding pages of chapter six.

The Community Chest or other umbrella agency for charitable groups in your community may have a list of social services agencies; canvass them to see if there are any employment opportunities there.

As Dan discovered, the local YMCA (or YWCA or YMHA) often employs older people in various jobs. The community center is another possible source of employment. Local institutions, such as hospitals, often need willing workers, especially during the busy holiday seasons. Entertaining children in hospitals or institutions can be especially rewarding.

One green-thumbed senior citizen we know in Maine works during the summer season for the local forestry department, which needs extra help then. If your area has a tourist service, perhaps you, as someone who knows the area well, could find employment there.

In general, survey the social and recreational services in your own community, think about your particular skills and talents, and see how they can be put to use either in a paid or volunteer capacity. One man had a large workshop in his cellar for woodworking, but was bored working alone. He realized that he could run a workshop Saturdays for youngsters whose fathers lacked time and talents to teach them. He put an ad in the local paper, called the schools about his project, and soon was busy afternoons and Saturdays teaching carpentry to eager students. Local papers are a good place to run ads offering your services after you identify your skills and community needs. Notifying the local schools, public and private, also is a good tactic. What are the unmet needs in your community that you could fill? Think of Hal Crane, who made a niche for himself shaving patients. Older persons tend to underestimate themselves and internalize the rejection they receive. You survived by your wits; use them to find a way to reengage.

A retired teacher, who was researching his family's history in this country, was paid by his town to take an historical census of all the old families in town. His ebullient wife, long interested in antiques, guides tourists around the historical house in their town.

Younger persons should consider what jobs they can offer lonely seniors. One academic couple, needing a baby sitter, deliberately sought out a bereaved seventy-year-old widow in their neighborhood. They admit they had some concern that she might not be a happy influence on their child, but decided to try her out. Much to their delight, she regained her zest for life as she took care of "her" baby. The paid "extra Grandma" was completely reliable.

The owner of a corner grocery store found the work too much so he called the local senior center to see if there was an older man who would like to help him out. He obtained a good part-time employee and also the patronage of many of the senior's friends in the neighborhood.

Two retired teachers who felt isolated from life had trouble paying the taxes on their large house. A friend pointed out to them that many working mothers in the community would welcome a safe and educational "after school school" for their children. These two women now operate an afternoon program that helps working mothers and helps them feel needed too. According to the Department of Labor publication *Working Mothers and Their Children* in 1976, 49 percent of all mothers with children worked.

In Boston, Massachusetts, seniors themselves run a hot line for seniors at the city's Department for the Aged. Perhaps in smaller communities other seniors could set up such services needed by other older persons or by the handicapped. One senior we know is paid to drive a person who is not sighted.

Another older woman attended a retirement course sponsored by her city's local Aging Committee. She let it be known that she could type and found several professional people who needed a good typist.

Many community-minded older persons work through their local Gray Panthers' networks to improve community life for both young and old: their slogan is "Age and Youth in Action." As of 1977, the Gray Panthers had networks in Arizona, California, Colorado, Connecticut, the District of Columbia, Florida, Georgia, Illinois, Iowa, Maine, Maryland, Massachusetts, Michigan, Minnesota, Mississippi, Missouri, Nebraska, New Jersey, New York, Ohio, Oregon, Pennsylvania, Rhode Island, Texas, Vermont, and Virginia. You can write to the national organization at: 3700 Chestnut Street, Philadelphia, Pennsylvania 19104.

Some of the seniors in this and other chapters heard about jobs because they were active in senior citizen groups. Get involved in the various organizations in your community. You are more apt to hear of jobs if you are out than if you are home brooding because you have nothing to do. Read in your local paper what organizations exist in your community and when they meet; or call the mayor's office or your town hall. And let people know of your abilities. You have a lot to give and seniors deserve visibility in our communitites. In short, identify your abilities and announce them wherever you can. Perhaps you will not get a job — but perhaps you will.

These vignettes illustrate that it is possible for some older persons to find a useful way of working in their communities. It also is true that a more systematic way of such job development also should be a responsibility of the communities themselves.

Notes

1. Dr. Edward F. Ansello of the University of Maryland Center on Aging reports that in nearly 700 books available to children throughout one local library system, only 16 percent contained any older characters and that the majority of these characters were one-dimensional stereotypes rather than full and accurate characterization. For a fuller discussion of the report of older characters in children's literature, see *New York Times*, January 7, 1977.

2. More than two-thirds of the workers in this country are covered by private pension plans at their place of employment. The workers whose plans include compulsory retirement had to retire at age sixty-five before the 1978 legislation. Forty percent of the workers studied were covered by plans restricting their employment by their company after retirement. This meant that companies adopting a pension plan with such a policy could not hire workers who were over sixty-five. This data is reported in "Pension Provisions Affecting the Employment of Older Workers," *Monthly Labor Review* 96 (4) (April 1973): 41-45, a study conducted by the U.S. Bureau of Labor Statistics. (For changes in legislation in 1978, see note 6, chapter one.)

   Many of these retirement restrictions are related to insurance on the workers that is paid by the companies. Many companies pay some or all of the health and/or life insurance premiums on its workers over sixty-five. To avoid having to pay large insurance premiums, many companies in the past adopted pension plans that mandate retirement at age sixty-five. The new seventy-year-old retirement law will not stop "voluntary" retirement with such pensions, only mandatory retirement.

3. The authors wish to thank Larry White, a student at Boston University, for his study of and perceptive comments on condominium living in Florida and living in an old-age apartment house. For further reading on segregated housing, see Ruth Harriet Jacob's article, "The Friendship Club," in *The Gerontologist*, December 1969.

Chapter Four

Second Careers Working With Other Aged

"If you have something to keep you going, you live longer."

Introduction

The axiom that you can help yourself by helping others is particularly relevant to the many senior citizens who have found new careers working with other older persons.

In 1975, 10 percent of the people in this country — about 22 million men and women — were sixty-five years or older.[1] Both figures — the percentage and the total number of senior citizens — are expected to increase, so that by the year 2000 the U.S. Census Bureau estimates that nearly 12 percent of our population, or more than 30.6 million individuals, will be sixty-five or older. The most rapidly growing age group of senior citizens consists of people over age seventy-five, as indicated in Figure 4.1. These senior citizens can benefit the most from help willingly given by other senior citizens.

Already, more than one million people serve the aged,[2] and more services and facilities will have to be developed, especially for the people over age seventy-five.

Many senior citizens now derive great satisfaction from helping other older people.[3] The mutual advantages in this situation are threefold: First, working with other older people can give a retired person perspective on his own life. As one man said, "Whenever I start to feel depressed, I just look around. Lots of older folks are worse off than me." Second, old people also benefit from having other older people around.

Figure 4.1: Number of people over age 75 in the United States, 1900 - 2000 (projected)[a]

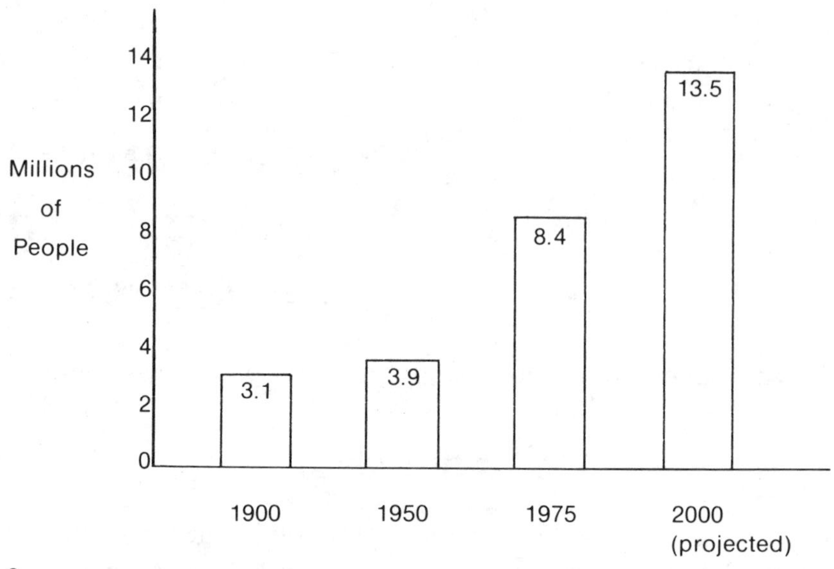

[a]Source: United States Bureau of Census.

Retired people working with the elderly are good examples of what older people can do to be useful. Growing old is the one life situation for which we usually lack preparation. Some older people literally are at the end of their rope because they have no examples of how to live at their ages. They have outlived their parents' age and often their friends as well, and times have changed. An actively engaged older person can be living proof to them that old age can be productive and worth living. Third, older persons best understand what it means to be old and so can relate to the needs of other elderly. Even though young people often empathize well with the aged, the elderly themselves know first hand what the problems are.

The seven people we will meet in this chapter all have put their knowledge to good use. They all are committed to leading active lives, as their statements reveal:

"I didn't want to retire."
"I hate to stay home."
"I like to mingle with people."
"I like to help others."

In one way or another, each of these people managed to side-step the depression stage that sometimes is part of the retirement cycle. Whether voluntarily retired or retired by organizational policy, each person believed in the value of work. Therefore, the end of one job naturally meant seeking another occupation. Also, even before fully retiring, several people had shown their interest in other elders by working with them in an unpaid, volunteer capacity. Their need to be with other people led them to an old age career.

Since this chapter focuses on elderly people who have re-engaged by working with other elderly people, each person has two stories to tell — his or her own experience of retiring and re-engaging plus a description of each job with other elderly people.

Abe Ginsberg

Abe Ginsberg is a retired man who has re-engaged with a plan. At age sixty-six, he works for a social service agency, where his job is to find jobs for older, needy people who also have some disability.

Abe is a short, somewhat portly man with a deep voice and a self-assured, friendly manner. His own retirement story gives us some insight into how he handles his second career.

At age sixty-five, Abe sold his clothing manufacturing company to a large corporation. He had founded the company thirty-five years before and had been very successful but now thought he wanted to retire.

He played golf for several months, but soon got bored. His interactions with other retired men convinced him that he did not want to stay permanently retired.

"A lot of people go out there and play golf every day, but I didn't want to do that. I know too many men who are bored to death who haven't anything to do. They go into the community building and they play cards all day. They come about 10:30 in the morning and stay 'til four. They have nothing else to do.

"I wanted something to do," he said. He had given a lot of serious thought to finding a second career that would suit his abilities.

"I always had a good relationship and rapport with my employees and I think I knew how to handle them, so I thought

I ought to get into counseling personnel, using common sense. I thought I knew how to counsel, and it's proven that way."

Abe is not bragging; in his matter-of-fact voice he is accurately appraising himself. He also is an ambitious, energetic man who likes to try new tasks and is used to being successful.

"I wanted some exposure to the employment field, so I took a job with a professional employment center in the city. It's a very fine concern. I did a very good job with them. I was a senior counselor, but I didn't need the pressure to always do the sales, sales, sales. So I resigned and went back to doing counseling. Then this social service project came along. When I heard of it, I accepted it as a challenge. Every time I talk to a company now I have two strikes against me because I'm not selling an able-bodied, twenty-five-year-old man just out of college, but I'm selling a fifty-five-year-old or more person who has a disability. The average age of persons that we place is sixty-eight. The oldest person we placed is eighty-one."

This job has taught Abe what so many retired people have discovered for themselves:

"It's difficult to find employers. Many organizations have this hard-and-fast rule that they will not hire anyone over sixty-five. We are continuously battling that. Someday, something ought to be done about it."[4]

Abe also has discovered that some places of business have more flexible, humane, and also complex rules.

"Some of the companies I have found are willing to work with us. Let me give you one example." He paused and searched for a folder on his desk. "Ah, here. For example, I placed Sam Maitland with a company that makes men's ties. When I called the company several weeks later, I found that Sam was not on the tie company's payroll, so I did some further checking and found that Sam is on the payroll of a temporary agency. The tie company pays the agency just the money for Sam's labor. This leaves the agency with the headaches of insurance and workmen's compensation. Why does the tie company do this? Insurance, primarily. If they have on their payroll some employees over sixty-five, then the health insurance rates go up, and the tie company makes less profit. But at least the tie company and some others like them are willing to work with us that way."

In this job, Abe frequently has seen other retired men go through the retirement cycle — leisure - depression - re-engagement — that we encountered earlier.

"Unfortunately, many people lose their pride in themselves when they retire. Many times a retired man comes in here feeling so dejected and so rejected. The first thing I want to do is pick him up off the floor. Make him feel that he can help himself. This is where my counseling background comes in. I find out what he has to sell, so to speak — what he can do. Then I get him to the point where he wants that kind of job. Incidentally, I never ask a man how old he is. Instead, I ask how long he has lived. That gets them thinking POSITIVE."

The phone on Abe's desk rang and he quickly picked it up.

"I've got just the man for you," he said, rummaging through the job applications on his desk. "Ah, here it is. Paul Scola, age sixty-seven. He was the manager of a laundry but he has a heart condition and can't stand the pressure there anymore. Yes," he answered into the phone, "a messenger for your law company sounds ideal; his doctor wants him to walk. O.K., I'll call him. Thanks a lot."

Abe feels that the transition from one kind of job to another is not difficult for most of the people he places.

"The type of job that we get them are types of jobs that can be done by people of normal intelligence without any special type of background."

The change in earning ability is another transition that retired people must make. Fortunately, most people are realistic, Abe finds.

"People are reconciled to think that by the time they reach sixty-five, they are not going to be able to earn as much as they did when they were in the prime of their life. The people who come in here feel that they are ready to accept less money. Of course, they want as much as they can get, but they don't expect to earn as much as they did, ten, twenty, or thirty years ago."

Abe Ginsberg, himself, is fortunate in that he has not suffered from self-denigration. One reason is that Abe did not need a late job just to make enough money for survival. He made a profit when he sold his company. Abe has kept intact a strong sense of worth as an individual by finding another meaningful activity.

"It's too bad if someone is driven solely by money. I was never driven entirely by money; otherwise, I wouldn't be here. There were other things that compensated me."

Jenny Swift

Like Abe Ginsberg, Jenny Swift, now seventy, got her new job because of her previous work. Until she reached sixty-five, she had worked as a dormitory director at Tappan College, a large suburban coed school.

"I had worked at Tappan for twenty years, even before my husband died. I was in good health. I knew I could do my job, but I had to retire as soon as I was sixty-five. They wouldn't even let me finish the term."

Despite her soft voice and composed manner, Jenny's anger is still evident. She is against compulsory retirement.

Jenny is a short woman with a trim figure. For the past five years since her retirement, she has been the manager of a senior citizens' apartment complex. She heard of the job through a service club to which she belonged for many years. She is paid through the philanthropic agency that supports and maintains the apartments.

"I am very pleased with my job,'" Jenny states. "The assistant director and I each have a lovely apartment here in the complex. I am supposed to work only forty hours a week. But I live here, so I'm really on 24-hour duty — just like I was in the college dorm," she adds with a smile.

"Part of my job is to have some of the older people into my apartment for meals if they can't cook because they aren't feeling well. I enjoy the companionship of having someone to eat with." Jenny has high praise for the agency that runs her apartment complex.

"The organization hires directors who live in. We can keep an eye on some of the people who need it. Like Mrs. O'Malley in Apartment 5-B. She's blind. Without us here to help her with some things, she would have to live in an institution. But this way she can stay independent in her own apartment. Believe me, that feeling of independence means a lot to her."

That feeling of independence also is important to Jenny.

Bessie Thomas

Bessie Thomas, like Jenny Swift, has a paid job working with older people in a senior citizens' apartment house. Bessie is a small black woman whose eighty-one years have been filled with purposeful activity since early childhood.

"I came from a group of people where you could never say 'I don't know; I don't know how.' Because you would get murdered. My father didn't allow us to say, 'I can't.' If he told you to go out there and cut a load of wood, don't you say, "I can't.' You just go and take the axe and start in. We didn't know what it was to have a rug on the floor. We had to scrub those floors."

Her family's insistence that everyone contribute left an indelible mark on Bessie's attitude and way of life.

"If you have something to keep you going, you live longer. But if you sit down, you die soon. Even your hands die, your mind dies."

Bessie came to her present job through more than fifty years of various volunteer activities, in addition to work experience for pay as a beautician and a caterer. Bessie, now a widow, married young. When her only daughter, with whom she is quite close, was small, Bessie put herself through night school. When her husband, a veteran, was alive, she served as president of the American Legion auxiliary. She also volunteered for seventeen years in her local Veterans' Administration Hospital, where she worked with many elderly bed-ridden veterans. Bessie also always was active in the Pastor's Club at her church and, as her daughter was growing up, was a Girl Scout leader for twenty years.

"I know what it means to work," Bessie says "And I love to get involved with helping people."

After her daughter's marriage and her husband's death, Bessie's interests almost instinctively turned to working with other older people. When her local council on aging was taking a census of the elderly people in her area, Bessie volunteered her services.

"We canvassed door-to-door to find the seniors. People that we thought were gone because we never saw them, we found them by knocking on doors. Some of the houses we went to, there were difficulties because the people refused to open their doors, but we covered five thousand seniors. Imagine that! We knocked on the doors and told them what the council was all about, and tried to find out how many seniors were in the city. We did that for two years; every day we were knocking on doors."

Through one person she met while volunteering, Bessie was offered a part-time job helping seniors at a nursing home.

"Even though some of the work was difficult, I really liked that job. It was a lot like the volunteer work I'd done at the VA hospital years and years ago when my husband was living; but now I looked at it in a different light because I'm older, too."

Bessie was seventy-eight when she left that strenuous job and became a part-time group worker in the apartment building where she lives.

"The housing authority pays me to work part time, but people call me at all hours to help them and to chat. Of course, I can't say no. I'm not working just for the money, although it sure is nice to have. I took this job to try to help the people here; some of them seemed to be so lost.

"When I first came to work," she recalled, "the people living here were all so alone in their apartments all the time. I knew they should get to know each other. I thought they should have a club."

With her many years experience working with people, Bessie knew how to start. "I found all the people by knocking on doors. You can't just put up a notice in the elevator. I had to find the people in their apartments and tell them what the club was all about."

Bessie's enthusiasm and good humor were so contagious that the residents came out of their apartments and into each other's lives.

"We got together. The first thing I asked them to do was please respect each other. I said, 'We aren't all black and we aren't all white or born in America, but we are all here to help each other.'

"We had no money, just this room," she said, motioning around a large community room, "and some chairs and a few tables, but a lot of ideas. I explained to them that we were here to make the club be what it should be for us all and to work together. The first thing I did was to have a dinner. Each member helped buy and fix the food. We invited everyone in the building and charged just fifty cents. Our dinner was such a success. We didn't have enough food because so many people came down. Next time we bought more food and charged everyone 75 cents.

"We also had a Christmas party that was a wonderful success. The members made decorations and cookies. We gave each other little gifts. The best part was the singing."

Bessie went on to explain how she has gotten the group to work cooperatively.

"We have to make the money we need for our own projects. The members worked hard at planning dinners and bazaars and saving money all year, so we got to take three bus rides, all paid for. They decide where they want to go and make most of the arrangements. We've gone to an animal farm, to the beach, and to an amusement park.

"The ones who live here really love this place now and anything you ask them to do they are kind enough to do it. Honey, this house is supposed to be seniors, but this is the youngest group of seniors you ever did see!"

Bessie's commitment to the older people in her apartment building gives her a reason to stay healthy.

"Recently, I had to go into the hospital because I had some shortness of breath. While I was lying in the bed, all I kept saying was, 'Lord, just help me to get out of the bed so that I can get to the bazaar on Saturday. I did get out of bed, too, and the bazaar was a wonderful success. We took in $454. That was after clearing our expenses. The only thing I'm sorry about is that I had to go to the hospital. Medicare is paying an awful lot of money for me."

In an effort to prevent this problem from recurring, Bessie bought herself a humidifier.

"I figured that I had trouble breathing because the air in my building was so dry from the heating system. Now that I know, I can watch it. I sleep with the window open and I have the window open all day. I wasn't getting enough air in my apartment when I kept all the windows closed.

"Because I had felt so bad and had so much trouble breathing, I figured that probably some of the other people in the building did, too. So I went around and asked them, and sure enough, I found six other people who were having similar trouble and arranged for them to get humidifiers. One woman came back and told me that she was grateful that I spoke to her. She would just sit there and wonder, 'What is wrong with me' because she was so dry in the throat."

In another effort to look after the health of the people in her building, Bessie stopped serving so many cookies after the weekly twilight service. "We were all eating too much sweet stuff," she said, "so I thought that this would be a good place to start cutting down."

Her own needs are simple so she likes to use some of the money she earns as a group worker to purchase materials that she makes into gifts.

"I like to knit afghans and shawls, and to make little baskets," she says. "Being busy is much better than just making money. I've worked all my life, but I've never made more than $5,000 a year. Even now, with Social Security and the money from this job, my income is less than that. But that doesn't matter," she says. "Working the way you want to is what's important.

"I know what it means to work. I love it. Whatever I want to do, I do it and I don't want anyone to tell me that I'm doing too much.

"When they tell me I'm doing too much, it kind of hurts me. I don't ever want to hear that again. I don't appreciate it. Because what I do for you, I do it because I want to do it. And there is something that pushes me to do it. Everything that comes to me is always a success."

A strong, independent person with a wonderful ability to give of herself, Bessie is gratified that she was given the opportunity to share her enthusiasm with other older people, and that she has been successful.

"I have really enjoyed my life," she says. "I can't look back on too many sad days and I am happier now than when I was younger."

Elizabeth Green

Elizabeth Green is not so content about her retirement life. Elizabeth, who is now seventy, was an eighth-grade teacher for thirty years and then a school guidance counselor for twelve years until she retired at age sixty-five.

Because of her public school experience, she was able to get a part-time job doing psychological testing for a private school.

"I enjoyed that very, very much," she recalls, "but then the school hired a full-time psychologist and did away with my position and I had nothing."

Elizabeth lives alone, never having married; but she loves and needs people.

"I have always been with people and kept myself as active as possible," she says. "I was one of a family of five. But having them all so far away from me for twenty years, I think the world outside is my family more."

Elizabeth's doctor reinforces her own sense of needing to keep busy.

"He said, 'There's one good thing, Betty, you'll always be healthy. You're always pounding the pavements. I see you wherever I go.'"

Pound the pavements is what she did, after losing her testing job.

"I couldn't get a job in my own field, so I started looking around town. I never thought I'd have trouble finding a job. I went to practically every store in the center of town to see if I could sell or work behind a counter. I tried the bookstores and the drugstores, but at that time they had no openings and they said that when they did have openings, it usually went to members of the family or to high school and college young people who needed jobs.

"I especially wanted a job in a store to get some Social Security quarters to my credit. My job for the public school was covered by a pension, but I don't get any Social Security. And with inflation when I get older, the Social Security, even the minimum, will help a lot.

Betty's search for a job is hampered by her lack of transportation. "I don't have a car, and the buses are infrequent and not dependable. If I had transportation, I could have looked over at the shopping mall for a job."

Betty did find a job, although it is not entirely what she wants. The job came as a result of volunteer work.

"When I was working part-time I also did some volunteering at the hospital and at the Town Hall Senior Center. I served as a hostess. They called me and offered me a job at the center.

Elizabeth likes certains aspects of her job.

"It's only eleven hours a week. I like that. It doesn't tie me down on some days when I want to do other things. Also it's working with people, and I'm not happy unless I'm out of the house."

But she is not completely happy with the job itself because she cannot use her skills and training.

"If you ask me, I'm a glorified housekeeper. I do pretty much all the odds and ends that nobody else does. I usually have the hostessing and the general upkeep of the center.

"There is no one around on Fridays and so I do the dusting and vacuuming and upkeep. I also write cards and letters to people and do all of the buying. So I'm sort of a general custodian of the place. I'm not too pleased about that."

With all her psychology education and teaching experience, Elizabeth resents this kind of job.

"Actually, I should be using my training and not be doing this type of menial work and chores." She would prefer to be a counselor to the people who frequent the senior center. "There is a need here for a friendly person for these older folks to talk to. They don't need to go in for expensive psychiatry."

She thinks that one important function of a senior center has been lost — that of being a place for senior citizens to have someone with whom to talk.

"The center has grown so, there are so many different activities. I almost think that it has grown too business-like. We've lost that contact with people. I think that you can lose the human touch. I think this is where I could be of use. I would just have to be here a lot so the people could come and talk. I don't think it would work if they set up regular hours."

At this stage in her life, Elizabeth feels rejected as a professional person. "I won't stay much longer, I think. I'd like to find some work that's a little different from this and that will let me build up Social Security as this doesn't, being a town job."

But it is unlikely that at her age Elizabeth will be able to find a job in the overcrowded fields of teaching and counseling or that the town will pay her to counsel seniors. She is wise enough to realize that working at this job probably is better for her than staying home alone and waiting for the perfect job.

Helen O'Brien

Unlike Elizabeth, Helen O'Brien is very happy with her job. She is seventy-five and for a year has been the director of a sheltered workshop.[5]

"Before I got married, I worked in a grocery store. Then I got married and had four kids. I stayed home and cleaned and worked until my husband died. Then I had to get out of the house, somehow. My kids were all older by then. So I started volunteering. I volunteered to take care of sick people.

"I was the organizer. I could see who needed help and then send someone out to the home. I would also go myself.

"I also kept busy at the Church. I helped the priest a lot. Oh, I could never stay down. Seventy-five years old, the first day of February, but I can't stay home five minutes. I live in a two-family house. One of my daughters lives upstairs. She has five kids. I love those kids, but if I was home they'd be on me every single minute."

Helen has been involved with the workshop since she was sixty-five.

"I volunteered to help the director. I collected money at the lunch bar. Then I worked up to a paid job. I was the assistant director for two years and now I direct the place."

Like Bessie, Helen's job is supposed to be part time.

"I'm supposed to work only four hours a day. But I never rush home if there is something to be done.

"I'll work as long as I can. I'll die in this office chair. I'll work as long as they need and want me. I've been with them so long that I guess they just can't get rid of me."

Like many women, she outlived her job as wife and mother at an age when she still had great energy and a need to contribute. Unlike some older women whose lives are empty when their husband dies, Helen was able to find a niche. Many other older women who try to re-engage experience rejection and end up with despair and illness caused by their loss of a valued role. Like Helen, they need opportunities to give.

Bud Cahill

Bud Cahill is seventy-three. He gets up early every morning at six for his first job: a neighbor pays Bud to drive him to work. Then Bud goes to his own morning job in the legal department of his city's Council of Elders. He is paid a small stipend provided by a national senior citizens' organization.

Bud has been a hotel owner, a gas station owner for thirty years, and most recently a cab driver. After ten years of driving a cab, he retired.

"I didn't decide I should retire," he says emphatically, "my wife did. There were too many killings. It was too dangerous. And besides, I hadn't been feeling too well working nights. She said to me, 'I don't want you to drive a cab any more,' and that's how I left."

Bud also had been active with senior citizens. "While I was still a cabby, I belonged to a senior men's group. When I retired, an officer in the group sponsored me for the legal aid job. He knows I've had a little college and that I like to work with people."

Bud is lean and restless. His clothes fit very loosely and his hands are always moving.

"The legal aid department as a whole tries to improve services to the elderly. They try to change the laws that effect and will raise the day-to-day living standard for senior citizens. They are working on a guaranteed minimum income for seniors and are working on getting more police protection in public housing. That issue is quite important, for in many projects for the elderly, there is a great deal of vandalism against old people. My job is to help handle various incidents. If a building doesn't have electricity, I try to do something about it. If a building is rat infested, we have it cleaned out or condemned. Some of the places around here are not fit for human habitation," Bud says emphatically.

It is clear that Bud Cahill enjoys his job. He feels that he is working to help other elderly people who are not as well off as he is. He also enjoys learning new things in his old age. "It's nice to graduate from a cabby to an almost lawyer."

Charlies Jones

"I'm not supposed to get into the rocking chair, am I?" That is how Charlie Jones, at age seventy-five, views retirement.

Charlie is a large man with a booming voice. He was a truck driver for a bakery until he was sixty-eight.

"I didn't have to retire at sixty-five," he explains, "because my boss was the only owner of the bakery. He let drivers stay as long as they could drive the trucks. Boy, I tell you, I felt sorry for some of my pals other places. As soon as they was sixty-five, out they went. And there they were, with nothing to do, and not really any different, just one day older."

Charlie knew when it was time for him to retire; his body told him so. When he was sixty-eight, he had a frightening experience.

"One hot afternoon, I was drivin' and started to sweat real bad and then felt weak and kinda dizzy. When I got to one stop to deliver some rolls, I could hardly stand up. Someone called my boss and a substitute finished my route. An ambulance took me to the hospital. The doctors said that I was dehydrated. I had lost all the sodium in my body. When I got out of the hospital, I told my boss I was quitting. I said to myself, 'Charlie, this is the handwriting on the wall. I'm not driving anymore.' And that's how I left. If I'm going to go I'm going to go; but while I'm here, I'm going to enjoy myself while I can."

Charlie enjoys himself by keeping busy. "I can't just sit," he says. "I walk a lot, sometimes four or maybe five miles a day. I play pool. I have a lot of friends and sometimes we just get together and just shoot the breeze. We go to the track and the dog races. The wife and I like to go dancin', too. I'm a great dancer!" he adds.

Charlie also belongs to a senior men's group. One man he met in the group told him about a job opening and now Charlie is a handyman in a fraternal home for the aged.

"I enjoy it," he says. "It gives me something to do. I go

around and help the people who have to live there, fixin' radiators and sinks and stuff. I talk to the people, too. Some are real lonely. Even though I'm reachin' the age of seventy-five, there are a lot of people worse off than I am, and younger, too. I like to cheer them up. It's a real pleasure and an eye-opener to get out. I always mingle with people, you know, socialize, and I have a little private money now to play the ponies."

An important aspect of Charlie's job and of his many activities is the feeling of masculine independence as well as usefulness he gets. He expresses that strong feeling clearly when he talks about his wife.

"I tell her I'm going out — that's it. Why should she know what I'm doing? Do you think she should know everything that I do in the course of a day? I didn't tell her when I was younger, so why should I tell her now? It's the same with my two kids. It's none of their business what I do with my time or money."

For Charlie, 'sitting home' would mean the loss of valued independence and autonomy. He has seen many older men gradually lose their zest when they retire. Charlie is determined that this will not happen to him. He keeps busy and he keeps his own private sphere. He does not have to try to keep busy by moving into his wife's tasks. Although some retired couples enjoy sharing household tasks and shopping after retirement, many bluecollar workers like Charlie have a strong sense of 'woman's work' and 'man's work' and take pride in staying out of the kitchen and in a 'man's role.' Most senior centers are inhabited largely by women and the Charlies of the world feel uncomfortable in such places.

Conclusion

Despite their diverse backgrounds (from cab driver to teacher, from hairdresser to company owner), the people whose stories were told here share a fundamental love of people and activity. Their abilities to work with people in the jobs described came from a lifetime of human interactions and a disposition to help others. Human relations skills came from their own experience.

Betty Green was disappointed only with the nature of her job — the housekeeping chores that were beneath her professional capabilities. She liked working with other older people and had thought of a way to create a job for herself that would benefit them. She cleaned the center in preference to staying home and mourning the loss of professional opportunities.

Jenny Swift expressed another note of disappointment.

"Why did I have to retire from the college? I could still do the work."

Should Jenny and capable people like her have to retire to make way for 'young people who need jobs'? Society now is re-thinking this issue, and legislation has been passed extending to seventy the age of involuntary retirement for most people. However, there are now many older people already retired who are interested in re-engaging.

Recall how the people in this chapter found their second careers. Abe Ginsberg deliberately looked for work in employment and counseling because he knew that he was good in these two areas. He was interested in retirees because he himself had been retired for a brief time, without much happiness. His background and experience in business helped him find a good job.

Jenny Swift found her job in the Senior Citizens' apartment house through a service organization to which she belonged. Like Abe, her previous job experience qualified her to handle the job as apartment manager.

Other people found their new jobs working with seniors through their involvement in senior citizens' groups to which they belonged or in which they volunteered their services and time. Unlike Abe and Jenny, their new careers were unlike their old paid jobs, even though several had done similar volunteer work. All of the people in this chapter found their jobs by word of mouth. Other people may not be so lucky. More systematic ways, such as clearing houses or newsletters, and preferential treatment, need to be provided for seniors who would like second careers serving other older persons. Senior services should have younger persons involved. However, an interesting question arises: In the future, will jobs working with older people continue to be available as second careers for older people, or will these jobs become professionalized out of existence?

Today, growing old is more than just a physical process. It has become gerontology — a scientific study of the aging process. Gerontology has become a double-edged sword.

Young people are going to college and graduate schools to learn about aging and to get credentials for working with older people. This trend is good; knowledge and training are important. But these young people will soon need jobs. What will happen to the older people themselves? Most have no formal education in gerontology; in fact, only 7 percent of people now over age sixty-five are college graduates. They have instead the background and experiences of sixty-five years and more of living and working. It seems ironic to think that in trying to help older people, many professional people inadvertently hurt them by taking jobs away from them.

This, of course, does not have to happen. We believe that as programs for elders increase in response to the needs of this rapidly growing age group, certain jobs in all-new programs should be specifically given to capable older people. These people can be trained for the jobs in educational institutions and on the job itself. Perhaps it is time to add to recreational and intellectual courses for seniors, courses in working with elders that could be given at many local community colleges. These wise adults know first-hand the problems of retiring from work and of aging. They need the feeling of self-worth that comes with working and they can provide valuable skills and commitment. And most people are willing to work part-time and for small pay. Even that small amount of pay can add to life's comfort and satisfaction.

Suggestions

Working with other elderly people can be rewarding, both for you and for them. If this kind of job sparks your interest, you can begin by inquiring about what courses on working with the aged are offered in local adult education programs and colleges. Through these courses you may meet people who can give you ideas on where in your area to work. Many schools give free tuition to people over age sixty-five.

See what programs in your community are being offered for elder persons. Your state department of elder affairs or your municipal or area department, if one exists, will supply lists. Perhaps you can obtain employment in one of these programs. If you find programs sadly lacking, perhaps you can work with local social workers or churches or other organizations to obtain a grant under the Older Americans Act and start a program. The Older Americans Act has funding for various programs. Further information may be obtained from your state office of the federal Administration of Aging or from the U.S. Department of Health, Education and Welfare Administration on Aging, Washington, D.C. 20201. An overview of A.O.A. and its funding programs under the Older American Acts is provided by fact sheet number 76-20084 available free from the National Clearinghouse on Aging, Administration on Aging, U.S. Department of Health, Education and Welfare, Washington, D.C. 20201. You also can get information from your area agency on aging; agencies exist in each of the fifty states, and also in the District of Columbia, Guam, Puerto Rico, Samoa, the Trust Territories of the Pacific, and the Virgin Islands.

You also can contact private charitable agencies in your community that have programs for the elderly, including homes for the aged. Nursing homes frequently will use older workers, though these jobs often are difficult and low paying. As will be discussed in the next chapter, sheltered workshops are needed. Perhaps you could help start one in your area.

Notes

1. These figures, actual and projected, are from a recent report of the United States Bureau of the Census.
2. For an interesting description of these careers, see the *Occupational Outlook Quarterly,* Fall 1976, the special issue "Working with Older People." This publication is available from the U.S.

Department of Labor, Bureau of Labor Statistics, Washington, D.C. 20212, or at regional offices of the Department of Labor.

3. This attitude is in direct contrast to the many older and younger people who prefer the company of younger people. Their rejection of other older people is their way of denying that they themselves are aging. They also have internalized society's glorification of youth. Hence, we see some older women with brightly dyed or bleached hair wearing fashions more suitable for their adolescent granddaughters and complaining that other old people are senile. (See chapter eight for a manifestation of this phenomenon in the story of Joe Tierney.)

4. This interview with Abe Ginsberg was conducted before the mandatory retirement changes in 1978.

5. For a fuller description of a sheltered workshop, see chapter five.

Chapter Five

The Sheltered Workshop

"Who needs a nagging mother around his neck?"

Many older people do not relish the leisure activities available at senior citizens' centers, even though they may enjoy the atmosphere and companionship. For many people, old and young alike, work is the best recreation. The sheltered workshop provides the important work situation, plus much more, for some needy or depressed men and women who are the least able to find employment in the traditional marketplace. Ordinarily, these lonely elderly people often are considered unemployable because of their age; their lack of skills, experience, and poise; their appearance; or merely because of a lack of energy to sell themselves or a lack of jobs.

But being able to work often counteracts the debilitating depression that can lead to serious mental and physical illness and ultimately even to suicide. In the comfortable, relaxed social atmosphere of a sheltered workshop, these people often derive remarkable benefits from the stimulation, interaction, and income provided by the work situation. They become less dependent on physicians and psychotherapists and more dependent on themselves.

In addition, the many people who need to supplement their Social Security or SSI can put an end to penny-pinching with the income they receive from working. The sheltered workshop provides pleasant companionship, dignity, extra money, and a reason to get up in the morning.

Throughout the United States, fewer than 100,000 people are employed in sheltered workshops for handicapped people of all sorts, including the aged.[1] Thus, the actual number of older people working in sheltered workshops is much smaller. The need for many more such workshops is pressing; many older people who eagerly apply for work in existing workshops must be turned away.

This chapter describes one such workshop for the aged[2] — The Independence Sheltered Workshop,[3] located in a large town that has a sizeable elderly population of diverse ethnic backgrounds and religious affiliations. The Independence Workshop is run by the town's Association for Rehabilitation. The association hires a director and several assistants for the workshop. In addition, two men, both with business backgrounds and contacts, work part time specifically to get jobs and contracts for the workshop. By telephone, letters, and personal visits, these men canvas industry, businesses, and nonprofit organizations (including colleges) in their town and surrounding municipalities looking for suitable tasks that people over age sixty-five can do in the workshop. When the jobs are found, the Association sends a driver to the factory or store to pick up the work and deliver it to the workshop. When the work has been completed, the driver is notified by the workshop leaders and returns the completed job to the factory, often picking up another project at the same time.

One standing job that the workshop members perform is sewing bra straps. The workshop possesses several sewing machines that qualified older women use. Other jobs include stapling raffle tickets for a large company to use in a promotion and collating and stapling booklets for a local college to use during its reunion week. One small machine shop asked the workers to separate thin wires with hooks from thin wires without hooks.

The Independence Sheltered Workshop is housed in one large room of a senior citizen's apartment house. Because the apartment building is owned and run by the town, the rent charged to the Association is minimal. The workshop is in a large, sunny room on the first floor of the building. The Indian print drapes on the large windows add color to the room, whose walls are painted yellow. Most of the room is taken up by six long tables, which are surrounded by a melange of folding chairs. Several comfortable armchairs and rockers line one wall, and the table nearest the door holds the workshop's coffee maker. Near the sink are the supervisors' desks and chairs.

Arlene, the workshop director, is a woman in her mid-fifties. She and her two coworkers, also middle-aged women, are dedicated to the workshop and have tremendous enthusiasm and love for the project and the people in it.

Arlene, who enjoys talking with people about themselves, relates how she became employed at the workshop.

"When I heard about their starting this place, I thought it was a terrific idea to help older people get out into the work world and feel useful again. I needed something to do also, as my kids are all grown up. I've been here for eight years already, since the place opened. I love it!"

Arlene has accumulated much knowledge about the workshop and about elderly people in her stint as director.

"A lot of people who work here," she explains, "were referred by mental health staff doctors who had them as patients or by psychiatric social workers. Others heard about the workshop from friends or neighbors. We have a long waiting list of people who would love to work here, but we don't have the spaces, unfortunately."

One important aspect of the workshop is that it is just that — a Workshop. The older people are paid for the work they do. Each worker is paid according to how well he or she performs the various tasks. Sheltered workshops also may receive waivers from the minimum wage regulations in order to employ people who could not earn minimum wages.

Arlene mentions that the wages paid must be small because profits are small and "so as to avoid interfering with their Social Security benefits." Yet, for many of the workers, this small sum can mean a better apartment, good nutrition, or occasional money for recreation. She hastens to add, however, that the actual amount of money earned is not the important aspect of the workshop for most of the people; it is that they are worth something. Also, the work itself, amidst the companionship of other older people, is therapy and an antidote to isolation and self-denigration. The older people are once again back in the work setting and feel that they are again contributing to society.

This productive feeling combined with the close friendships that develop give the workshop a strong sense of community and vitality. The workshop day starts at 8:45 AM, but most of the workers arrive by 8:00 or 8:15, even in rain or snow. The thirty or so people present, mostly women, are all working and chatting at the same time. Their faces are animated, their eyes bright with interest. Twenty-seven people regularly attend the Independence Workshop — twenty-four women and three men. The three men are alone in life. One man was divorced and the other two had never married.

Of the women at the workshop, two have husbands still living; the other twenty-two women are alone. Five had never married and the remaining seventeen are widows. It is interesting to note that there are no divorced women and no widowers at the workshop, illustrating the fact that a higher percentage of women live to age sixty-five and older. Simply put, in American society today, women over age sixty-five outnumber men over sixty-five and widows predominate.[4]

Most of the workers are attractively dressed in clothes that suggest any other work setting. The women wear neat dresses, skirts and blouses, and even pant suits. Some hairdos are beauty shop styles. Each woman pays close attention to what the others are wearing. They are quick to spot a new dress, piece of jewelry, or hairdo and to offer a compliment. Arlene and her assistants also receive comments on how they look.

"Once I made the mistake of wearing the same dress two days running," recounts Arlene, "and three of the ladies had something to say to show that they noticed. Now I'm very careful about how I dress."

Most of the women wear some makeup, usually lipstick and face powder, and several pieces of jewelry. The grandmothers among them are partial to gold charm bracelets and necklaces that boast small silhouettes of grandchildren.

The men also take pride in their appearance. One man wears tan sport slacks and a long-sleeved flannel plaid shirt. The other man, who is tall and extremely thin, wears a black dinner jacket, a light green shirt, and brown corduroy trousers. His clothes are old but obviously well cared for.

After saying good morning and making a personal remark or two to each worker and starting them on the day's task, Arlene and her assistants do some paper work and then prepare for the morning ritural: the ten o'clock coffee break. They plug in the coffee pot, set out the cups, milk and sugar, and arrange on a china platter any cookies or bakery products that have been donated that day by a worker who is having a birthday or celebrating a happy family occasion.

"Last week," says Arlene, "Mrs. Berkowitz brought in homemade apple strudel. She had just received a letter from her son in England saying that he and his family were coming to visit next month. The pastry was her way of having us all join in her happiness."

Food is an important aspect of the workshop. The people like to spend part of their earnings on what they call "goodies" for all to enjoy. It is their way of having their friends and coworkers share part of their lives and happiness; this sharing enhances their self-worth. Too many older people feel frustrated because they can no longer give to anyone else.

Psychologically, the link between food and happiness is forged early in most people's lives, usually in childhood when mother soothes hurt feelings or a scraped knee with milk and homemade cookies. Most of the women at the workshop, now widowed, have spent many years as full-time homemakers. To these exnurterers, food holds a special importance. When they see people enjoying a homemade apple pie, or even a hand-picked bakery apple pie, they feel satisfied, loved, and needed; by feeding other people, they have been important to those others.

In their apartments alone, many of the workers do not eat nutritious, appetizing meals because there is no one else for whom to prepare a meal or with whom to eat. Some workers often admit they do not bother to eat at all when they are at home alone. But when they get together, they enjoy the food and each other's company. Good food is a symbol of good company and good times.[5]

The coffee break thus is a highlight of each workshop day.

"I don't have to ring any bells or watch the clocks at coffee time," Arlene says. "They come get their coffee at different times, there's never a rush, and they're very good about sharing the goodies. If they see that one person is still working, they're sure to save her a pastry. After about fifteen minutes, they all go back to work and we clean up."

The workshop day lasts until noon, "But it's usually close to one o'clock before I can lock the place up," Arlene says.

"Some of the people hate to leave, especially on Friday or before a holiday when the workshop is closed. They are very slow about putting everything away and getting on their coats"

For many of the workers, the Independence Workshop is their only contact with other people. They live alone, in small apartments, in a room in someone else's home, or in rooming houses. These people depend on the workshop and look forward to going every Monday through Friday morning. In the cold weather, when the buses never seem to run, many of the workers spend their money on cab fare, just so they can get to the workshop.[6]

Gussie Berkowitz

Gussie Berkowitz, at age eighty-four, is one of the oldest workers at the Independence Workshop.

"I have worked here for three years, and I plan to be here as long as my physical condition holds up. I'm not getting any younger, you know," she adds, with a wide smile.

Mrs. Berkowitz — "Call me Gussie," she insists; "it's easier" — is one of the several people who work at the workshop for reasons more intangible than money.

"The money I get for the workshop does help," Gussie admits. "It helps supplement my Social Security and it is welcome." But she quickly adds, "We don't work just for financial reasons. The few dollars that we get at the end of the week is ten times its value. It's what you've done yourself that amounts to something."

Companionship and a congenial place to go to avoid staying home alone all the time also are Gussie's reasons for appreciating the workshop. She is sensitive enough to realize exactly what the workshop does for her and articulate enough to express her feelings, both about the workshop and about growing old.

"You feel like a person again when you have something to do. The problem of old people not knowing what to do with themselves is not funny. I feel the workshop lays a foundation for the day. Really, what old person gets out of bed and is raring to go? Not too many of us! But the workshop gives us a reason to get up and get dressed."

This comment was made by many of the workshop people who depend on it for a reason to keep going. After holidays, when the workshop has been closed, many of the workers admit that they didn't bother getting dressed all day because they had no place to go.

"The workshop really is miraculous, I think," Gussie continues. "The companionship is very special, for one cannot help but feel lonely at times."

Gussie feels sorry for the older people who think that going to the workshop will be demeaning. "Many of the people living in this housing unit do not go to the workshop. Some of them feel above that work. They think that it's beneath them. They pity us; they think that we only go for material reasons. But there are so many other reasons that bring us to the workshop."

But Gussie also remembers that at first she hesitated to go to the workshop. "I didn't know very much about it. And I'm fundamentally a timid person in a new situation. I guess many people are. But my daughter-in-law kept asking, 'haven't you tried the workshop yet?' She said this on several occasions, so finally I went over, and I took to it right away."

Gussie's mention of her daughter-in-law's support underscores the important point that family support toward working after retirement is important to older people. Perhaps the people Gussie mentioned who look down on the Independent Workshop do not have family support that can help them more willingly accept new work situations.

Gussie "took to the workshop right away" because she is an outgoing woman who thrives on work and companionship.

Gussie's husband was a pharmacist. She helped in the

family drug store while her only son was growing up. After her husband died, when she was only fifty-four, she continued to work.

"I worked downtown in a department store for many years in the ladies' wear department. Then when I retired, I still worked. I took care of children while their parents went on vacation. I also took care of some elderly people while their children went on vacation. That's when it hit me. These old people who stayed alone all day had nothing to do, nothing to live for. Maybe's that's one reason I think the workshop is a great place for older people who can still get around."

After her husband died, Gussie went to live with her married son and his young family. "But I wanted to be self-sufficient. I always worked. I never wanted my children to support me. I think the things you earn yourself are of more value to you."

Gussie lived with her son for twenty years, but then decided she needed more of her own life. "After staying with some of the older people who lived with their families, I decided I didn't want to be a burden to my own family. And thank God I could still work and get around, so I found a little place of my own. I call it my little palace." She has a small, tidy apartment in a low-income complex for the elderly. "I have several friends who live in the same complex, but after being in the workshop all morning, I find that the company tires me more than being alone. I love to sit home alone and listen to the radio. With the radio on and the delightful music, I find that the hours fly by."

Rebecca Franklin

Rebecca Franklin is a striking woman. She wears her long, graying hair pulled tight into a bun at the nape of her neck. Her eyes are a dark blue. A thin gold wedding band and large cameo brooch pinned to the collar of her well-tailored pant suit are her only adornments. Rebecca is seventy-two, and until two years, ago she had been a business woman.

"After high school, I went to business school. That was very unusual in those days," she adds. "After I graduated, I went to work in the office of a small laundry and the next year I married the boss! My husband and I ran the laundry until he died, when I was sixty-three. We did very well, too. We managed to put our three children through college, including one through law school. But then everyone starting using laundromats. After George died, it just seemed natural to me to keep on working but the laundry business, as I said, went way down and I had to give that up. But it was awful being without something to do. I kept getting nervous. My doctor sent me here.

"It's funny to think that I'm now on this side of the fence," she commented about her present work. "When I owned the laundry, I was the boss."

Because her background is different from most of the people at the workshop, Rebecca reacts to it first as a business person rather than as another worker. Her praise of the workshop, and especially for its leaders, is unqualified.

"I think the most important thing to say is that the workshop would not be nearly as successful without these leaders. They are very capable, sympathetic people and they know how to understand elderly people's problems. They have to know so much about business. We are doing this for the companionship. They don't have to make a profit on things like that. We all understand we have to do the best we can to keep the quality up. I think it's such a marvelous program.

"The pay varies according to your ability. They start everyone at the very lowest and some people don't get very much above that. But each person is considered as somebody who accomplishes something and it gives them a sense of pride. We don't start working until 8:45 and here it is only half past eight and they're here already and they're working. Some of these people have to to walk about three-quarters of a mile. Not too many of them, but some do. They have to cross main streets and everything, which isn't too easy for elderly people."

Rebecca goes on to relate how a typical day procedes.

"We have a coffee break at 10:00. They don't ring a bell. They just call coffee and people continue working to finish something if they want. They walk around and talk to friends. It's usually not more than a quarter of an hour and every one is back working. There is not a bell to limit you. As I say, it has so much to do with the leaders. It would be difficult to find people like them for other places like this. Arlene, she knows just how to get people to work. She has had business experience in the past."

Rebecca herself admits that she enjoys the workshop for three important reasons: companionship, money, and watching the goings on at Independence.

"I've stayed on here becaue I've made a little extra money.

"Now that rents are going up and food is going up, I find that the money comes in handy. I am trying to have the work here pay for my food for the week. It's interesting how I have cut down on some food and luxuries and things that aren't needed. I don't always keep to it because sometimes I eat out, but I find that the money I get here comes in handy. I know that many women here depend on their wages," she observes. "A lot of them find it a lot easier to have that little bit what with rent going up and food going up. Some live in subsidized housing and so they're helped a lot in their rent. Take Mrs. Sweet, for example," she says, discreetly inclining her head toward a slim, pale woman with wisps of gray hair. "They call her 'Honey' and she gets the biggest kick out of that. Now *she* needs the money she makes. She's been here for four years. Poor soul, she has no family; her husband died and they never had any children. She needs the friendship she finds here as much as the money."

As Rebecca pointed out, her own doctor sent her to the workshop because of her nerves. She could not cope with idleness after the laundry was gone. At the workshop, she functions well and nothing escapes her.

"I do enjoy watching how a thing like this affects people, how it affects me. I almost look at this as an observer rather than as a worker, even though I work here, too."

Her way of thinking allows her to separate herself from her surroundings and then to offer valuable comments on what she observes about the other workers.

"You see how they come here in the morning. They're all dressed and neat and some of them mention taking a bath in the morning before they come in. As I say, this keeps them up and some of them when they first come are real quiet. Some are a little mentally disturbed. Some don't know how to meet people. Some aren't the sociable type. After living alone, they don't know how to mingle with people. But before you know it, you see them sitting at the table and chatting away about little things, some of the personal things about their grandchildren and they take pictures out to show them. They liven up. And they enter into the conversations. It's wonderful for them."

Rebecca feels that the relaxed and easy-going feeling in the workshop contributes to the workers' happiness and love for the place, including her own.

"This is a lovely environment here. Yesterday we had a special anniversary party. Oh, it was delightful. I don't know if a lot of them went home and slept all day because we had so much to eat. Wonderful appetizers and cakes. It's a kind of relaxed atmosphere. If you have a dentist appointment or something like that, they let you off. And if you're only gone for an hour or so, they don't dock you. They never make any fuss about it. When I first came here, I said that I'd like to come only a few days a week because sometimes things came up. The leader said it would be all right. I do find occasional things come up. You don't feel that you're going to get fired if you stay out a day. These people always make arrangements if they're not going to be here. If they're ill or something, they call up in the morning. Like yesterday, two people could not even come for the party. They must be very ill because people hardly ever stay out," she says with a note of concern in her voice.

Once hired, each worker is allowed to work at his or her own pace and ability and the work is assigned according to ability.

"There are certain kinds of work that are given to the ones who are not quite capable to do harder or more skilled work. They get to sit at the same table. They are on a kind of plane. If you put a few fast ones at the table, sometimes it will make the rest work a little faster. One keeps the other moving at a good pace. Sometimes it makes some of the slower ones go faster in an easy way. And then of course you have a few people who use the sewing machines. The ones on the machines are marvelous."

In some ways, Rebecca sees herself as a leader at the workshop, both because of her business experience and also because she is younger and more mobile than many of the other workers. At seventy-two, she still owns and drives a car.

"I sometimes take some of the people out for rides to some of the shopping centers or for a scenic drive. We were thinking of going on a long ride, but I told them we would have to miss a morning because by the time we get out of work and drive, it would be too dark when we got home. Some of them, including 'Honey' Sweet, said that they could not go because they couldn't afford to miss a day."

Rebecca was the only person interviewed to mention that she sensed a difference between herself and the other workers.

"Although I'm seventy-two, I have always had a young feeling. I have always been interested in younger people and doing things with younger people. Sometimes when I'm with a group of elderly people, I feel out of place and then I laugh at myself."

Nelly McMinn

Nelly McMinn is seventy-seven.

"I taught second and third grades in this town for nearly forty years. I'm now seventy-seven," she adds, "and I have been coming to the workshop for 3½ years.

"One afternoon while I was in the market near my apartment, I ran into a woman I used to know when I taught school. She had been a seventh-grade teacher at the junior high school. We talked about the old days and about some of the students we both had known and how well many of them had turned out. Then she told me about how she was working at the workshop and how nice the people were and how nice it was to have a special place to go. Unfortunately, my friend no longer comes. Her arthritis is so bad that she has difficulty moving. But I am grateful to her for introducing me to the workshop.

"Most of us here heard about the Workshop from friends or from doctors. Priscilla Powers, the plumpish woman with the pink sweater around her shoulders, has a wonderful story about how she came here. Pris is seventy-seven and lives alone. Her husband died years ago, and, poor things, they never had any children. Four years ago she got hit by a car. After she got out of the hospital, she went to a nursing home. When she got home, she had to have therapy. Finally, her orthopedic doctor told her that she should come to the workshop and get paid instead of paying for a lot of fancy therapy. She loves it now because it gives her some place to go. She used to come in a cab but she now manages to take the bus, canes and all; she has real courage."

Nelly is one of the seven people at the workshop who never married. She has no brothers or sisters or other family living and she lives alone. Thus, more than some members, she depends on the Workshop for social contacts.

"Priscilla says it even better than I do. Just the other day, we were talking about being alone. She thinks loneliness is like an illness. She said to me, 'When you are first alone, there are great pains but after a while, the pain subsides. But you have to help yourself.' I say, big girls don't cry. You can't just sit and fold your hands and say I don't want to play anymore with this lousy life. After you swallow the pill of loneliness you do feel better. And it's a big pill to swallow. But the workshop has been a great help. That's why I'm always talking about the workshop."

Nelly feels fortunate that for the past year she has lived in the senior citizen apartment house where the workshop is located.

"All I have to do is go downstairs. Thank God I still am able to walk without any serious problems. I can walk to the store and I feel exercise is good for me. Some people do not realize it, but walking is very healthy for elderly people."

But Nelly knows what limits to put on herself.

"I used to belong to a lot of organizations and clubs, especially when I was teaching, and just after I retired. But I can no longer do that. I would be interested, as I love to be with all kinds of different people, but I have to limit myself in what I can do. It's enough to go down everyday to the workshop. I find that by the time I come back upstairs I have had enough socializing and activity for the day. But without the workshop, many of us would never get out at all.

"We do different things. The ladies in charge give us things which don't require keen eyesight which at this age we don't all have. Others can use the sewing machines. If they had experience using one before, they are quite adept. Most of us can do work with our hands. I never learned to use a sewing machine, but thank God my fingers can still move pretty well and my eyesight is still good with my glasses on so I can do a lot of close work that some of the others can't."

Because of her long experience as a teacher and her years of living alone without any family, Nelly is one of the workshop's most independent people. And conversely, because she has no family, she relies on the workshop for social contacts more than many of the other members who have their children for additional interaction and moral support.

Summary

For the older people in this chapter, the Independence Sheltered Workshop is important for two reasons: companionship and a sense of self-worth. It is the sense of family, of belonging somewhere and to someone, that makes the Independence Workshop so special to Gussie, Rebecca, Nelly, and others.

Most of the workers who regularly attend the workshop are alone in life. Many are widows or widowers or have never married. Some, like Gussie, have children who live and work far away. Others have no children.

But the workshop is much more than a social club that could serve the same function and offer the same companionship. As an employer, the workshop gives these older people tasks within their abilities to perform for pay in a congenial setting. The elderly people know that they are working for real companies that need the work done, that they are not being given 'pretend' tasks to do. This knowldge, plus the money at the end of each week, add to each worker's pride in self and in his or her ability to continue to be a contributing member of society.

Arlene explains what she feels is the major value of the workshop.

"Look, we are all going to get old some day. Society has a tendency to cast aside the old. Here, we seek to build up their morale and make them feel that life is worth living. You have to realize there is a big difference between the senior citizens who are working here and those who can get jobs and are out working in industry. They aren't thrown into the cold hard world with people who don't care about them."

The mutual caring and support that the sheltered workshop engenders is perhaps the most important feature. The work done is only one aspect that helps older people to realize that others care. The continued contact with other people in similar situations reassures the older people that their anxieties, difficulties, and problems are not unique but rather are shared by other people who also manage to survive.

Gussie Berkowitz recounted an exchange she had with a woman new to the workshop. "One day we were drinking our coffee and one of my friends came over and said, 'You are all going to have to get used to me; I am getting cranky in my old age.' So I said to her, "So, aren't we all, but we don't have to go around talking about it. I don't feel sorry for myself and neither should you. So we're getting old. Everyone does at some point in their life.'"

Several years at the workshop and prolonged contact with other people with similar problems have given Gussie a larger outlook on life and an acceptance of what her life brings her. What the Independence Workshop has proven is that given a place to meet on a regular basis and some meaninfgul work to do, seniors can do the work and at the same time can help each other and themselves.[7]

Other small experiments in organizing groups of senior citizens to perform a task reinforce this conclusion. Recently, a large philanthropic home for the elderly, in an economy move, asked some of its more able residents to fold and staple the home's newsletter, sent monthly to families and supporters. When asked to volunteer, the first response of most of the older people was negative — they did not feel up to it and did not want to change the passive existence that they had settled into. In short, they were reluctant to extend themselves to try anything new.

Finally, a crew was gathered, instructed in the folding and stapling procedures, and spent several mornings working together on the project. "It was remarkable to see," an executive commented, "how people who had spent their time dozing in front of the television suddenly came alive. They organized the project themselves," he continued. "After being told what had to be done, they decided how the material would be passed down the line, who would staple it, and who would fold it.

"The problem and at the same time an encouraging note, however, was that when the newsletter was done, these residents came around to our office begging us to give them some more work to do. They said that they had such a good time that they didn't want to wait a month for the next newsletter. It was amazing to see that in the short time of four mornings together these six people had suddenly become a special group with common interests and needs. The unfortunate part is that we were not set up to give them more work."

Another similar occurence was related by a recreational therapist at a nursing home. She decided to have the patients help bake and frost cupcakes for an upcoming party. Many women who had run their own homes, and some men, too, were delighted to have a chance to get back into a kitchen. They all had a wonderful time baking and frosting and talking together. For them, the party took on a special meaning.

But the inspector from the Department of Health learned of the project and told the therapist that the town's sanitation rules prohibited such activity. A patient was not allowed to frost any cupcake except the ones that he or she would consume.

With a little organization, some contact with and cooperation from the business community, and some committed leadership, more facilities could develop workshops on their premises for their own residents.

In addition, some senior citizens also could organize and develop sheltered workshops within their own communities.

To accomplish this, however, business, industry, and public service organizations must make a commitment to providing tasks for such workshops. Before this commitment can be made on a large scale, businesses and communities and all citizens must be made aware of what a sheltered workshop is and what it can do. Although this will raise hopes when spaces are not available, continued publicity for thriving workshops, such as newspaper articles and television spots, as well as access to information about them, are musts. Religious and charitable organizations have started some successful sheltered workshops. For the past seven years, a workshop in Chelsea, Mass., has operated under the sponsorship of the Associated Jewish Community Centers of Greater Boston. Now it also is possible to get sheltered workshops funded under Title V of the Older Americans Act, administered by the federal government's Administration on Aging.[8]

Some of the best publicity comes from the workers themselves. One lively eighty-eight-year-old widow spoke at length about what the workshop means to her: "This is the happiest I've been in five years. Some people I know in their seventy's would not come here. They think the work is menial and would not want to waste their time. I don't think that at all. Where else could I sit around, work and talk? Not many people will pay you to talk! I've met lots of people here. We all have a lot in common, so I enjoy talking. You know, it would surprise some of my friends, we have interesting conversations. With so many people from all walks of life, we have a varied group and it makes for interesting discussions.

"Working here gives us something to look forward to every day. The four hours is the best part of the day. They should have more places like this for senior citizens. It makes us feel useful to society. What we do is simple and isn't much, but still it is important to us."

Another possible avenue for publicity is to give some young people first-hand experience with what happens at a workshop. For field work in sociology, one student, Pat Kramer, was given a job at the Indendence Workshop. Her presence added another dimension to the worker's lives; she became an instant granddaughter to many of the people who loved to fuss over her and offer free advice. Conversely, all that Pat saw and learned has done a lot to make the workshop better known.

On another level, high school students also can learn about older people in general and workshops in particular by visiting a sheltered workshop and talking in class and with their parents about what they have seen.

One woman at the Independence Workshop relates what happened when a group of high school students came to observe: "They thought we were mentally retarded or disturbed. You could hear some whisper, 'They're not so bad; they're pretty good for retarded.' I suppose that when kids hear 'workshop for the aged' they naturally associate it with sickness. We were doing what would seem to them to be meaningless tasks. What they probably did not realize is that this is what keeps us from being disturbed. I'd go crazy if I wasn't here, or if I did not have some work to do during the day. I'm busy and I have a grand time. The best time of the day is when I'm here. It's wonderful, especially for people with no family. I don't like to bother the children. Now I keep myself so busy. Who needs a nagging mother around his neck?"

To the casual observer, the workshop seems to be a group of congenial, outgoing and even fun-loving people. In a sense, their workshop activities serve as therapy that helps them re-engage in life.

The physical work itself does not provide the therapy; rather, the therapy occurs in being given a chance to do the work, which leads to the feeling of again being a useful, contributing member of a work-oriented society. The work thus is therapy in an indirect but nonetheless very important sense.

The work, and with it the workshop setting, become the core around which new friendships are made, a community develops, and self-confidence replaces loneliness and despair.

Notes

1. Unfortunately, the aged are included here under the general term "handicapped." This figure is based on an estimate appearing in the *Socioeconomic Newsletter* of the Institute for Socioeconomic Studies, White Plains, New York. Sept. 1977.
2. For their extensive help on obtaining the material, the author offers her special thanks to Ellen Friedman, her research assistant, and to Patricia Ann Kramer, who wrote her senior distinction thesis for Boston University on the Independence Workshop.
3. Like the names of all of the people in this book, the Independence Workshop is not the real name of the workshop reported here.
4. For a more complete breakdown of the statistics on the number of men and women who live to age sixty-five and longer, see Part II of this book, "Re-marriage," chapter eight.
5. When seen in this light, the valuable hot lunch program provided seniors under Title VII of the Older Americans Act assumes even greater importance.
6. The original study of the workshop included in-depth studies of seven female workers. But because their enthusiastic comments often echo each other and because many of their living arrangements and family situations are the same, we have illustrated here three women. As you read their stories, however, note the comments of their workshop friends.
7. For further examples of how senior citizens can build their own "communities," see: Jennie Keith Ross, *Old People, New Lives: Community Creation in a Retirement Residence.* Englewood Cliffs, N.J.: Prentice-Hall, Inc., 1975; and Ruth Harriet Jacobs, "The Friendship Club," *The Gerontologist,* winter 1969.
8. You can write to the Administration on Aging at the Department of Health, Education and Welfare, Washington, D.C. 20201. A book on grants available for elderly programs can be ordered from Adelphi University Center on Aging, Garden City, N.Y. 11530. Also, further information about sheltered workshops can be obtained from the Rehabilitation Division of the United States Government, Department of Labor, in your area.

Chapter Six

People Unable To Get Work

"There you have depression upon depression."

Not all retired elderly people who want to work are as fortunate as those in chapters two through five. Many older people lose their jobs before they reach age sixty-five. Although they never formally retire, they soon discover that they cannot find work. Employers often prefer to give what jobs they have to younger people who may be less expensive to hire and who have longer futures in which to be productive.

It also is true that there are not enough jobs for all Americans, especially older men and women. Added to the tight job market are reasons that make it even more difficult for elderly people to find jobs. In this study, we encountered many people over sixty-five who could not work because of a lack of jobs and age discrimination, as well as personal predicaments, including the lack of education, flexibility, social support, and job information.

In this chapter, we will meet four people who are unhappy when not working, but who were unable to find work that they either could or wanted to do.

Carlo Anthony had absorbed the stereotypes that people of age sixty-five should retire to the rocking chair; but when his vigorous body and mind rebelled at this change in his life, he stifled his anger and became depressed. Unfortunately, his well-meaning family continued to believe that retirement meant staying home and relaxing, and thus they could offer him no support in his search for a way out of his stultifying retirement existence.

Joseph Tierney wasted a lot of time and energy trying to get the kind of job no longer available to him at his age. His efforts to find a job were complicated by bad references from his previous employer.

Joshua Harris was doubly deprived. Having been denied education in his youth because he was black and poor, he is now is a poor, unemployed old man who does not get the federal benefits to which he is entitled because of his pride and a lack of skill in dealing with agencies.

Like many older people, Florence Hammond did not complete her education when formal training seemed less important than working, so she now lacks credentials, as well as safe transport home at night.

These four people, then, illustrate some of the problems of older people who would like to re-engage but cannot because of lack of opportunity, skills, and help from others.

Carlo Anthony

For the first time in his long busy life, Carlo Anthony, at age sixty-seven, was depressed and deeply unhappy.

"I've only been retired for two years," he said slowly, "but it seems like an eternity."

Until then, life had been good to Carlo and his wife Vera, whose families had come to this country from a small fishing village in Italy. He and Vera had set out together to raise a family and build a good life. Using his natural talents, Carlo prospered at various mechanical jobs and finally had saved enough money to open his own repair shop.

"I did it all for my family," he said. To his pleasure, both of his sons expressed interest in working in the repair shop.

"I sent them both to a technical school," Carlo says, "and now they're the best in the business when it comes to fixing TV sets, stereos, and radios."

In this strong family tradition, Carlo was determined not to stand in the way of his sons' future success. "I gave them notice that at age sixty-five I would walk out. That seemed to be the magic number, so I walked out. If I stayed, what initiative did they have? This was my own thought. They would have thought they were dependent upon me. I had enough money to live on, so I couldn't let them live under that. So I left," he repeated.

But almost as soon as he had turned over the keys and books to his sons, he regretted his decision, for now he had nothing to do all day. In American work-oriented culture, with a growing family to support and love, Carlo had never had the impetus, inclination, or time to develop any hobbies or interests other than his work and his family. Now there was no work of his own to do, and his family had families of their own. His two daughters were married and living out of state, and his two sons led busy work and social lives.

Carlo longed to go back to the shop and work a few hours a week, but he didn't; his pride and his strong sense of family would not let him.

"I said I would leave the store when I was sixty-five and I couldn't go back on my word. Besides, I think it would be the end of the family."

Carlo, still healthy and vigorous, felt the need to be out working. "I wanted, oh so much, to do something. I decided to look elsewhere immediately."

The longer he stayed in the closeness of his home, however, the weaker his resolve became.

"I just didn't get around to looking for something," he admitted. "Although I read the ads in the papers religiously. I would find something and then my wife would say, 'What do you want that for?' She's a very wonderful person, but she would always say, 'What do you want that for?' There would be a few jobs to find as far as the paper is concerned, and I haven't got the push. My wife wants me home. Saturday, I was talking to her about this very thing. I wanted to do something. I asked my wife if there was anything in the world I could do for her to make her life better. I said, 'Tell me, how is it possible for a woman to have a man under her feet all day? Now, you know that isn't right. It's not right for the man and I know it's not right for the woman.' She said, 'Have you heard me kick? If you could put up with me for forty some odd years, then I'm not going to kick even the devil himself.'"

"My daughters think I should take it easy, too," Carlo complained. "So you see, I have no one on my side."

With family opinion so weighted against his own, Carlo found it difficult to implement his decision. In the end, he succumbed to his wife's entreaties and never actively looked for work. His decision illustrates one of the significant points in many of the stories throughout this book. Elderly people, like Harry Lewis the bundle boy, and Rose Bernstein, whose spouses and/or children support and even initiate their search for meaningful re-engagement, tend to be more successful in finding and keeping jobs than do people like Carlo, whose family urged him not to seek work.

Vera's feelings, and those of the many women like her, are motivated by love. "He worked hard all his life and has made a good living, thank God, and has given me a beautiful home," Vera says. "So why shouldn't he relax a little, take it easy, and not worry about every little thing at a job working for someone else?" Vera does not seem to realize what the bundle boys, for example, discovered — that working for someone often means not bringing home any worries at all. She also thinks it would be demeaning if her husband, who had owned his own business, went to work as an employee at a lesser job.

In not following up on what appears to be a strong resolve to find work, Carlo is expressing his own ambivalent feelings about looking for work after reaching sixty-five. Perhaps Carlo (like Anna Armanian, who was offered a job in a market) is anticipating some of the rejection and discrimination he believes he will experience when he goes job hunting. The Anthonys have more than enough money on which to live comfortably.

In addition, Carlo, like others we have met, is afraid that he will have to give up his hard-earned Social Security benefits if he finds employment. Carlo voiced his concerns as he conjectured about the finances of what he called 'a theoretical reasonable fellow,' whom we can assume to be Carlo, himself.

"In my opinion, there is another entire field of the over sixty-five which should be looked into. What about the fellow that is going to get Social Security? Let's say that he draws roughtly three-hundred fifty dollars a month. Now he is a reasonable fellow, smart and conservative, and he also has another income of two-hundred fifty a month, say through the stock market, naturally. Now he has six hundred dollars. But if he works, he won't get anything. Financially, he will get nothing. Because of his tax bracket, he will lose right away. That fellow says that he will go out and work, but when he realizes he would be working for nothing, he might not work at all."

Due in part to Vera's opposition, his own anxiety, and his financial situation, Carlo has stayed home, now fully retired, but not completely satisfied with his life.

Carlo's ambivalence about working is obvious in the story he tells about his neighbor:

"I would like to take you to see the man across from my home. At sixty-five, his employer let him go. Gave him a big handshake and a small pension. Now this is five years ago. Sam has never left that house. He's become a partial invalid. I know his wife. I speak to her and Vera speaks to her. He was so badly hurt that he wasn't wanted. Now here is a man that they have made a Zombie of. Now he is a Zombie and that's all he is. It isn't his life only but it's his wife's, too. She was talking to me. She said, 'I don't know what to do. Everyone tells me to put him in a home.' She said, 'I can't do that. He was a good husband. I couldn't put him in a home.' I said, 'Call me; I'm across the street.' She can't lift him. She said, 'I wouldn't want to bother you.' Here was a fellow that was probably much more capable than myself. I don't believe he ever lost a day from work, probably in an hour early, according to his wife. One of those fellows; that was his life — his work."

Carlo's nostalgia for his own work is clear as he tells this story, as is his fear about what could be his fate if he were to follow the same path in retirement. And so, despite all of his and Vera's reasoned arguments for not working, Carlo, after two years of retirement, has become very depressed. With nothing to do tomorrow, he reminisces at length about yesterday and about the successful business he built. He thinks about the past because he assumes that for him there is no future.

"When a man gets up to sixty-five, I know this from experience, his drinking is over, his sex life is over, his going out to a ball game is over — he'd rather watch it on TV. Everything is over for him and then there's the loss of that job. That is just the frosting on the cake."[1]

Carlo's family cannot understand his feelings of emptiness that inexorably led him to depression. Carlo knows it for what it is and tries to fight it, but he has neither weapons nor allies.

"I don't know anyone who would accept depression. But you take a fellow who has nothing and there you have depression on depression," he says, speaking in the less personal and vulnerable third person. "I had awful days," he continues. "Many, many times I would scare myself. I say what the hell do I go on for. I could take a handful of pills and a bottle of Scotch and I'd never know what hit me. I would go to sleep and never wake up. I have been that depressed. I'm not better than anyone else; please don't get me wrong. I'm humble and I want to be. I swear it. But it's so easy for the depressed fellow to go off the deep end. Because I've sure had the thought many times. That's why I know about pills. The doctor told me to take them. In fact, he prescribed four a day."[2]

Unfortunately, Carlo's physician, like many doctors who treat older people, treated the physical complaints only. That is their job, but a person in Carlo's situation has other needs. Doctors rarely have the time or knowledge to offer the counseling that helps.

His commitment to life and his belief in God were too strong to let him take his own life or become like his neighbor, the living dead.

He has pulled back from the edge and has looked within himself and to his religion for strength.

"I don't take those pills," he emphasizes. "I want to beat it by myself. That's all a part of being sixty-five. I am as confused today as I was two years ago when I retired. I want you to know that because that's certainly going to help you understand. I feel terrible about my retirement. As I say, I'm confused. Something will happen. It's only by the grace of God that I'm here. I don't know the answer to this."

In his depression, Carlo has turned to his religion and to the family priest for solace. His fantasy illustrates his desire to escape from the old age he has found so painful to accept.

"I believe that if I could be given a child and I could go every day and work with him, calling God for help, through the help of God we could make a retarded or mentally disabled child better. If I could see myself making any progress as a Catholic, I would take the child up to the shrine in Canada."

Contained in this fantasy is the seed of an idea for Carlo — volunteer activities working with children, perhaps at a local hospital or through a school for special children.

"Working for nothing wouldn't bother me," Carlo said when discussing his Social Security dilemma. "And if it's going to be for nothing, for charity, I'd rather go over and take children to help."

One possibility for Carlo is SCORE, the Service Corps of Retired Executives. Service in this organization would give him the opportunity to use his business experience.

Carlo still has a long way to go. One hurdle to be overcome is his family's insistence that he sit at home. Perhaps with some hindsight and support, Carlo will be able to remain firm against these well-meaning entreaties.

Another hurdle is to find a job. With determination, perserverence, and some luck, he may be given the chance.

Joe Tierney

At sixty-eight, Joseph Tierney, a widower for ten years, is a robust, handsome man with blue eyes and thick white hair. Well educated, articulate, and charming, he often is outspoken, but humor softens this.

Joe has been unemployed since he was sixty-four. "I am an engineer and I have a good license and for years I used to work for big companies. But it seems as though once you reach sixty-five, no one wants any part of you."

Joe would like to find a steady job, but in three years he has had little success. One reason for Joe's difficulty is the way he left his last employer:

"When I was sixty-four, I went to a conference on my vacation, where I met and took off for California with a rich widow. We liked each other. I didn't ask permission of my employer. They would have refused extended leave. Lots of my troubles are my own making. When you're pushing sixty-four you're really not supposed to act like a school boy. It was the last caper. And it probably was worth it," he adds with a wide grin.

He defied the system and took one final fling at youth and romance. The memories are warm, but reality is harsh. When Joe returned from California, he tried to get his job back, but could not; he was fired. So he looked elsewhere.

"I was practically on the payroll at another company. The head engineer okayed me and I passed the physical. I just don't know what happened, but I didn't get that job."

The new company undoubtedly checked with his previous employer and found that Joe had left without notice for California. Unfortunately, he now has been branded as unreliable, despite years of experience on many engineering projects.

Joe bitterly blames the system for his difficulties in obtaining a good position. Many places to which Joe applied never even bothered to check his previous employment record once they knew he was over sixty-five.

"Usually, companies come right out and say they can't hire you. Discrimination is still very strong. Discrimination is pretty cruel. They all say that it's on account of insurance — it would affect the rates if they had old people on. Old people are more of a risk, if they drop dead on the premises of natural causes. They always pitch that at you. They'd be subject to a lawsuit if you dropped dead."

Despite his many experiences of discrimination, Joe faithfully scours the Help Wanted section of the daily papers looking for job openings.

"Most of these jobs I applied for," he explains, "if there's an ad, they're hiring engineers, it will say in fine print at the bottom, an equal opportunity employer. That means everything but people over sixty-five. They will consider a black person. One place they were hiring and they wouldn't even talk to me. I usually go right in and apply. At a power house last summer, they were short-handed and they wouldn't put me on because they have a rule they don't hire over sixty-five. I used to go there to inspect machinery. I have all the qualifications. I'm in fairly good health and I might get by their doctor, but they don't want any part of you. At one place," he continues, "after the fellow asked me my age, he began tearing up the application, right in front of me. And in their ad, in very fine print, it says, 'We are an equal opportunity employer.'

"Companies all think you should have a buck or two by the time you reach the age of sixty-five. That doesn't work out that way. The average family had three or four kids and they will all probably end up going to college and you have to take out little loans to pay the interest on big loans and the kids feel no obligation to you once they're out. And nobody would want them to. If they hadn't come along at that time, you might have had quite a chunk of money in the bank, and be ready for retirement, but nobody is. And another thing, too. Most of these places, they enroll you in their pension plans. But they fire you before sixty-five and you are right out in left field and sometimes, too, the firm folds. Or they move and they just dump their help out on the street. I think about 90 percent of the people arrive at sixty-five with no pension plans, just Social Security. Even people who have real good high-salary jobs, very few of them ever have a buck."[3]

In his frustration and anger at not having the money he feels he needs, Joe lashes out at his own family.

"My son brought up the subject of funeral money a few months ago. He said something about my not having an insurance policy to take care of my own funeral. Gee, that burns me up to think that he'd be so cheap to bring that up. I have equity in the house and I figure that they could always make a buck on that. I want a cut-rate out, either to be cremated or to give the carcass away. I have all the forms for the kidney organization, but I think you have to be processed by an undertaker and that costs money. I don't want to be a burden to anyone. They tell me funerals run into hundreds of dollars."

Joe's preoccupation with death is evident in most of what he says about trying to live and work.

"When I pick up the paper, I look at the jobs before I turn to the obituaries. In the obituaries today there is a doctor who died and I went to school with him. You find all your classmates are pushing up daisies at this time. It's quite a trick just to survive. I went to the fiftieth anniversary of my class at prep school. Only four other guys showed up. It shows what can happen."

Joe's preoccupation with death is related to his not being

able to find work. He feels unneeded and separated from the important world of work. The part-time summer jobs he has been able to get do not have the same meaning to him as a full-time job would have.

"It seems as though once you reach sixty-five, no one wants any part of you. They will hire you for vacation work or I got one nice little job for a man's place who was in Europe for the summer. But nobody wants you on their regular payroll. Anyone over sixty-five, they think you should be completely retired or dead. They just don't want you. The last couple of years, I can't pick up anything."

Aside from job hunting, which he feels compelled to do, he has nothing to keep himself occupied and interested.

"If I had lots of money and lots of hobbies, I could stay busy. I could work on my house, but I run out of materials and keep running out of money. And you have to wait until you pay off your debts before you start another project. Life is rather boring unless you have an awful lot of hobbies."

At one time Joe had a hobby that cost little money — writing. "I used to think it would be great to have time on my hands so that I could write. I'm one of these compulsive writers. I've never been published, but I've written a novel and countless short stories. But I've only received rejections. I don't know what the answer is; why it doesn't go over."

Now that he has all the time he needs, writing no longer appeals to Joe. It adds to his feelings of rejection by society, so he rejects it.

After years of working hard at good jobs, he finds it difficult to stay home. Like many other retired American men, he cannot adjust to being at home day after day. Joe has no place to go[4] when he is not out job hunting.

He has not joined a senior citizens' club. His intense feelings of being rejected because he is sixty-five do not enable him to identify and associate with other seniors. In psychological terms, Joe identifies with the aggressor (here, society's rejection of the over sixty-five) and turns against others his own age, repeating all of the usual stereotypes against the old.

He says, "I think it's totally unfair to want to stuff people away in an old men's homes. This segregation for the old is as cruel a method of treatment as segregating people because of their color. In our town, we have two colonies for oldies. I'm on the waiting list of one of them, but only because of the cheap rent," he hastily adds. "I think everybody's entitled to good housing, not just old people. But to be stuck in with a bunch of oldies who are walking on canes or are in wheel chairs, that's no good for you. That's a pretty cruel attitude that they have. Society has that attitude. They think that oldies should be swept away in one spot. I have a hunch that if I were in one of those old age places, I would be bored stiff. You wouldn't have that much in common with most of them. They are not your kind of people. They wouldn't laugh at the same sort of things. Some of them are half dead."[5]

After a difficult three years, Joe must begin to realize that interesting work may lie in directions other than that of another full-time engineering job. He must learn to find and accept the occupations that are available. He now is thinking of doing some volunteer work, perhaps as a way of finding and working into a paid position.

"Yes," he predicts, "I will probably work at some type of social work or something. If I could help retarded people, I would work for nothing if they would give me the carfare."

Through his depression, Joe is beginning to see himself in terms of the assets he can bring to a job rather than of society's discriminatory policy.

"There is a good thing about getting old," he says; "actually, a person over sixty-five would be better on most jobs than a youngster. You do accumulate knowledge over the years. And you know the right thing to do at the right time. I'm in good shape physically, though, for an old guy. I don't have these pains or arthritis. I can do things; why, I shingled the roof on my house last summer."

Perhaps Joe Tierney will make it down the road to active re-engagement in the world of work; but for him it will have been a long, difficult journey.

Joshua Harris

Joshua Harris probably will not get work. At sixty-six, he has many more strikes against him that Joe's California indiscretion. Josh is a black unskilled laborer who never had the opportunity to attend school. For nearly fifty years, he had worked at a variety of unskilled jobs, never staying very long at any one place. He had worked past his sixty-fifth birthday at a difficult construction job:

"I carried heavy bags of cement up and down flights of stairs. That's the only job I could get, and my back gave out on me. The work was actually too heavy even for a young guy."

Because of his age, color, and lack of education, Josh feels the full weight of discrimination as he searches for a job.

"Blacks are more discriminated against in employment than others; old black men end up getting jobs that are too hard even for a young person. The unscrupulous businessman, he can't get a young person to do heavy work; sometimes he'll take an old guy and the work will kill him."

Josh needs to find a job in order to feel secure as he gets older.

"It's not only a question of living," he says, "but I need a little money for a bank account. I have enough for rent and food, but it's really not enough. I need a little in reserve."

He needs the extra money to repay a large debt to friends who loaned him enough for funeral expenses when his brother died.

"They don't bother me much for the money, but I'd like to be able to return it to them, just the same."

Without a job, Josh has no money coming in at all. Even though he is over sixty-five, he is not covered by regular Social Security since he never worked at any job long enough to build up enough quarters. And because he finds it very difficult to go through procedures of filling out required forms, he does not receive Supplemental Social Security Insurance.[6] Josh is one of the many older, poor, and under-educated Americans who have slipped through the cracks of the Social Security system.

Because he receives no government benefits, Josh thinks of himself as a 'nonperson.' "A nonperson is somebody that's outside the scheme of things, beyond the pale, you might say. Like I say, there's probably countless millions that are in my category and worse off than me, and yet they are not getting any help. It's the kind of situation where you're going to have to find somebody generous, but where are you going to find generosity in the system today?"

Aside from his few friends, Josh is alone in life. He never married, and two sisters went their separate ways many years ago.

Josh spends most of his time job hunting.

"I read the papers every day and then go looking. I usually go to the various places because they won't listen if you call. They want you to waste three or four hours, three or four dollars on carfare, coming down. They know that they are not going to give you the job. I waste half a day and a few dollars and get nothing."

He also has frequented some temporary agencies, but finds them both depressing and misleading.

"It's sad to see some of these poor people looking. You see them down there of all ages, poverty stricken with rags on and shoes falling off their feet, hopeless looking, hoping for a job. It gave me such a feeling of misery, to see my fellow human beings in misery. You look at the night life, and see all the cars and luxury stores and think that everything is beautiful, but beneath the surface you see all this misery and poverty. You go to these places, and you see maybe a hundred people waiting. You're supposed to report at six in the morning. The whole thing is a game in that aspect in that it's at the expense of the worker. Usually the employers are looking for cheap labor for a short period of time."

Josh has gone to several employment agencies in the past.He now avoids such places because "they make you fill out forms. They promise you the world. They are so glad to see you. They also want a big labor pool that they can fall back on. They are the same as the employer. They want a lot of human misery that they know they can pick out of. I got kind of tired going to those. I just look in the paper now.

"I also tried to get kitchen work at hospitals, but the hospitals don't want you unless you fill out a form. The same as Social Security; they want everything in order, or they don't want you, either. They want references. Where did you work the last eight years? State the time you began and the time you ended. I take a look at those forms and sometimes I make an effort to fill them out. I get no anwers anyway because they take one look at my age. Of course, naturally, I don't tell them that I'm over sixty; you can't do that when you're looking for a job. But they can take one good look at me and are able to tell that I'm no youngster. That finishes me right there."

Josh then looked for work at some supermarkets.

"I tried some and they aren't interested. I went to one supermarket and they had more forms to fill out than any of the jobs I've been to yet — three or four pages. I've tried the smaller places, too. They just take one look at me; yet, they have a sign outside the window that says 'help wanted.' They say, 'We don't need anyone now,' after looking at me; 'We have the position filled.'"

Josh says that these places never told him that they would not hire him because of his age or color.

"No, they're too smart for that. They hint around. They don't actually refuse you on account of age. What are you going to do when they tell you that the unemployment rate is 7 percent when probably it's as much as 10 percent. They don't know everybody that's unemployed.[7]

"Well, as a matter of fact, the elderly who are in need shouldn't have to go around and look for this type of unskilled work. The government should provide a place where they can go right in and get it, without begging for it and without making inquiries into where to get it or without having to compete for it. I don't think that enough is being done for them in that direction at all.

"This matter of helping the needy aged," he continues; "let's say that for the aged that are in need, there shouldn't be any red tape. It's a matter of, if they need help, give it to them, whether it's food or a job; they should give it to them automatically. There are a lot of old people that are too proud. They would rather starve to death than come begging for work. They are so disgusted they don't want to explain. They are fed up with everything. They just sit and wait for death. If you are going to help these millions that have given up, you can't expect them to go out and look for help. You have to have some place for them to go where they know that they can get help, maybe meal tickets, even twenty dollars a week. The least you can live on is twenty dollars a week, and then you are on a semisurvival basis right there. I'm not talking about donuts and coffee. I don't call that food."[8]

Charity is not a good solution, Josh feels, because it does not provide enough. "So what is charity doing? For a person's self-respect, I don't think that is enough. A person's respect demands more than just to subsist. You need a little extra besides that."

Josh is anxious to build up some reserve funds in the event of illness. "What are you going to do if you get sick and are in the hospital? If you don't have the money to keep up the hospital's profit, you will be left to die. They pack them poor people into wards like sardines and let them die off one by one. Most old people don't want to see the unpleasant reality. It's a sad thing that that's all they have to look forward to, just survival itself. They are going to pay for it. They will end up in one of those wards and die a slow, horrible death. Up in the hospitals, I have seen the poor dying like sardines. Dying from neglect. Once you've been lying there for a week, you can't get out of it, because your muscles get weak. They get semiparalyzed. They just have to wait there and die."

Although he did not speak in the first person, Josh's fears are obvious. His feelings are not completely paranoid. Better, more sophisticated health care is given to elderly people who have both money and family, not to indigent black people like Josh who are alone in the world.[9]

Despite his fears of a 'slow, horrible death' in a hospital, Josh remains independent. Once he gave up a good job because for him it meant hurting others. "I worked as a watchman, at one time. It was a nice easy job, but a bunch of kids came in one time. They were only playing, a little mischief, but they smashed about $30,000 worth of property and stole a few things. So the boss bawled me out the next day for not calling the police. I said, 'Well, if I have to put a couple of kids in jail who are just looking for fun, then I quit.' So I quit. He tried to get me back, you know. I said, 'Nothing doing because it would happen again.' There was a job I could of had for life. The very fact that I would have put someone in prison — that they probably did not deserve — would ruin their lives."

At sixty-six, with a bad back and little money, he remains his own person; he refuses to give up or plead for charity.

"A lot of these old people, like I say, won't even tell you their problems. They just give up. But I go this way, and if I hit a blind alley, I'll retreat and try another way. The survival problem, I've got that mastered. My needs are so few. A lot of old people are satisfied to rot. Their mind doesn't function beyond a point. But somebody like me who can think and has the urge and the drive wants a little more. I confront a lot of older persons who are quiet and disgusted. Not me. I speak up.

"I would love any kind of job that is an unskilled job, like construction worker, dishwasher, porter. I know I could be useful, but I don't know anybody that could use my usefulness."

Perhaps in this age of paperwork and red tape, government agencies should adopt special approaches for people like Josh who do not benefit from the existing social service agencies. His depression is evident when he says: "You say to yourself, it can't be this bad in other places, so you go other places and find that it's worse. Unemployment, poverty. It's bad all over. It's a problem nationwide." It is a special problem for Josh Harris, a problem of survival in his older years.

Florence Hammond

At seventy-two, Florence Hammond's hair is the same color as the starched hospital uniform she wore for many years. But Florence ('Floss,' as her friends call her) has not worked as a nurse for several years and has not worked at all since she was seventy.

She retired from a full-time position at an urban hospital when she was sixty-two. "I am not a registered nurse," she explained; "and the hospital was getting strict about registration at that time." She could have continued to work at the hospital, but chose not to.

"I was determined that I was not going to be a nurse's aide. With all the training I had and the other courses I had taken, I did not think it was fair for me to do only aide's menial work, so I retired early and took my Social Security."

Until she left her job at the hospital, Florence had worked full time since she was twenty-seven.

"My husband died when my daughter was young, so I had to get a job to keep us going. I'm a high school graduate and had some nurses' training and got a job in the hospital. In those days, a high school diploma and some training in a hospital school meant more than they do now. Now you really need to be a registered nurse to get the good jobs. I wish I had become a registered nurse. If you are registered, you can work until you're ninety on private duty work!" Looking back, Florence now realizes that she should have gone to school for her RN when her daughter was grown. At that time, however, she had an excellent position and did not anticipate the changes in the nursing profession that would ensue.

After she left the hospital, Florence tried other work. "A friend of mine said to me, 'Why don't you do commercial work through an employment temporary agency? They will keep you busy every minute. You have to pay them 10 percent of what you make, but that isn't so bad.' So I signed up at a temporary agency and I did get some jobs typing."

But Florence soon discovered that she missed the active hospital routine. "After a few temporary clerical jobs, I did lower my pride a little by working as a nurse's aide. I worked in a nursing home for older women. It really is a retirement home that also has an infirmary. I didn't like that place very much.

"Women sometimes became disabled and went into the infirmary, but I didn't think that they were very well taken care of there, and I wanted no part, I never have; I have always been a fuss-budget. I never wanted to work in a hospital that didn't take excellent care of the patients. I stayed in the nursing home only a few months."

Her description of the inadequacy of this nursing home is accurate and not the result of inflated standards or fussiness. Of the ten thousand nurses who answered a questionnaire in the journal *Nursing,* many had critical statements about such institutions throughout the country.[10]

There were other reasons for leaving the nursing home. Florence was offered only the least desirable night shift. And like many older people, she lived in an apartment in a decaying area of the city.

"I worked the 3:00 to 11:00 PM shift. By the time I got home, it was about midnight. You know, all the old winos hang out on the banks of the river near my apartment building and then there are a lot of bums there. I was absolutely petrified when I came home so late. So I said to myself that I would stay just long enough to make it worth my while. About a year ago, a woman was killed in the entry of a nearby apartment. Then on the same day, close to my place, someone else was killed. I thought maybe it was just as well that I didn't stay on any longer. Maybe God took care of me. I'm afraid of after-dark work now."

Since leaving the nursing home, Floss has had only one job. "Two years ago, I got some working typing in a rectory. It was a lovely rectory. So I took the job. The priest didn't ask me how old I was. He had me come for an interview. He told me about the girl he had before. He wanted an older woman. He had a youngster before and she didn't behave herself. She ran around all the time; she was never there. He said, "You look like a settled woman.' He still didn't ask me how old I was. He was a very kind man. A few days later he had to make out the government form. He said, 'How old are you?' I said 'seventy' and he nearly dropped dead."

Florence liked her typing job at the rectory because of the pleasant surroundings and the safety of working during daylight hours.

"I was depressed when the typing was all done. I asked the priest, but he said they didn't have any more work for me to do."

It has been nearly two years since that job ended. During this time, Florence has not been able to find any work that she considers both safe and suitable, even though she has answered many newspaper ads.

"I have turned down several jobs," she says, "because they involved doing only domestic, menial work. I don't want to be somebody's maid or housekeeper and I don't like to work with unintelligent people, either."

High standards clearly stand in the way of Florence's finding work. Unlike many of the people we interviewed (notably, the men employed in the supermarket as bundle boys), Florence cannot bring herself to compromise and to accept a less prestigious job if she is to work at all. Yet, she still yearns for some useful occupation. Her dilemma is not unusual. It is unfortunate that senior citizens often must accept the least desireable chores in order to work at all.

Florence now busies herself reading. "I get six books at a time from the library," she says. Although she also would like to take a knitting course and learn to play bridge, she so far has not registered for any adult education courses in her neighborhood — perhaps because they are given only at night, when she does not want to be out alone. Such courses might be useful to get her moving in a new direction.

Florence needs counseling to bring new job possibilities to her attention, to suggest viable alternatives to sitting home alone and reading, or to help her adjust to leisure pursuits. A good counselor would help her continue to use her nursing experience; perhaps she could nurse other older persons. This would be possible if door-to-door evening transportation could be arranged or if she could obtain a live-in nursing job in a good institution or in a private home.

Valuable talents and needed skills of many people, including Florence Hammond, are going to waste. Elders often become lonely and depressed, feeling unwanted and isolated. This need not happen.

Summary

In microcosm, Carlo Anthony's dilemma is the contemporary version of retirement. People retire and are retired earlier in order to provide an opportunity in the labor force for new recruits. Social Security, with its promise of a guaranteed income for life for not working, has made this situation possible. Even though Carlo worked in his own small shop, rather than in a large corporation, he nonetheless felt society's pressure to follow the mandate: Retire at age sixty-five and give the next generation a chance to work on its own.

But what about all of the people like Carlo who for a lifetime have clung to the American work ethic? As Carlo and the others illustrate, they cannot be deprogrammed to stop believing in the value of working and making a useful contribution to society. One response to this problem has been to raise the mandatory retirement age to seventy for most people.

Another positive response is retirement education — education that begins long before a person blows out the sixty-five or seventy birthday candles. When they are younger, even in primary and secondary schools, people in our work-centered culture should be encouraged to develop interests, hobbies, and recreational activities that will stay with them throughout life.

In some measure, this "training" for retirement already is occuring. Recreational and leisure pursuits are booming. More and more Americans are buying recreational vehicles, are bowling, and/or becoming home carpenters, to name a few such activities. Other people are going back to school late in life and enjoying enrichment courses.[11] Perhaps for them, the transition from work to retirement will be easier than it has been for Carlo.

In the meantime, however, people who retired yesterday and people who must clean out their desks next Monday are still in need of help. In addition to counseling about re-engagement possibilities, many newly retired people need the reassurance that their problem is not unique. More and more of them are joining organizations of retired persons and becoming part of the "Gray Power" movement. More than 350 people attended the Gray Panthers' 1977 convention, and membership in the American Association of Retired Persons has nearly quadrupled in the past six years —from 3 million to nearly 12 million members. Publications of the AARP and similar groups offer valuable suggestions on how to make constructive use of postretirement years.

Business and government also have a responsibilitiy to help people prepare for retirement. In the concluding chapter, we will provide some suggestions to make retirement easier and postretirement re-employment more possible. For people like Carlo, however, who would benefit from volunteer work, here are some concrete suggestions:[12]

Much useful information appears in the *Fact Sheet on Employment and Volunteer Opportunities for Older People,* DHEW Publication No. (OHDS) 77-20233. This free 8-page booklet is available from the U.S. Department of Health, Education and Welfare, Washington, D.C. 20201.

There are a number of volunteer programs under the umbrella of ACTION, which is the central focus in the federal goverment for volunteer programs. People sixty years or older may become volunteers in the Retired Senior Volunteer Program (RSVP), of which there are 600 programs throughout the country. RSVP volunteers are placed in community activities that are suited to their interests, such as helping other older people or the handicapped. To find the one nearest you, contact your state agency on aging, or ACTION, Washington, D.C. 20524. More than 162,000 aging seniors already participate in this popular program.

Another program, Foster Grandparent Program, also administered by ACTION, is for people sixty years or older with low incomes. These volunteers are paid a small stipend to help needy, lonely children usually in institutions. There are 13,000 Foster Grandparents.

Retired businessmen who would like to help owners of small businesses may volunteer for the Service Corps of Retired Executives (SCORE), which, since its founding in 1965, has helped more than 175,000 enterprises. SCORE volunteers sometimes receive expenses but they are not paid. For SCORE information, write ACTION.

Older Americans also have been serving in the Peace Corps and Volunteers in Service to America, VISTA. Peace Corps Volunteers serve for two years in developing countries. They are paid a monthly living allowance. VISTA volunteers work for one year wherever poverty exists in America — in city ghetto areas, rural settings, and Indian reservations. They receive a monthly living allowance plus an additional stipend when they finish their service. For information on the Peace Corps or VISTA call ACTION, toll free, at 800-424-8580.

The U.S. Department of Labor also sponsors volunteer programs for older persons, including Green Thumb. Cosponsored by the National Farmers Union in twenty-four states, Green Thumb offers part-time work in beautification, conservation, and community improvement in rural areas and also in existing community service agencies. Volunteers should have a farming or rural background. Write Green Thumb, Inc., 1012 14th Street, N.W., Washington, D.C. 20005.

Senior Aides, administered by the National Council of Senior Citizens in thirty-three urban and rural areas, pays small stipends for part-time work in community service agencies. Write National Council of Senior Citizens, 1511 "K" Street N.W., Washington, D.C. 20005.

Senior Aides are trained to assume the role of ombudsmen — objective, accessible, and impartial advocates agents between individuals and agencies. The ombudsmen extend their knowledge of Federal, state, and local agencies, organizations, and services for elders to the community at large.

Elders who meet the income and eligibility requirements of the program are placed in host organizations by the area coordinator. Senior Aides work twenty hours per week (additional hours are optional if funding permits) at a pay rate of $2.50 per hour, thereby not exceeding the yearly earnings limitation for Social Security beneficiaries under age seventy-two. Senior Aides also receive fringe benefits, transportation reimbursements, and support services.

Senior Community Service Aides, sponsored by the National Council on the Aging, 1828 "L" Street, N.W., Washington, D.C. 20036, do part-time work in eighteen urban and rural areas in Social Security, public housing, libraries, hospitals, schools, and food and nutrition programs. The National Retired Teachers Association and the American Association of Retired Persons also have volunteer programs; you can write them at 1909 "K" Street, N.W., Washington, D.C. 20006. The Forest Services of the United States, Room 3243, South Agriculture Building, 12th and Independence Avenue, S.W., Washington, D.C. 20250, also provides volunteer opportunities in their regions, and many municipal departments of elder affairs and community service coordinating agencies also provide information. In many communities, elders are welcomed as volunteers in the public schools. Boston, for example, has an active program of Senior Volunteers in the schools. Hospitals and institutions often welcome older volunteers.

Write the Superintendent of Documents, U.S. Government Printing Office, Washington, D.C. 20402, requesting all current and new publications of information on volunteer and working opportunities for the elderly.

Preretirees can get some suggestions ahead for retirement from *Dynamic Years for working Americans fifty plus*, published by Action for Independent Maturity, an affiliate of the National Association of Retired Persons. *Dynamic Years* is published bimonthly at 215 Long Beach Blvd., Long Beach, California 90801.

Notes

1. Carlo is sadly misinformed about many aspects of aging. Many older people enjoy exercise and various recreational activities. People interviewed for this book like to walk, play golf, and fish. Many older people also enjoy active sex lives, as we will discover in Part II, Remarriage. But for some people, like Carlo and his neighbor, expectations become self-fulfilling prophecies —they think they can't, so they don't, thereby proving their point that they can't.
2. The suicide rate among Americans over sixty-five is phenomenally high. They account for 25 percent of the suicides in this country, even though as a group the over-sixty-fives comprise only 10 percent fo the total population.
3. Although Joe's 90 percent figure of people without pensions is an exaggeration, it is true that many persons enter retirement with no income but Social Security or SSI. Action for Independent Maturity, an affiliate of the American Association of Retired Persons, states, "Many people have reached retirement age to discover belatedly that pension income is far less than they had anticipated. In some sad cases, expected pensions do not materialize at all, due to a variety of reasons, including insufficient funding of the plan, business failure of the employing company or loss of a job before the pension rights became 'vested.'" AIM's *Guide for Financial Security*, p. 5. This useful guide is available from the Membership Dept., 215 Long Beach Boulevard, Long Beach, California 90801.

   In one survey of pension income, it was found that about

half of male wage and salary workers and 78 percent of women did not have any pension other than Social Security. See Alan Fox, *Earnings Replacement form Social Security and Private Pensions: Newly Entitled Beneficiaries, 1970. Preliminary Findings from the Survey of New Beneficiaries,* Report No. 13, Washington, D.C. Office of Research and Statistics, U.S. Social Security Administration.

In a recent look at pensions, economist James H. Schulz concludes, "Experience has shown that there are many problems connected with private pensions." In *Handbook of the Aging and the Social Sciences,* Robert H. Binstock and Ethel Shanas (eds.). New York: Van Nostrand Reinhold Company, 1976, p. 585.

Information about sources of retirement income is available for retirees in *Your Retirement Money Guide,* a pamphlet available from the American Association of Retired Persons, 215 Long Beach Blvd., Long Beach, Calif. 90801.

4. Some ethnic sections of American society, such as the Armenian-Americans in Boston, have a men's club that essentially is a retreat for retired men who need to get out of the house and have some male companionship. In their senior men's center, the older men relax and read their newspapers, drink coffee, and play cards. For a look at an Armenian-American center, see the article "Passing Time: Male Dignity in a Community Center for the Aged," by Ruth Harriet Jacobs, in *Geriatrics Digest,* May 1971, Vol. 8, pp. 7-15.

5. This same phenomenon also has been observed in old-age homes. In one study of a large old-age home, the author found that the older people who felt they had been pushed into the home or who had nowhere else to go turned on the other residents, referring to them as "useless and not worth talking to." Feeling totally rejected, these people sat isolated in the midst of agemates and potential friends, declaring, "Everybody here but me is senile!" This study, entitled "One-Way Street: An Intimate View of Adjustment to a Home for the Aged," by Ruth Jacobs, appears in *The Gerontologist,* Vol. 9, No. 4, Part I, Winter 1969.

6. Supplemental Security Income (SSI) for the aged, blind, and disabled now replaces the old "welfare" program that was formerly administered by municipalities or states. SSI is a federal program that pays monthly checks to people in financial need who are sixty-five or older and to people in need at any age who are blind or disabled.

   Under SSI, the basic maximum cash income in 1977 was $167.80 a month for an individual and $251.90 a month for a couple; but the SSI income, like regular Social Security, is increased yearly as inflation increases. People who have income from other sources receive less. In most states, a person who is eligible for SSI also is eligible for Medicaid and social services provided by the state. People may get these benefits even if they have never worked or have insufficient quarters under regular Social Security.

A free booklet on SSI entitled *Supplemental Security Income for the Aged, Blind and Disabled* is available from the U.S. Department of Health, Education and Welfare, Social Security Administration, HEW Publication No. (SSA) 77-11000, January, 1977. Application for SSI is made at any Social Security office. People eligible for SSI may get an emergency immediate payment when applying for this aid. They also should receive a booklet "What you have to know about SSI" from their Social Security office.

Josh, though undoubtedly eligible, is one of the many who fail to apply either because they do not know SSI exists or because they do not wish to take what they consider charity or, as in Josh's case, cannot cope with the application procedures. Social Security has made some attempt in the media to inform persons of their rights to this.

7. Josh is correct in saying that American unemployment is probably higher than the estimated official figure of 7 percent in 1977. Unemployment statistics are taken from people currently receiving unemployment compensation and actively seeking work through the U.S. Employment Bureau. Many people exhaust unemployment benefits, get discouraged looking for work, and drop off the official statistics. This is particularly true for older workers over fifty, many of whom are unable to get jobs and do not officially continue on lists of the unemployed or of retirees. One might call this phenomenon 'early retirement through unemployment.'

8. Josh's estimates of food costs are not excessive. The U.S. Department of Labor, Bureau of Labor Statistics, Washington, D.C. 20212 issued a news release in August, 1977, with estimates of the annual budgets for a retired couple at three levels of living in the urban United States. In the lowest budget, they estimated that food would cost $1,443 yearly for two people. An individual would require more than half of this because it is more expensive for a man like Josh living in a single room and having to eat out.

9. A bibliography on ethical issues is available from the Institute of Society, Ethics and the Life Sciences, The Hastings Center, 360

Broadway, Hastings-on-Hudson, New York 10706. Georgetown University Library has an extensive collection of bio-ethical material.

10. For a discussion of this questionnaire and the many negative replies by nurses, see *Time* Magazine, Jan. 17, 1977, p. 73.

11. In 1977, the Massachusetts Society for Adult Education devoted its annual meeting to a discussion of education for the older adult.

12. Reports on volunteer programs for seniors appear frequently in *Aging* magazine published by the U.S. Department of Health, Education and Welfare's Administration on Aging. This magazine usually is available in your public library or for $5.05 yearly through subscription DHEW Pub. No. (OHD/AOA) 77-20941 from the U.S. Government Printing Office, Division of Public Documents, Washington, D.C. 20402.

Chapter Seven
Conclusion

"In my dictionary, there is no word 'no'."

Many retirees are happy not working and spend their time in other meaningful activities and roles. These people should not be pushed into working. Many other older men and women seek to continue being employed. They prefer or need to work rather than to retire. The stories in Part I of both successful and unsuccessful efforts at re-engaging illustrate the complexity of obtaining employment late in life. Many factors, external and internal, obvious and subtle, influence whether a person re-engages. Two leading gerontologists, Robert J. Havighurst and Bernice Neugarten have logically extended this complexity to encompass the entire life of the older person.

"In attempting to understand why one individual copes successfully with illness while another does not or why one individual copes successfully with retirement and another does not, we shall have to peruse in greater depth the ways in which aged individuals relate their pasts with their presents, how they integrate their lives into meaningful wholes."[1]

Integrating a lifetime of work with retirement is not always easy, as the people in the previous chapters have shown. To see how they have managed, we will first review and summarize the conclusions we have reached about the many people who shared their retirement and re-engagement struggles with us.[2]

Their experiences varied. Some people had cheerfully retired, some had been retired involuntarily. Others had been encouraged to retire by their employer or spouse for benefits. Some had been fired or had left because they felt unable to continue to work. Some could no longer be homemakers.

Once out of the job situation (either paid work or housework), which had been their principal valued activity during adult life, most of the people we met in Part I felt lost without work's structure and rewards. Most, however, coped with the retirement crisis and grew creatively, despite prevalent stereotypes about the aged.

Many overcame tremendous barriers to get new jobs, sometimes even very late in life; they found the results worthwhile and so they adjusted well to the new conditions. Their work dissipated loneliness and also gave self-esteem and needed money. More than that, these people provided needed service, enriched their communities, and inspired younger people.

They contrast sharply with the unemployed, many involuntarily, whose repressed anger at enforced idleness, like Carlo Anthony's, led to depression and even thoughts of suicide. Some of these unemployed people had internalized negative concepts of aging and thus were self-defeating. In addition, many of the involuntary unemployed had few skills and less information, opportunity, or luck.

The importance of "luck" in finding jobs highlights the lack of information and counseling available for older Americans. Some people happened to be in the right place at the right time and so got jobs, like Anna Armanian, who found a job in a supermarket. Other people, after enduring many rejections, swallowed their pride and took work well below their ability. That they enjoyed this work indicates the importance of working in any capacity. For those who want to work, the opportunity to do so usually is more important than the type of job. In fact, all of the people we interviewed, with the exception of Betty Green, the exguidance counselor, accepted without reservation alternative kinds of jobs. Most actually welcomed the lower pressure. For example, Harry Lewis the bundle boy expressed relief that now he did not have to worry about decisions concerning large purchases for his company.

Among the benefits that the re-employed elders reported were companionship, having something to do, avoiding depression, keeping active, obtaining some income, getting out of the house, fulfilling a need, avoiding boredom, enjoyment, gratification, activity, avoiding loneliness, and building up needed Social Security quarters. Many said such things as, "It keeps me sane," and "I don't know how I could get up in the morning without this job." Most people reported that their spouses, families, and/or friends supported and even fostered their interest in their new job.

Despite the lower status of many of the jobs they held, the people who had re-engaged were remarkably cheerful and accommodating. They were flexible and had both a sense of humor and a sense of humility. They were active, aware, interested, and interesting people. Many of them participated in organizations and many more had various hobbies. They wanted to work, whether or not they needed the extra income.[3]

From the small group we interviewed, it is difficult to judge with finality the factors that make for successful reemployment in later life. But some statements can be made with a fair degree of certainty. Overall, the crucial factors seem to be the degree of gratification and importance of previous work; the degree of autonomy and dignity the individual retained in the retirement process from the preretirement job; the support of other people on a personal level and in the community, such as relatives, friends, and physicians; and the amount of information available (sometimes accidental information) about opportunities for work through formal and informal means, such as friends, clubs, and service organizations.

Relationship of new careers to previous jobs

The people who felt arbitrarily retired, most of whom had received signals from their supervisors that their working days were over, tended to accept this evaluation of the situation, at least at first. We all use influential people in our environment as mirrors in which to judge ourselves. Told by an employer, "Now it's time to rest," some people do so, thinking they have no other choice. With idleness, some then deteriorate or worse, as in the case of Carlo Anthony's neighbor.

Because we found the role of accident so crucial, we believe that many people would work in later life if they had some counseling on how to go about getting work.

We believe that preretirement counseling in depth is a social responsibility. We suspect that many older persons do not work because they receive neither encouragement nor information.

Some companies have preretirement programs, including those sponsored by AIM — Action for Independent Maturity of the American Association of Retired Persons. A few pioneers, like the International Business Machine Company (IBM), provide funds for persons over age fifty to re-educate themselves for retirement occupations. A few cities, like Newton, Massachusetts, provide retirement workshops for citizens. But by and large, people have to redefine themselves on their own, and it is difficult.

We believe that large companies should consider ways to rehire their able retired full-time employees on a part-time basis. As of now, most corporations have a policy of upward mobility only. Executives past age fifty often are encouraged to take early retirement. People are promoted or held at the same level, or fired or retired since they cannot be demoted. Perhaps company policies, procedures, and attitudes could be changed to retain older workers at lower level jobs or on a part-time basis. But, of course, downward mobility is a controversial concept.[4] Many retirees would prefer the lowered status and some pay to supplement Social Security to no occupational status and no money. Their experience would be of value and they might also provide younger workers with more positive attitudes toward the aged and the prospect of their own aging. We fear aging because we see few roles for seniors.

Relationship of postretirement work to persistance

Many of the seniors who shared their experiences tried and tried again to find work; they were not deterred by rejection. However, others who did not get work were discouraged by the way they were treated by prospective employers. Josh Harris, quoted in the previous chapter, was right when he said that many of the most needy seniors are made to spend money and time unnecessarily for dead-end and even cruel job interviews. Public and private employers and agencies should re-evaluate their practices. More flexible working arrangements and alternative means of transportation could be developed if there were a real commitment to involving the elderly in society.

As the situation is now, however, the elderly who are likely to get work are those who keep trying and who follow leads. It helps to know a lot of people and to be out where one hears about jobs. Sociologist S.M. Miller has pointed out that most people, old or young, obtain jobs through informal means, not through ads or employment agencies. It is unfortunate that the elderly who are the most isolated, perhaps having lost friends by death or geographic moves, are the very ones who are least likely to hear about jobs. For such seniors who lack helpful informal networks, it might be possible to develop in more communities the kind of job-finding service run by Abe Ginsberg, as described in chapter four.

Older women present a unique problem.[5] With the growth of their children and often the loss of a spouse, many older women lose their roles as nurturers. Some are successful in re-engaging, in helping others through paid or volunteer work. Many, however, compete for scarce jobs in overcrowded fields. Some of these women would be better off giving up their dreams of re-engaging in "nurturing" or helping jobs and instead seek training for other kinds of jobs. Some of the older women at the sheltered workshop described in chapter five were isolated and lonely before they found the workshop. Earlier, these displaced homemakers might have been re-employed in businesses of one sort or another if society had re-educated them rather than largely disdaining them.

Relationship of new jobs to support from others

People are influenced by the opinions of others. We have seen how most people who found postretirement work were encouraged to do so by their doctors, spouses, children, and/or other relatives.

Seeking postretirement work and being able to accept lower status jobs are possible when older persons are supported emotionally by those people around them whose opinions are important. One bundle boy was hesitant to put on the red coat until he found that his former business executive friends did not look down on him. Samuel Solomon, in chapter two, persisted in his search for a job and became a janitor; his sister objected but his wife felt that any honest work was dignified. Several older ladies were able to go every day to the sheltered workshop, despite their aches and pains, because their children were so proud of them.

If older people are treated with respect and dignity, they generally are willing and able to do menial low-paid work if they feel that the work is useful. Money, although handy, also is of symbolic value because society measures by it. Individuals often derive values from the overall culture. Families and friends frequently urge the older person, (Carlo Anthony, for example) to "take it easy" because that is what society has expected until recently.

Families should be concerned about the physical well-being of their older relatives. They should make sure that older people who appear withdrawn are not sick. Many physical illnesses often are passed over as being merely symptoms of the aging process. Often they are not; they are illnesses which, if not properly diagnosed and treated, can cause deterioration.

Relationship of volunteer work to postretirement work

Many seniors do worthwhile volunteer work. More probably would be willing to if volunteering were more respected in our society. Many people feel that those who do useful work should be paid for it, whether they are young or old, male or female. In a society that gives prestige in terms of money, is it surprising that the old as well as the young would like to receive a tangible token for their services? As many of our interviewees said, "When you are paid even a little something, you feel good."

For the old as well as the young, volunteer work often leads to paid work as a result of the contacts and opportunities that open and the experience gained. Many of the seniors who volunteered their services or belonged to organizations eventually got paid work.

Federal programs such as Foster Grandparents and Retired Senior Volunteer Program (both mentioned in the previous chapter) recognize this and offer payment to seniors who do social service work. These programs, however, should be expanded and made suitable for more elders of many backgrounds and abilities. This point was made well at the recent conference on "Older Persons, Unused Resources for Unmet Needs," sponsored by the Gerontological Center of the City University of New York. Many speakers pointed out that older people could make a valuable contribution if jobs were available. Alice Brophy, Commissioner, Department of the Aging of the City of New York, reported that 1,300 seniors were employed under a federal grant to help staff human service agencies in New York City. The average age of these valuable employees was seventy-four. Miss Brophy reported that many seniors want to work: most of them never wanted to stop working and said that they value work so much that they would earn beyond the Social Security limit if they could.

At this meeting, three Congressional leaders discussed the difficulties caused by retirement. They called for more federal programs to combat despair among elderly people who feel useless. Senator Harrison Williams of New Jersey commented, "There may be no more important thing in the decade ahead than to find new roles for the aging. We must open more doors. The service areas can be met by people with a little training."

Congressman Augustus Hawkins of California added: "It is a great mystery why we have tolerated as a society not using the human resources of the aged; the burden should be on the government, not on the backs of those least able to bear it." He referred to the fact that we should provide opportunities for all citizens to contribute. He declared, "We have become so obsessed with a balanced budget, our productive facilities are vastly under used."

Congressman James Scheuer of New York extolled elderly workers and called for a CETA[6] training program for the elderly. He declared that we have vastly underestimated the role the elderly could play. Elderly people who are well, for example, could take care of frail elderly, many of whom are lonely rather than ill. This could save on staggering health costs. Older people could be employed in family planning and counseling. Scheuer reported on successful senior health aides in the Bronx section of New York City.

Nelson Cruickshank, President of the National Council of Senior Citizens, said, "We should not be trapped into saying what kind of jobs old people can do. They can do anything anyone can do. You get the job and you can find an old person to do it."

By presenting in this book various jobs, many of low status, that older persons obtained, we have not meant to imply that persons over sixty-five can hold only such jobs. Many self-employed elders, many professionals, and many academics continue at their life-time careers into extreme old age. There are, of course, many world leaders of advanced age. Seventy-seven-year-old Claude Pepper was the moving force in Congress to extend mandatory retirement, for example. We have attempted to show here that some average seniors who lost their former work have courageously re-involved in work and in life in the jobs that were available to them.

But there are not enough jobs to go around now. The people who lose work before sixty-five and take early Social Security benefits must survive on reduced benefits. We heartily agree with the legislators quoted above and with Cruickshank: the aged can be used outside the market economy if the society has a commitment to this use and to social service. According to Cruickshank's estimate, there are now relatively few senior aides on all the federal projects employing elderly; much more funding is needed if this is to be an avenue for senior accomplishment in substantial numbers.

As Congressman Scheuer pointed out, "Even though there may be sporadic and miniscule programs for elderly employment, . . . there hasn't been a comprehensive program for aging."

This is where we stand today.

Suggestions and Possibilities

After reading the stories in the previous chapters and the comments in this concluding chapter, an older person seeking a job might ask, "What have I learned that will help me?" Here are some possible lessons. Some have been mentioned earlier, but it is useful to see them here as part of the entire list of possibilities. The list also includes some suggestions by the authors and others on steps that the larger society might take to assist elders who want to re-engage in the world of work.

1. First of all, make sure your health is as good as possible. Never assume that any problem is just old age. "Think treatable," as Knight Steel, M.D., Boston University geriatrician, reminds his medical students. You can work better when healthier and you look better.

2. If your well-meaning relatives or friends tell you that you should take it easy when you yourself want to work, tell them politely but firmly that what you do with your life is your decision. Get support from your physician and/or clergyman if you can.

3. Do you want to try to hang on part time or as a consultant to the job from which you have been or will be eased out? Would you like to get a similar job? Or can you think of some alternate kind of job, perhaps something you have never done before?

4. If the latter is true, can you identify some interests that you have not expressed in work that might lead to a job? What are your talents, hobbies, skills? Or what skills and talents could you develop? You know more than you realize. You have a lifetime of experience.

5. Can you investigate training programs available in your area that will prepare you for a late-in-life career? (Check with educational institutions and associations in your locale.)

6. Are you sure that you really want a paid job, or would you just as soon do volunteer work? If the latter, check out the federal, state municipal, and voluntary agencies in your area that use and place volunteers. Also, review the suggestions at the end of the previous chapter. Even if your ultimate goal is a paid job, volunteer work can provide experience, contacts, and a chance to try out.

7. Inform everyone you know that you are looking for a job; tell them that you are open to any idea. You never know who will turn up what. Be flexible; try things that may seem unusual.

8. Read your local and metropolitan newspaper ads. Check with public and private employment agencies, including those like AARP's Mature Temps, which specialize in placing older persons. List yourself with temporary agencies even if you really want a permanent job. Temporary jobs sometimes develop into permanent ones and at least you will get out of the house.

9. Remain or get active in organizations, including senior citizen organizations. You may hear of positions through these organizations or the members you will meet.

10. Accepting a job below your level of competence probably is better than sitting home worrying about how useless you feel and how empty life is. The money and social contacts you will make may be worth lowering your standards a bit. Besides, you won't be under too much pressure at work.

11. Try to get service organizations in your community to help you develop jobs for yourself and other older persons. Nag political and community leaders to hire you and other older persons as part timers or full time. Nag congressmen to get federal programs to employ seniors.

12. Try to figure out the peak periods for businesses when students might not be available. Offer yourself as some-

one who can fill in at these periods, especially during the holiday shopping rush, for example.

13. Keep an eagle eye on bulletin boards. Don't hesitate to put up ads in such public places as laundromats, churches, temples, supermarkets, etc., offering your services for pay.

14. If you have graduated from any school or college, no matter how long ago, you are still entitled to use its employment service. Sometimes the jobs that students reject or are too busy or proud to take may appeal to you. You have enough self-confidence to keep your dignity while starting again at the bottom.

15. Write a résumé geared realistically to the kind of jobs you are going to be able to get at your age. Send the résumé to all agencies and businesses in the community for whom you might like to work. Send it to all relatives and friends, too. Follow up with phone calls.

16. When you look for a job, present yourself well and don't complain. Don't talk too much or clam up. Relax. You know you are capable.

17. Use the telephone when you can to save yourself time and carfare, but make the effort to present yourself in person when that will be useful. Have the judgment, however, to realize that answering some ads is a waste of your time and money. Some people or companies are just not going to hire you at your age, but others may give you a chance. With time, you will learn how to judge the possibilities.

18. While you are looking for a job, do other things, too. Many schools offer free tuition for people over sixty-five. Take a course. You might get ideas for a job from the other people in the class and anyway you'll probably enjoy the course itself. Above all, don't sit home and brood. Go to events at your church, senior center, community center. Search out whatever is available for recreation in your

community. Local newspapers are a big help.

19. If you have additional ideas to those offered here and at the end of the previous chapters, please share them with us and with other older persons in your community. Do not be like some of the older persons we met who have rejected themselves and other seniors.
20. Realize that accident is important. By being out in the community, you may see or hear of something. Anyway, you'll get fresh air and exercise.
21. Read some of the books, articles, and magazines suggested throughout this book. You can get many of them at your community public library or use a university library near you. Librarians can suggest other books and magazines that also are good.
22. Think of what services you could offer persons older and less healthy than yourself or the handicapped. Could you shop, drive, cook, clean, garden, entertain, serve as a secretary? Many people will pay for such services. Advertise your services in the local paper. Also check out jobs with organizations and agencies that serve the aging and handicapped.
23. If you like children, think of services you could offer busy and employed parents and advertise. Remember, half of the mothers of small children work today. Parents also like to vacation sometimes without children or may need a trustworthy person to water their plants and check the house in their absence.
24. If you are not getting much support from your friends or relatives or have lost them, organize a support group among other elders in your community who also might like to work and are having trouble. Gripe sessions may help — suggestions and group action or pressure might emerge. Maybe you people could pool resources to start a small business or service company.
25. If you would like to work in a sheltered workshop but there are none in your area or they have long waiting lists, put pressure on social service agencies in your community to

start one. Perhaps you could start one, getting others to help, of course.

26. Get a list from the community council or Red Feather agency of social service agencies. See if any of them have possible jobs or suggestions.
27. Check out such places as nursing homes and hospitals and other around-the-clock places that usually have trouble getting people to work odd hours.
28. See if there are institutions for exceptional children or the mentally ill who can use your wisdom and love, if this interests you. Many such places use case aides who are given on-the-job training.
29. If you experience rejection when you first start looking for work, realize that it is inevitable and that there is nothing wrong with you — that ageism is a fact. In other words, don't take it personally so that you curl up and give up. Keep trying. Don't withdraw from life if a job isn't immediately available.
30. If you keep trying and there are still no jobs, you may be in a bad area. Again, do not assume you are at fault. Rejection is hard to take, but there is a lot of unemployment in this country among people of all ages. It is, of course, worse for older people and you may be unable to get work no matter how hard you try. Be angry openly about this. Don't turn it inward and become depressed. Write letters to the newspaper editor and to all of the legislators who represent your area, both state and federal. Write to the governor complaining. Do something to get out your justifiable anger. Join the Gray Panthers and work with young and old to change society.
31. When you finish reading this chapter make your own list of possibilities. Revise it every few months.
32. If you have enough money to live on comfortably and can't get a job, please realize that there are other ways of being human than working. Take a look at older persons in your community who are terribly busy doing other things. Keep your sense of humor. You may find you can manage to have a very happy life without a job. You are still *you* and a

worthwhile human being even without a paycheck. Get over the American hangup that only paid work is important. Look for new friends to replace the people who filled your worklife. Help others in your community. Swim, or do what you enjoy. Live a little. But if you really want and need a paid job, good luck. We will keep agitating to make more jobs available for older persons and we hope you will, too.

Notes

1. Robert J. Havighurst and Bernice Neugarten, in *Adjustment to Retirement: A Cross-National Study.* Robert Havighurst, Joep M.A. Munnichs, Bernice Neugarten, Hans Thomal, eds. The Netherlands: Van Gorcumt Co., N.V., 1969. Chapter 9, p. 146.
2. Many people were interviewed for Part I of this book. In the interests of space and to avoid unnecessary repetition of retirement situations, only about one-third of the cases were included and some others were presented in condensed form, as in the chapter on the Sheltered Workshop. Nonetheless, the input and comments of those people not mentioned are a valuable part of this book and we are grateful to them.
3. While doing research on a senior citizens housing project, we were made aware of the tremendous value of money to older people. The weekly bingo games, which the housing authority did not approve of, were very important to the residents. Bingo was their only way of making money and thereby achieving some measure of status among their peers. See R. Jacobs, "The Friendship Club: A Case Study of the Segregated Aged," *The Gerontologist,* Winter 1969.
4. Many people feel that "downward mobility" could become a way to exploit working people.
5. For an elaboration on the position of older women who had been primarily housewives and mothers, see the article by Ruth Harriet Jacobs, "A Typology of Older Women," *Social Policy* (November - December 1976).
6. Comprehensive Employment Training programs are now geared mainly to younger adults.

PART II
REMARRIAGE

Chapter Eight
Introduction

"Senior citizens and their concerned relatives need more information on remarriage as an acceptable life style."

As has been emphasized in Part I of this book, the proportion of elderly people in the population of the United States is rising. In sheer numbers, the elderly population has increased about sevenfold — from three million to twenty-two million in this century. At the present death rates, the older population is expected to increase 40 percent to thirty-one million by the year 2000. In the relatively short ten-year period between 1956-57 and 1966-67, the death rates among persons aged sixty-five and older declined in the United States, with somewhat larger decreases among females than among males. Thus, the older the age group, the greater percentage of females it contains (see Figure 8.1, p. 144).

As the numbers of older people in the population increase, so do the numbers of widows and widowers, who are, after all, the pool of potential late-life brides and grooms. In 1970, there were more than six million widows and a million and a half widowers in the United States. These figures represent a sixfold increase in the number of older widowers since 1900. From 1974 to 1985, the number of single females in the United States is expected to rise by about three million, and the number of single males by about seven-hundred thousand.

Concomitantly, the number of marriages between elderly men and women also has increased. More than thirty-five thousand marriages now occur annually in which at least one of the participants is sixty-five or older. A comparison of numbers of old-age marriages in the United States Marriage

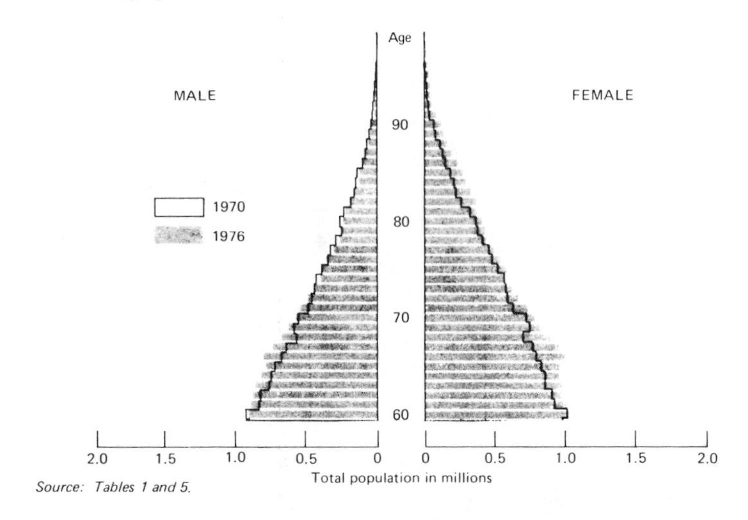

Figure 8.1: Changes in the numbers of older men and women: April 1, 1970 - July 1, 1976. Note especially:

1. The large increase in the number of older women in every age group, especially in the upper sixties and mid-eighties.
2. To a lesser extent, the increase in the number of men in their late sixties.
3. A decrease, or lack of increase, in the numbers of men in most age groups above age seventy-three.

Adapted from Series P-25 N0643, from U.S. Department of the Census, January, 1977.

Registration Area (forty-one states and the District of Columbia) between 1960 and 1973 reveals that the number of brides age sixty-five and older has more than doubled to more than sixteen thousand and the number of grooms has almost doubled to more than thirty-three thousand.[1] Statistics for late-life marriages in Mason and Sumner, the towns from which we chose the couples whom we interviewed, show the same trend.

Although there is a barrier to an increase in old-age marriage, namely, that there are between four and five single women to every unmarried man in the population over age sixty-five, there are several reasons to believe that in the future marriage among older people will be more prevalent. First, most people sixty-five and over are independent and not incapacitated. Only one in twenty reside in any kind of institution.

Among the noninstitutionalized population of the United States, only a very small percentage are not able to prepare a meal, do light housework, or wash themselves. Most older people, therefore, are physically capable of activities associated with courtship and marriage. In addition, medical advances undoubtedly will enable an increasing number of elders to enjoy a healthy old age.

Most widows and widowers prefer to live by themselves rather than with children or other relatives. Although older people are not isolated from their families — they generally live nearby and there is visiting and mutual aid — the growing trend to single residence is substantiated by statistics, our own interviews, and other studies. In the twenty-year period from 1950 to 1970, the proportion of older people living with relatives fell from more than 20 percent to 12.5 percent. For the most part, older people live with children only when necessary, mainly because of poor health. Such arrangements often are the last step before institutionalization.

Because an increasing number of older people are living by themselves, it can be predicted that the chances for remarriage increase. Elders living alone have the independence and freedom to form new relationships. But loneliness often is the silent partner of independence.[2] Thus, people living alone not only have the freedom, but also often have the motivation born of loneliness to seek out another mate.

Finally, attitudes toward old-age marriages seem to be changing. For one thing, the notion of sex in old age has gained considerable interest in recent years, stemming from the pioneering work of Masters and Johnson. According to geriatric psychiatrist Martin Berezin, the knowledge that old people are capable of sex and even have the *right* to a sex life is "filtering down to the masses."

Although it often is assumed that society looks with disfavor on old people marrying, we did not find any concrete evidence to substantiate this view. An informal poll we took of some college students showed that even though there may be prejudice against a "dirty old man" or woman who marries a much younger person, there is almost no negative feeling against the remarriage of two elders.

Increased awareness in the media and increased consideration by researchers to problems of the elderly seem likely to result in more positive sentiments towards every aspect of life in old age, including remarriage. Now, however, many of the elderly, as a minority group, accept negative views of themselves, as is the tendency of all victims of prejudice. Studies have shown that many older people self-stereotype — they incorporate negative characteristics that younger people attribute to them.

Elders and their relatives often are confused about the advisability of remarriage. A study conducted by sociologist Helena Z. Lopata revealed that many widows felt that remarriages were bound to be unsuccessful or that they were "too old" even to think about remarriage. Senior citizens and their concerned relatives need more information on remarriage as an acceptable life style. Professional people who work with the aged, as well as social and economic policy makers, also need information on remarriage.

As this information becomes available and as society's attitudes towards the elderly change, it seems likely that attitudes of older people themselves also will change. Lopata found that only one-fifth of the widows she interviewed expressed a wish to remarry. A future group of widows probably will show a more favorable attitude toward remarriage as they are able to gain more positive responses from the environment.

In the 1970 census, more than eighteen thousand couples over age sixty-five listed themselves as unmarried and living together. Some of these couples would like to remarry but have been unable to do so because of economic policy. A widow usually must give up a pension when she remarries; her Social Security benefits usually have been cut in half. Thus, changes in economic policy will mean changes for the better in the lives of these often conflict-ridden people.

Legislation recently passed in Congress will allow widows to retain the full amount of the Social Security benefit they received as single persons when they remarry. The enactment of this amendment to the Social Security finance bill on January 1, 1979, undoubtedly will encourage remarriage. In fact, remarriage actually will be rewarded by the government: a remarried couple will receive higher payments than a couple married since youth because the woman will receive a full allowance rather than a dependent's benefits.

Selecting and Interviewing Remarried Couples

The people themselves are the primary focus of this look at remarriage — their feelings, satisfactions, disappointments, and activities.

Obtaining information about their remarriages from older people themselves, although difficult in certain ways, is a valuable undertaking. Statistics are important, but as the authors of a recent statistical paper on remarriage state, "We have yet to tap the rich social meanings and . . . motives which surround late-life weddings."[3] We have little information about the human beings who make up the statistics; we know little about the process involved — about people's thoughts and feelings, about what factors were important to them, what influences they felt. We have some statistics, we have some information about the physical aspects of sex in old age, but we have had almost no information about the relationships between people. The following chapters contain such information. This material comes from in-depth interviews with twenty-four couples who were married late in life.

How, specifically, did we find the twenty-four couples and how did we obtain the information? First, we recorded the names of older couples who had applied for marriage licenses in two Massachusetts communities, here called "Mason" and "Sumner." By obtaining names in this impersonal way and not relying on recommendations of people we knew, we avoided biases that might have made a personally chosen group either "special" in some way or unrepresentative of most later-life marriages. By contacting *every* couple on our list — those who met our age requirements and had married in certain years — we became acquainted with many different kinds of people. Some were rich, some poor, and most were in between.

Mason is a medium-sized Massachusetts city that in 1970 had a population of about ninety thousand. The city has a higher than average number of senior citizens — more than 14 percent, compared with a national average of 9 to 10 percent — and includes a cross-section of social classes and ethnic groups.

The town of Sumner is primarily a summer resort area and a residential suburb. It had a 1970 population of about thirteen thousand, five hundred and borders the city of Mason. Sumner also has more older people than the national average and is more affluent than Mason. Forty-four percent of the families in Sumner have an income of $15,000 and over, as compared with only 18 percent of the families in Mason.

Of the twenty-four couples we met and talked with, eighteen were listed in the Mason records and six in the Sumner records. Not all were living in Mason or Sumner when we met them, although most lived nearby. Some couples had held their wedding ceremony in one of the communities and/or lived there when applying for a marriage license, and had subsequently moved. The farthest couple lived forty miles from Mason at the time of the interviews.

We do not claim that these couples are representative of the older population of the United States as a whole. Perhaps our results would have been different in some respects if we had interviewed people who lived in southern or western states. We do say, however, that because we contacted or attempted to contact every couple who met our criteria, these couples are representative of Mason and Sumner on the American northeast coast.

Our first criterion was that one spouse had to be listed as age sixty-five or older and that the other person had to be sixty or older. Since this is strictly a study of remarriage among older people, we did not want to include any May-December marriages of seventy-year-olds and thirty-year-olds. On the other hand, eliminating all marriages except those in which both spouses were sixty-five or older would have limited the group too much. Since men usually marry women younger than themselves, we could include a number of couples in which the husband was in his middle or late sixties and the wife in her early sixties. The final group of people we interviewed contained only one age "reversal" in which the wife was sixty-five and the husband under sixty-five.

In addition, we did not try to contact any couple in which one spouse was married for the first time. We felt that being married for the first time at an advanced age would create special problems. Such people would be different in some respects from second- and third-time brides and grooms.

With the assistance of the local telephone company, we determined that most people in the older age groups have telephones. We therefore decided to call the couples to ask their cooperation in providing information. Because of the topic itself and the desire to save time, we did not want to knock on doors unannounced.

We were not able to contact every couple on our list. Seventeen couples had simply "disappeared" — that is, we could find no current address or telephone number. Eleven couples have moved out of state, too far to be interviewed. In ten cases, one of the spouses had died, and three couples had unlisted telephone numbers.

Of the forty-four couples we contacted, more than half (twenty-four couples) accepted our proposal to be interviewed. Because we had used marriage license records spanning a five-year period, all of the couples had been remarried between two and six years when we interviewed them.

In an interview study such as this, the question arises that perhaps the people who refuse are different from those who accept, that perhaps they have special reasons for not wanting to give information about themselves. Here, we might suspect that the people who refused had unhappy marriages — that they were reluctant to discuss negative feelings with a stranger or to admit that they had made a mistake. Although there is no way of knowing absolutely, we believe that the couples who refused were not so different from those whom we interviewed. Of the twenty people who refused, eight people did say that they had good marriages, or were "very happy." The feelings of the other twelve people probably varied; they did not say how they felt. Furthermore, not all the people we *did* interview had positive feelings about their marriages, as we shall see. Several people welcomed the chance to vent feelings of frustration or hostility, or to complain about little things that bothered them. Although most couples were satisfied with their marriages, there was a range of feeling from ecstatically happy to miserable.

Each couple was interviewed three times — first together, and then husband and wife separately. Meetings were held in the couples' homes, where the participants could feel most comfortable and where they could be interviewed most conveniently.

The tone of the interview was conversational, since we wanted to avoid cut-and-dried question-and-answer sessions. Because we were particularly interested in certain areas, the interviewer used an "interview guide" that listed certain topics as reminders and contained specific important questions we wanted to ask during appropriate points in the conversations. Most of the people told us their stories at their own pace, emphasizing whatever aspects they considered important. We asked questions about particularly interesting areas, things we did not understand, or topics that people had not broached themselves. Obtaining information in this way has been called "focused" interviewing. We developed a feeling of warmth and friendliness toward each couple, which we hope was mutual.

The first joint meeting generally was a get-acquainted session. The couple was assured that their names would not be used and that their responses would be identified only by number. All of the names we use here are fictitious.

The second interview allowed us to get to know husbands and wives even better, as we spoke with each separately. The interview alone was particularly valuable if one spouse were reticent and/or if one partner had monopolized the conversation during the first visit.

Most of the couples made us welcome, offered refreshments, and were delighted to give a tour of the house or apartment, which looked as if it had been tidied especially well. Almost all of the people were well-groomed and looked as if they had made a special effort to look nice.

Each interview varied from about one-half hour to more than three hours, depending on how loquacious the informant was. In all, we spent a total of two-and-a-half to nine hours with each couple, usually on two days.

Interviews were recorded on tape. The small unobtrusive recorder with a built-in microphone did not seem to bother anyone. No one objected to its use, or even took much notice of it.

After transcriptions were made, we had a word-for-word record of each interview. Thus, we did not have to rely on hastily written notes or sometimes faulty memories. Using the transcriptions, we categorized responses for almost 150 different topics and obtained frequencies of response for men and women together and then separately. Especially interesting were the differences in the men's and women's statements.

The findings in the following chapters include the results of categorizing frequencies of responses, and the results of statistical procedures done with the help of a computer. But our emphasis in this book is on the words of the people whom we met. We hope that recording their feelings, experiences, and anecdotes will give a sense of immediacy to the question of remarriage in later life.

We told the older married couples that they would be helping other older people who might be contemplating remarriage, the families of these elders, and people who work with seniors. We sincerely hope that this is so.

Notes

1. Authors of a recent study of remarriages among the elderly, based solely on statistical information, emphasize that the *proportion* of old-age marriages relative to the total number of marriages in the United States has not changed in the last decade. See Judith Treas and Anke Van Hilst, "Marriage and Remarriage Rates Among Older Americans" in *The Gerontologist* of April, 1976. We came to the same conclusion after working with similar data: in 1960, brides sixty-five and older constituted approximately 1 percent of all brides in the Marriage Registration Area of the United States; in 1970, elderly brides still constituted only 1 percent. Likewise, the proportion of elderly grooms remained the same at 2 percent. Treas and Van Hilst state that this level is not

likely to rise. Even if the *percentages* of old age marriages have not risen in the last decade, however, the rise in the *numbers* of older brides and grooms indicates that this phenomenon warrants study.

2. The author of one large-scale study found that more than half of the elderly women she interviewed cited loneliness as the overriding burden of widowhood. See Helena Z. Lopata, *Widowhood in An American City,* Cambridge: Shenkman, 1973.
3. See Judith Treas and Anke Van Hilst, "Marriage and Remarriage Rates Among Older Americans," *The Gerontologist* 16 (April 1976): p. 134.

Chapter Nine

Portrait of a Remarried Couple

"I thank my lucky star for finding such a good wife."

As we got to know each couple individually in the course of our interviews, it became impossible to cite any one couple as most "typical" of remarried elders. All of the couples had something unique or unusual to contribute.

The following four chapters give a picture of the progressive phases of remarriage. They are arranged to tell the couples' stories chronologically, showing changes and transitions from one phase to the next. The generalizations are based on characteristics common among the twenty-four couples. The findings become real when we hear the couples speak about themselves, their feelings, and their new life.

Each chapter discusses and analyzes a circumscribed time period of the marriage, and within each chapter each general finding is enlivened by quotations from some of the couples. It therefore is difficult to delineate the complete story of any one couple's remarriage experience. With these constraints in mind, we have composed a portrait of a represenative pair of newlywed elders and will relate their story from beginning to end in terms of this book. Although they do not correspond to any one couple we interviewed, Lou and Irene Miller typify the most prevalent characteristics of our group of late-life brides and grooms. (The chapters following will deal more specifically with each of the factors mentioned.)

Irene Grant is a large-boned, energetic woman. Her tightly curled brownish hair bounces about her head as she walks around her house, occasionally humming to herself. In 1972, Irene was living alone in a small, white frame house on a side street in the town of Mason, Massachusetts. It was the same house to which she had moved with her husband, Dick, after his promotion, when their children were in high school almost twenty-five years ago. Hard to believe that Joey was now thirty-nine, with three children of his own, and Elizabeth, a few years younger, had two. It sometimes came as a shock that she was sixty-seven years old. She certainly didn't *feel* sixty-seven! And could it really have been six years ago that Dick had died? How long that year of nursing had seemed before his death from lung cancer. But the years since then had gone by quickly. Of course, the first year had been very difficult; and she still felt lonely, especially at home at dinner time and in the evening, watching television or reading by herself.

Soon after Dick's death, Elizabeth had suggested that Irene move to Sumner and occupy their spare bedroom. Irene had never seriously considered it. "You have your lives and your friends," she said firmly to her daughter, "and I can get along fine by myself." And she *had* managed to be active and busy with her family and good friends. She felt lucky. Both Joe and Elizabeth lived in neighboring communities, so she saw them and her grandchildren often. They all liked to visit Grandma, just as she liked to have them liven up her quiet house.

Her friend Stella had lost her husband the year after Dick died, and they had taken several trips together. Their boat trip one summer across the Great Lakes had been relaxing and enjoyable, despite her initial qualms about not liking the boat's motion. Irene liked travelling with her cheerful friend Stella, even though it was not always easy to divide up the dinner checks.

In addition, Irene still had many old friends, some from the early years of her marriage, with whom she often went out shopping and for dinner. Three afternoons a week she volunteered at the local library. The calm feeling of orderliness in the reference room as she alphabetized the cards and organized the dictionaries and catalogs seeped into her, giving her, too, a quiet sense of order as she moved through life.

Although there had been a man or two in the six years who had been interesting and who might have been interested in marrying her, Irene had not seriously considered remarrying. How could she go through another sickness like Dick's? And, besides, she told herself, she had as much happiness and contentment as she could expect at this time in her life.

Lou Miller is a quietly efficient man with a shy almost boyish smile, despite his seventy-four years. In 1972, he was living in the town of Sumner in the apartment he had shared with his wife. She had died six months ago, only a few months after her terminal illness had been diagnosed. Now he was all alone after forty-three years of a good marriage. Sometimes, as he wandered through the quiet rooms, he thought the loneliness was almost unbearable. Sure, he had quickly learned to make himself a simple meal and to keep the apartment reasonably neat, and his daughter, Louise, kept an eye on him. But it certainly wasn't the same without Julia. Sometimes he even thought about going back to work just to get out of the house and see some people. But, he thought, who would hire a seventy-four-year-old retired pipe fitter? So, he filled the time as best he could by driving downtown where he bumped into his old pals, visiting his younger daughter and her family in Vermont, fishing occasionally, reading the newspapers, and avidly following the baseball, hockey, and football games on television and radio.

No one could take Julia's place; but maybe if he met the right woman, he might feel happier again.

On one of his trips downtown Lou ran into the Blairs, old friends of his and Julia's. Since Julia had died he had not seen them very often. "Why don't you come for dinner on Friday? Our friend Irene is coming from Mason and we'd love to have you." Okay, he thought; why not? It would be good to discuss fishing with Fred Blair again, and Molly was a terrific cook. He didn't even think about meeting their friend Irene.

The week after he met Irene, Lou would think of her every so often. And Irene recalled the evening as one of the most pleasant she had spent in a long time. She had to admit that she had enjoyed Lou's conversation.

"Well, the worst that can happen is that she'll say no," Lou said to himself, as he picked up the telephone and dialed Irene's number. As they chatted, he asked if she would like to go for a ride the following Sunday afternoon. When she accepted with what sounded like enthusiasm, he was almost surprised to note his own pleasure. They each looked forward to Sunday, albeit with some nervousness.

As she smoothed her hair and checked her lipstick before Lou arrived, Irene felt more like seventeen than sixty-seven. "But I needn't have worried," she thought later that night after Lou had brought her home. They had had a lovely, leisurely drive on quiet country roads.

After a few weeks, both Lou and Irene took it for granted that they would go for a drive every Sunday and would stop for supper before returning home. Both looked forward to their meetings. They seemed to be able to talk about anything together. "Lou is most attentive and kind," thought Irene.

She invited him to her home for dinner one evening, taking great care as she cleaned the house and cooked a chicken dish that she knew he liked. He was pleased with her delicious efforts and felt very comfortable in her tidy home. Soon afterwards, they began to talk on the phone every day and to see each other more than every Sunday. When Lou left to visit his daughter in Vermont for a week, Irene realized that she missed him.

On his return, she was not surprised when Lou told her he had thought of her often. She had become very important to him, he said. After an awkward silence, he said that he wanted them to marry. Irene had mixed feelings about such a step. She knew that she felt a great deal of warmth toward Lou; in fact, she hadn't felt so *alive* since long before Dick's illness. But hadn't she said she would never remarry? What would her family and friends think? How would her life change? With all of these questions weighing heavily on her mind, she told Lou that they should wait before deciding anything definite.

Lou and Irene socialized more frequently with their friends and families. They often played cards with the Blairs and were invited for dinner at their children's homes. Both were pleased that their children had favorable things to say about their parent's friend.

Three months after Lou first broached the subject, Irene, too, decided that they should marry. Her misgivings had become more and more insignificant compared with the thought of spending the rest of her life with someone she now realized she loved. She was certain that her children and most of her friends would approve of her remarriage—but, regardless, she would do it anyway! Lou was overjoyed. They would marry in two months, he said; there really was no reason to wait any longer.

One year after meeting, Irene and Lou were married in the small chapel of Irene's church in Mason. All of their children and grandchildren, a few brothers and sisters who lived in the area, and Irene's two best friends attended the ceremony. Afterward, they celebrated with dinner and champagne in a local restaurant. Everyone had a happy time.

After five years of marriage, Irene and Lou are very satisfied. Soon after they were married, Lou sold or gave away most of the furniture from his apartment and moved into Irene's house. At first, he felt out of place in what he considered her home. Now, however after doing many repairs and some painting, he thinks of it as *their* home.

Both Lou and Irene now see their children and friends less often, although they still keep in close contact. They are happy with each other's company and do not need to rely on family for close personal ties. Lou had not been to any parties sponsored by his men's club in years. Now he and Irene like to go to dance a little and to socialize. He enjoys trying the new recipes she prepares, and they sometimes go fishing together. After Lou's cataract operation last winter, Irene cared for him when he returned home from the hospital.

Although Irene often thinks of Dick, she has never regretted her decision to remarry. When her daughter, Elizabeth, and her husband had a serious problem with their own marriage, Irene felt relieved at being able to discuss her worry and concern with Lou. Lou sometimes tells people that he "thanks his lucky star for finding such a good wife."

When Irene remarried, her Social Security was halved, but with Lou's Social Security and his pension, and his no longer having to pay rent on an apartment, they manage very well. They both enjoy travelling and are saving for a trip to the Bahamas.

This year Irene was delighted when her friend Stella re-married. Irene hopes that the example of her own happy second marriage may have contributed to her friend's decision and to her happiness.

Chapter Ten

Phase I: Being Alone

"I used to think I'd make a pretty good hermit, but it's not for me."

The time between losing the former spouse and meeting the present husband or wife is important to both men and women as a period of adjusting to a new way of life and of examining attitudes toward other people and toward life itself.

In recalling this phase of their lives, the remarried people talked openly about their previous marriages, their relationships with relatives and friends, their feelings of loneliness, their activities, and their relationships with the opposite sex. Their discussions emphasized the differences between the men's and the women's experiences and feelings, which came through strongly as the couples talked about themselves.

Previous Marriages

All of the men and women we interviewed had been married before. Because so many people spoke at length about their previous marriages, we believe this topic warrants some discussion here, even though it is outside the main focus of remarriage.

For most of the people, the present marriage was their second. The men's previous marriages averaged thirty-nine years, and the women's averaged twenty-six years. Almost everyone described their former marriages as "excellent" or "good." "If my previous marriage hadn't been so good, I don't think I'd have wanted to try again." This feeling was expressed in one form or another by many of the remarrieds.

Seventy-one-year-old Jim Cunningham stated, "I used to think I'd make a pretty good hermit, but not for me. Not after being married happily once. So, I went out and did it again. Lucky she had me," he laughed. "I'm lucky in love — that's one thing I'm lucky in. It's funny; there are so many marriages in trouble nowadays."

Jim's sentiment that he had been "lucky in love" twice was a widely shared one. Only two women and four men described their previous marriage as "fair" or "poor." Eighty-four-year-old Bob Johnson was one of the unhappily married men.

"My first wife always talked about her sons — 'my Henry, my Billy' — but she didn't treat either of them right. She always wanted to fight with the neighbors. *We* fought every day for twenty years. All my life I couldn't talk to another woman. She'd swear I had a date. But I put up with it. Came pretty near to separating a couple of times, but I took my vows and stuck to them." Three months after her death, Bob married his first wife's sister who, although in a wheelchair, was eager to keep house and to help him to recuperate from a serious operation. "I didn't want to live alone," he admitted. "She agreed to come down here to my place and we've never been sorry. After six years of marriage, she's still my sweetheart."

Eighty-six-year-old Helen Johnson's remarks about her first marriage are more typical of the comments made by most remarried older people. "It was good, a very good marriage. My husband was a good provider, a hard working man. He never got cross. He'd start to whistle instead."

A few of the men and the women had been married twice previously. Typically, the women, when quite young, had had a first short marriage that soon ended in divorce and was followed several years later by a good marriage of long duration. Such was the situation of Pearl Whelan.

"My first husband got a girl in trouble. I kicked him out. The second marriage was wonderful, wonderful. Of course, at first he didn't have any money. He was on the WPA, and then he got a job at Morton Electronics. He came home with his envelope every week and he laid the money on the table, paid all the bills, and what was left, we went to the amusement park.

We walked on the beach and everything."

Two men followed this pattern of brief first marriages followed by long second marriages. Conversely, two other men had had long first marriages followed by brief second marriages. Frank Lane had been happily married for more than forty years when his wife died. After her death, he started to drink heavily. Eventually he joined Alcoholics Anonymous, cured himself, and became a popular speaker on the AA lecture circuit. At a convention in Chicago, he met an attractive sixty-year-old widow from Milwaukee. "We wrote a lot of long letters back and forth," Frank says, "and then I went out to visit her on my vacation. We had a swell time together and decided to get married. She had a lovely modern house," he continued, "with a lot of fancy furniture and a big new car." Frank was awestruck by her lifestyle and all of her possessions, which were far beyond what he had ever been able to provide on his salary as a machinist.

"When I first went out there, of course, she was attentive, but then after we were married a while she would not get up in the morning and fix breakfast." After some awkward hesitation, he acknowledged, "She was a little oversexed, you know. Even at sixty-five you're not as young as you used to be. I tried to fulfill my obligations in a way, but it was too demanding." Their marriage ended after one month.

Most of the married elders had known in advance that their previous spouses had not long to live; most of the spouses had succumbed to terminal illnesses. Often the spouse (husbands as well as wives) had nursed the sick partner and run the household as well. As Helen Johnson remarked, "My first husband was sick for quite a few years. I took care of him, the house, the hens, the cows, and the garden. I worked very hard."

John King cared for his wife for six years before she died.

"She got diabetes, and from that she got high blood pressure. Then she got glaucoma. So I was pretty busy, you know. I calculated out what her meals should be — the carbohydrates and proteins and fats — and tried to make her a good meal. I did that every day. And then, of course, I gave her her insulin shot every morning. And I tested her urine now and then to see how it was. She'd pass out, you know, get unconscious. We went to the New York World's Fair with the Golden Age Club, and while we were down there, we were taking the tour and when we got in the bus, she started to 'go,' see. So, I had to leave and get back to the hotel. I checked her to see if she needed more sugar, or less sugar and she finally got out of that all right. But you never knew when you went someplace whether something was going to happen, so you had to be on your watch all the time. We didn't call on relatives to help when she was sick. We didn't want to disturb anybody, see. So, we made the best of it.

"One day, we went to Mason Hospital for her glaucoma. We went up on the bus. So, when we came back, she came up the street here, and sat down in that chair, and died. She was a wonderful woman. She was really nice," he added wistfully.

Dave Somers also had cared for his wife, who had had a serious progressive disease, until she became completely incapacitated and required hospitalization in an institution for the terminally ill. Every day for a year, he visited her in the hospital, knowing that there was no hope for her and seeing her become worse and worse. "My neighbors helped me out a lot during that time," Dave recalls, "especially Ruth; she was a widow who lived near us. Every so often she would drive me to the hospital and back home again. And she used to invite me to dinner once in a while. So, a year after Ida died, Ruth and I were married." "How could I go wrong," Ruth Somers interjects, "when I knew how wonderful he'd been to Ida?"

Seven women and two men had coped with the sudden deaths of spouses. After the death of his first wife, Gil Norton remarried a woman who had been her good friend. "Shirley and I were married less than a year. I went out to get a newspaper," he said, "and when I got back I found her slumped down in a chair. I tried to do something, but it was too late."

Some women praised their present husbands by contrasting them with their first husbands. A few women made an uncomplimentary comparison of the present husband with the previous mate. Flora Williams, for example, chose to remember and speak about only the positive aspects of her two previous husbands and to compare her present husband's behavior unfavorably. "Percy, my first husband, never complained" she stated. "Everything was always wonderful. No matter, even if it was just leftovers he'd say it was such a good meal. And he always made you feel so good, you know. Harold, my present husband, never says anything tastes good. Just the exact opposite. Roland, my second husband, was very complimentary, complimenting on the meals and what you wore and like that. I don't think Harold would notice if I had a new dress on every day."

Most people were familiar with both the facts of their spouse's previous marriages and the feelings of the mate toward a former husband or wife. As one perceptive man commented, "How can my wife forget someone she lived with for thirty-five years and who was the father of her children?"

Time Alone

The length of time between the death of a spouse and the subsequent remarriage varied greately between men and women. Two years alone was the shortest time for any of the women in the sample; three remarried after this time. Nearly half of the women had lived for ten years or longer as widows or divorcees before remarrying. Men remarried much sooner: more than half rewed in a year or less. Only three men were alone for ten years or longer. On the average, women were alone twice as long as men — six-and-a-half years versus three-and-an-eighth years for men.

Why do men marry after much less time alone? One important reason is demographic: in 1974, there are between four and five times as many widows as widowers. A greater percentage of women than men live to be sixty-five and older. Eighty percent of the women in this country, versus only 65 percent of the men, reach age sixty-five. This 15 percent difference in the survival rate greatly increases the ratio of women to men. Also, the women who do reach age sixty-five can expect to live about four years longer than men the same age. Statistically, women will live another seventeen years, whereas men will live about thirteen years more.[1]

A man who wants to remarry probably can find a willing woman either in his age group or a younger one. On the other hand, a woman who wants to remarry probably will have difficulty finding an available man. As a result, she usually will resign herself to a life alone and will compensate for the loneliness by involving herself in other relationships and activities.

Moreover, men are more motivated to seek remarriage. Most have less close relationships than women with relatives and friends, and they have acquired fewer skills for independent living than women have. Also, traditional patterns of courtship encourage men to take the initiative; women wait to be sought. These factors will be discussed in depth later.

For the older people we interviewed, there was no relationship between the type of death of the previous spouse (sudden or following a long illness) and the length of time before remarriage.[2] Many older women may have been ready to remarry as soon as a year after their husband's death but had to wait longer for an eligible spouse. Other women who had rejected the idea of remarriage at the end of a year had apparently accepted the idea by the time they became acquainted with an eligible spouse.

Relationships with Family, Friends, and Work

Although nearly all of the men and women had at least one child,[3] most people chose to live in separate dwellings during widowhood. The only exceptions are the two women who had unmarried children living with them. One woman lived with her divorced daughter and her child, and the other with an unmarried son.

Many people emphasized the importance of maintaining a separate, independent existence apart from their children. "They have their own lives to lead and their own families" was a remark we heard often. Wilma Lane lived with her daughter's family for only a few months before moving to her own apartment. "Never try to live with your children: it's no good. I stayed there at my daughter's house a couple of months and I couldn't stand it. The kids, you know, have to do what they want to do. When I was listening to my TV, they were playing games on the other side of the living room. My daughter has a husband you can't take to, you know what I mean? The minute he came home, I went upstairs and I stayed there."

Another man, Paul Brooks, moved to his daughter's house in another part of the state shortly after his wife died. "I used to help her put up the drapes and do little things around the house, but I really felt like a fifth wheel." He bought his own television because he was afraid of imposing his preferences on his daughter and her family. According to Mary Brooks, his present wife, his daughter waited on him "hand and foot and had him an old man."

Even the decision to move near a child proved to be unsatisfactory for two people. One man and one woman had uprooted themselves after the loss of spouses to live in distant states so that they could be nearer to children. Both were unhappy with the arrangement and found it difficult to adjust. Each one subsequently returned to his or her former area after meeting the spouses while visiting the former home towns.

Even though they did not live with their children, these elders were not isolated or estranged from them. Of the people who had children, nearly everyone had at least one child close by during widowhood. Most of the women and nearly half of the men had at least one child in the same or a neighboring town. Naturally enough, the people whose children lived nearby saw them more frequently than the older people whose children lived further away. Only one woman and two men did not have a child who lived within the distance of a day trip up and back.

Nearly half of the men and a few more of the women either saw or spoke to a child every day or almost every day. Men most often mentioned having meals at a child's home or discussing business with sons, especially the three men whose sons had taken over family businesses. Women most often mentioned shopping with daughters, inviting children over for meals, and discussing family problems. Mary Brooks had two sons who "looked in on me every day after work — not to tell me what I should do or anything, but just to make sure everything was all right."

Overall, women tended to live closer to children and to see a child more frequently than men. The women also usually were more involved with their children than were the men. Only one-third of the men said that they felt "very close" to at least one child, whereas about half said that they felt "fairly close" or "not close at all." In comparison, fully half of the women stated that they were "very close," whereas only a few were fairly close or not close at all. The women's greater involvement with their children was obvious in their spontaneous discussion of children and families. Women often spoke at length about their children and grandchildren, but many men never mentioned their children spontaneously.

A conversation with Doris Field brought the topic of relationships with children into sharp relief. Doris was quite concerned about the potential break up of her son's marriage. She loved her two young grandchildren whom her daughter-in-law had threatened to take to Arizona. Doris felt close to her son and his problems yet powerless to do anything to help him.

"I've had an awful hard time. You can't tell tham anything. I say to my son, 'Gee, Bill, why don't you do this, do that.' 'Oh, Ma!' That's all you get is 'Oh, Ma.' I love my son. I get along very well with him. He's a nice kid. But now that he's married he's definitely on his own. Nobody can tell him or her anything. I call up my son and find they've got a problem or something. I get upset over it because I worry about them. And I say, 'Well, how are they going to solve this?' And my husband says, 'Leave them alone. It's theirs. He's married and he's out of here. Just forget it.'

"My husband has been through this before. He used to live upstairs from his son. And he used to see them often. He would try to tell the kids something, and off they'd go. So he's learned. He said, 'I told you not to call up. When you don't call up, you don't know.' I'm learning good by him. He knows more about it than I do. He's been through it."

Interestingly, more than one-fourth of the women and three of the men had never had any children. Previous research has concluded that children cannot take the place of a lost mate — the relationships are qualitatively different. Although these elderly widows might have felt a particular void in their lives for a close, intimate relationship, they did not say they were any more lonely or needy than those people who had children. Many men and women had close relationships with a brother or sister or with another relative. Two men had lived with sisters while they were widowers. Frank Lane explained his situation.

"We had always lived near to my brother and his wife. So after my wife died, it seemed natural that I'd see them a lot. Every day I'd drive my brother to work and sometimes I'd take my sister-in-law food shopping. They don't have a car and I'm retired and had the time on my hands. At night, if the weather wasn't too bad, I'd usually go over there to play some cards. And sometimes we went visiting together."

Because they are in the same age group, siblings often have much in common, including similar life styles and commitments. Men often talked more about their brothers and sisters than their children. For many men, siblings and their spouses were their only friends.

Only one woman said she had no close relatives. All the other women had a sibling or other relative with whom they had a warm relationship. Childless women especially valued the close relationship with a brother, sister, or other family member. Shirley Norton was close to her niece. "Janice is like the daughter I never had. We go on vacation together every summer. We rent a house by the ocean and have a terrific time. Her two children are good kids; they call me Auntie Shirley, but I feel just like their grandmother. After I got married we moved just across the street from Janice and her family." Another woman who had neither children nor siblings described herself as being "as close as a sister" to a cousin who lived in a neighboring town.

Patterns of friendship during widowhood were similar to relationships with children. Women were more involved with friends after the loss of a spouse than were men. Half of the women had "many" close friends or "more than seven," as compared to only a few of the men. Many women described close friendships that had endured most of their lives. None of the women reported having no friends during widowhood. One-third of the men, however, reported that they had no friends. "At this age, all of my friends have passed away," was a prevalent response to a question about the number of friends. Two men had many acquaintances, but no real friends.

As mentioned earlier, one important reason that men have fewer friends is demographic: there are fewer widowers than widows. Since older women outnumber older men, and since men marry younger women, a sixty-five-year-old widow usually can find companionship in a society of widows. No cmparable "society of widowers" exists because widowers are not in the majority until after age eighty-five.

In general, the world of work had been of greater importance in the lives of men than it had in the lives of women.

Although as many women as men in the sample had worked full time while alone and, indeed, more women than men had worked at some time during widowhood, the women typically had moved in and out of work during their working years. Most of the men had retired before the death of the previous wife and did not work at all while they were alone.

Women, especially those who had lost the spouse during middle age, most often went to work out of financial necessity. Some had worked in family enterprises while married to the former spouse and continued to work after his death. "My first husband ran a variety store," said Wilma Lane. "I used to go in to help several days a week, especially at lunch time to make the sanwiches. After he died, I still went in. Someone had to make the sandwiches, and I needed the money." A few women went back to work "to fill the time," as one woman said. Only two women had never worked, and four had worked only when young, before their first marriage. For most women, however, work was not as significant as it was for men. Even though some women received a great deal of satisfaction from work, they also expended considerable energy in both other activities and relationships.

Ruth Somers had worked as a part-time librarian during the ten-year period between the death of her first husband and marriage to her second husband. She identified herself as a housewife, however, and only peripherally, while discussing another subject, mentioned that she had worked. She talked at length about her son and daughter and their families. Dave Somers also discussed his son and their closeness, but when he spoke about the wholesale toy business he had founded, his sense of pride and the commitment he retained were unmistakable.

For men, involvement with kin and friends had been secondary to work activities. After retirement, a man whose work was the nucleus around which his friends clustered usually finds that now he has no close friends. Such was the case with Bob Johnson, a retired shoe worker. After he retired at age sixty-five, Bob, like Pat Sullivan, one of the bundle boys in Part I, looked forward to his weekly drives to visit his old friends at the shoe shop. When failing eyesight prevented his driving, he rarely saw his former friends and became quite frustrated. He says: "After I sold the car I sold my whole 'goings.' If I had my eyesight so that I could drive, I'd be the happiest man in the world." Says Helen Johnson, "That's all I hear, that he'd like to go back to work, although, of course, he can't because of his bad eyesight and other ailments." If available, a sheltered workshop (as described in Part I) might help Bob Johnson alleviate some of the frustration he feels at not being able to work.

Loneliness

The time between the loss of the previous spouse and remarriage was lonely for both men and women. It was especially lonely for the men. As the previous section shows, the men we interviewed were more socially isolated than were the women. Three quarters of the men said that they had felt loneliness "very much"; only half of the women responded in this way. Conversely, more than twice as many women as men said that as widows they had felt lonely "not at all" or "not much."

Statistics concerning suicide support the conclusion that

men find their situation alone more difficult than do women. As studies have shown,[4] men who no longer have a spouse and a job, who lack close relationships with friends and family, and who do not belong to organizations have the highest rate of suicide in the country.

Loneliness is felt most keenly by people whose loss is more recent. A man or woman who was alone one year was more apt to report a feeling of intense loneliness than someone who has been alone for ten years. Thus, the people who had been alone for a longer time (usually women) said that they felt less lonely than people whose remarriage had been sooner (usually men). A woman, no matter how lonely she had been, rarely was able to remarry quickly because of the lack of available mates. A very lonely man, however, could more easily assuage his loneliness by remarriage.

Interestingly, even though most people lived near children and saw them quite often, the relationships with children did not diminish loneliness to any great extent. The remarks of the Somers show this. This couple was more articulate than most and their statements were typical of the feelings of many couples.

Dave: It's the companionship, love, and the affection, the interest and the attention that you give each other which is truly living a married life.

Ruth: Yes, your children can't do these things for you. You love them dearly and they love you, but they have their own lives and, while I'm sure they love both of us very much, 'cause they're good kids, they still have their own families.

Children could not meet affective needs that only a spouse could fulfill.

Friends were more successful at easing loneliness than were children. Siblings or other same-age relatives often served the same companionship function as did friends. People who had more friends were less lonely; and it is easier for women to retain friends than for men. After his wife died, Ralph Kane, for instance, found himself in a position not unusual among single men. "See, for many years we lived in Bolton. We had many friends there. Then we moved out here [to a condominium in a community about thirty miles from

Bolton]. I didn't have anybody who I wanted to sit down and discuss my problems with. Somehow, my friends from Bolton, I just got away from them. It was my own fault."

Because he did not realize that wives are the social secretaries of families and become more involved with friends than do husbands, Ralph blamed himself for not retaining his former friends. He continued, "My first wife, my late wife, somehow or other kept me with my friends. When I lost her, I lost my relationship with friends."

Typically, Ralph's present wife, Alice, had many good friends during her six years of widowhood, especially one who "lost her husband just a few years after I lost mine. We went to Europe together." Upper middle-class and middle-class women mentioned that they had enjoyed travelling with friends or going out to dinner or a movie.

Women in lower income brackets most often mentioned close relationships with family members, which resembled friendships with unrelated people. "Every Tuesday night I'd go to my daughter's for supper then we'd go down to the church and play bingo," said Wilma Lane. "I'm pretty good; I'd play eight or ten cards at a time and I used to win all the time."

Marie King related her social experiences as a single person. "My sister, who was also a widow at that time, she and I used to go places together. We have lots of cousins who live in some of the towns around here that we'd see. And of course we saw a lot of my children and her children. Once we drove to Chicago to visit our brother."

Working, either full time or part time, eased the feeling of loneliness for some women. Greta Hayes had been a high-school teacher who loved her work. "Teaching kept me very busy," she stated. "The type of work I did kept me from being lonely. It really was wonderful that I had my teaching to go to. I had adjusted, you know. I had a very happy life by myself. I had some very good friends with whom I enjoyed doing things. So, we always had something to look forward to. We were always planning and taking trips or going out to dinner."

The more prevalent attitude toward work was that even though it directed one's thoughts in a different direction for a while, the loneliness returned. Doris Field, whose husband had been killed in an accident, described her loneliness as "an awful feeling when you're all by yourself. You're used to somebody all the time, and all of a sudden you're alone." She worked all day in a shoe factory and felt especially lonely coming home to her empty house "at night when you know there's no one there." Ralph Kane also mentioned the loneliness of "coming home to an empty house" after work. "Working [in a retail store] gave me a chance to not just sit on my problems, you know. I'd get up early in the morning. Then I'd come back home about six, make myself a meal, and that was it."

Ralph was one of several people who stressed that in the months following the death of a spouse, he had little interest in any social contacts. "For quite a while I wouldn't even go down to the clubhouse in the condominium. But then I kind of snapped out of it."

Sam Gold recalled that "for three months or so after my wife died, I really was kind of miserable." He refused all social invitations and resented friends for "trying to marry me off." After a time, however, he accepted some invitations to go out for dinner with married friends and relatives and soon met Mildred, his present wife.

About half of the men and half of the women mentioned forming relationships with the opposite sex other than the person they married. Ralph Kane recounted his experience with dating. "I started chasing around a little bit, and it wasn't the type of life I cared for. Somehow I think I was meeting the wrong type of individual. You know, when you're married and you're out of circulation for approximately forty years, and you start going out, it was quite a difficult thing. I don't know. You have to make sure you say the right thing at the right time because the woman is an older woman — I didn't go out with thirty-year olders — and they're all widows. You know, trying to put myself into circulation, it was rather uncomfortable."

But several other men seemed to enjoy "playing the field." As Morris Singer recalled, "Everybody was after me. You know, when you like to dance and go out and be happy, everybody was after me. They knew me, they'd call me."

His seventy-two-year-old wife, Margaret, also had some dating experience, which she recounted in her German accent: "A few people were very interested and wanted to push. But I told them right away, 'I go out with you to a concert or something, but if you think of marriage, no.' Because I see somebody once or twice, I know already it's no good for me."

Margaret Singer, who had left Germany during World War II, openly discussed her feelings during widowhood: "I was very lonely. Loneliness is a big thing when you get older, anyway. I had a very hard time during the war, then I had a very happy time [during her first late-in-life marriage] and then I came back to being alone, and I got a lot of responsibilities. My husband had real estate and all kind of things I had suddenly to take care of. I had a very nice home I lived alone in. My only sister lived so far away [in Argentina]. I had a few relatives. But you know how it is, I didn't want to hang on to people too much. I drive, thank God, so I was independent. And I did some part-time nursing work. But I never could think to go through the rest of my life like that. I was still not so old and the loneliness was very fearsome."

Despite the "fearsome loneliness," Margaret was luckier than many of the widows in that she had been left an adequate income, in addition to her 'very nice home.' She was one of seven women who were financially secure after their husbands died.

"My husband knew he was very ill," said Alice Kane, "so we consulted our lawyer and made plans. I've been very fortunate financially. We had money saved and we set up a trust fund. I imagine it would have been terrible if I'd had to worry about money matters, too."

Many widows did worry about their loss of income after their husband's death. One-third of the women said they did not have enough money during widowhood and wished that their financial situation "could have been better." Only one woman was able to live on Social Security alone; half of the women worked or received a pension plus Social Security.

Only three men said that they did not have enough money as widowers. But despite their more fortuitous economic position, single older men had a more difficult time than older women. Women were able to ease loneliness by keeping busy at some activity. Women who had a hobby such as sewing, gardening, or organization work were less lonely. Men were lonely even if they had interests or hobbies.

Furthermore, most of the men were retired. They were doubly bereft, having suffered the loss of both spouse and work. For these reasons, men were more positive about remarriage before meeting their present partners than were women. Twice as many men as women said that they had hoped to remarry someday. A man's need and desire for remarriage and an end to his loneliness apparently outweigh any apprehension he may feel. Conversely, more than twice as many women as men admitted to feeling uncertain about the decision to remarry before the wedding.

Before her first husband died, Greta Hayes had nursed him for nearly a year. "I never wanted to go through that kind of an ordeal,again," she emphasized, "so I thought I'd never want to get married again." Several other women made similar remarks. But the women's attitudes toward remarriage while single seemed to have little bearing on whether they eventually remarried. Finding a companionable, eligible spouse who wanted to marry was more important to the women than were the fears or doubts they harbored.

In conclusion, widowed elderly men are fewer in number than their female counterparts, and they are more unhappy and lonely as widowers than women are as widows. A widower, who typically lacks close family and friendship ties, needs a wife more than a widow needs a husband. He more openly wants to find a new mate and frequently is more successful in the pursuit than is a widow.

Notes

1. All data from the Administration on Aging.

2. Ira O. Glick, Robert S. Weiss, and C. Murray Parkes, in *The First Year of Bereavement,* indicate that women who had some preparation before their husbands' death were more inclined to think positively about remarriage at the end of the first year after his death.

3. The average number of children for women was 2.4 and for men was 2.0.

4. For a discussion about the high rate of suicide among older isolated and desolate men, see the article by E. Wilber Bock, "Aging and Suicide: The Significance of Marital, Kinship, and Alternative Relations," *The Family Coordinator,* 21 (January, 1972): pp. 71-79.

Chapter Eleven

Phase II: Meeting and Courtship

"The more we saw of each other, the better we liked each other. It just worked into something."

Meeting

The courtships of the remarried couples did not always begin with the meeting of two strangers. Six couples had known each other for many years during their previous marriages, including Bob Johnson, who married his first wife's sister, and Dave Somers, who married his solicitous neighbor, Ruth.

Most of the couples who had not known each other before were introduced by a mutual friend or relative. Such a meeting often was arranged with the expressed purpose of fostering a meaningful relationship, as in Bill and Pearl Whelan's case. Seventy-year-old Bill Whelan, a tall, lean, quiet man, was a retired draftsman. After his wife died, he sold his house and moved into a small apartment. Meals often presented a problem.

"I never was much of a cook myself," Bill confessed. "If I wanted a good meal I went out to a restaurant. Besides, I liked to get out of my apartment, where I could talk to someone. It got so I knew the manager at this one place, Todd's Grille, where I used to eat a lot."

Pearl Ryan had worked in a bakery around the corner from Todd's Grille since her husband died. "After leaving work at night, I used to hate going home to my empty house," Pearl said, "so many nights I'd stop at Todd's and have supper before going home."

In her hoarse voice, Pearl related how she met Bill. "We were both friendly with the manager. One day Bill was down there at the restaurant and said how lonesome it was without his wife, you know. 'Well,' the manager said, 'I know a girl. She's awful lonesome, too. Someday when she's in here, I'll introduce you to her.' So, one day when I went in, he introduced me to Bill. Bill brought his tea over, and we talked. He said, 'Someday maybe I'll give you a call. Give me your telephone number and where you live.'" After checking her address and occupation in the city directory "cause he's very fussy you know," Bill called and they began to see each other regularly.

Other such introductions by a mutual friend or relative were accidental, in that the introducer did not intend to bring the two people together. For example, Paul and Mary Brooks were introduced by Paul's daughter. Mary had come to visit Paul's daughter, with whom she had worked. While visiting, she met Paul, nine years older than she, who was living with his daughter after his wife's death. The four of them (the daughter and her husband and the Brookses) went out to dinner. Says Mary, "I knew how loved he was by his daughter and her family; we didn't have to get acquainted." When she returned home, Mary invited her friend's father to escort her to a family wedding. What she missed most when single, she says, was not having anyone to escort her to family parties. "I had to rely on my brothers-in-law for dance partners!" she says. The invitation encouraged Paul to see her again, and soon he was spending much of his time with her. When asked what his daughter's response to his announcement of the impending marriage had been, Paul replied, "I guess it was a shock. She said, 'I didn't imagine you'd get *married!*'"

Two couples met in a public place frequented by older people (one in a dance hall and one in a cafe.) One woman had been persuaded to go to the dance hall with a friend. The man she later married loved to dance and went there often.

Three couples met in settings expressly provided for Senior Citizens. The Shores, for instance, met at a Golden Age Club activity. As Mrs. Shore related in a Yiddish accent: "He was sitting near me at the Golden Agers, and I didn't even know him. He was looking so depressed. You could see that the man needs something. The trouble is, when I see someone lonely, I want to know what's the matter. He was sitting just like a chicken without a head. After that, he went his way, I went my way. So, the next time I went there, he was sitting there again. So, my friend said, 'Let's sit down with him. It will warm him up a little.' It was awfully windy. We sat down, and then we started to talk. You know the way it is...."

Five couples met in various other ways, including one through the "personal" column of a local advertisement booklet. George Field was looking for a used car when he spotted Doris Field's request for an unattached companion of the proper age. "Her notice caught my eye," George said; "so I wrote to her and we arranged to meet and then we got married about a year later."

The ways in which people met strongly suggest that people who are active, who get out of the house and are involved in social networks have a greater chance of meeting a mate than those who remain housebound.

Most of the people were able to keep active because they were in fairly good health. A full two-thirds of both the men and the women claimed that they had no physical problems, even minor ones, before their recent marriage. Some men and women had chronic or serious physical problems, but only one woman — eighty-one-year-old Helen Johnson, who had married her sister's husband — was incapacitated and in a wheelchair. The other people all were mobile and, for the most part, unrestricted in their physical activities. Although health generally tends to decline with age, even the people in their eighties were quite active when they met their spouse.

Eighty-five-year-old Harry Nolan, for example, recalled that "after my first wife died, I used to drive a great deal. I didn't go anywhere in particular. Anything that would amuse me. Sometimes just go for a ride. I remember one Sunday afternoon I drove about one hundred miles and didn't go anywhere. Just to see the country." While visiting his son, he remembered Marion, whom he had known as a young girl; she had been a friend of his first wife. Because he was in the same area, he decided to call her.

First Impressions

Most couples did not fall in love at first sight or see the proverbial thunderbolt. Only a few men and women mentioned being very interested in the spouse when they first met. John King said that there seemed to be a "magnetic line" between them. Most people were moderately interested or had at most a friendly feeling toward their future mate.

Two of the women were definitely not interested, but in their cases, male persistence paid off. As Claire Paulsen related: "Wednesday nights the girls at work went bowlin' and they used to go up to the Mayflower Club to have a nightcap before they went home. Everybody knew everybody else. I got introduced around. And I had a real nice time and really enjoyed it. That's where I met Earl. He was livin' with his sister. And he came over and asked me to dance. I never went out with anybody. I didn't want to. He kept after me I don't know how many weeks. Week in and week out. Askin', you know, did I want a ride home. One night I was dancin' with him and I said, I'll surprise ya!' He was always askin' me if I'd go out for steamed clams, and I hate clams. I never bothered to tell him I didn't like clams. After that I'd see him once in a while and we'd go someplace. Then he got a little boat and he asked me to go fishin'. So I went. I liked that; it's very relaxin'. And I really enjoyed his companionship because I didn't realize how lonesome I was. He had a car; we'd go for a ride. He was a great one for going out in the country and seeing foliage, which I'd never noticed before. A great outdoors man. And I liked that, too."

Most people were attracted to their spouses by their desire for companionship; others mentioned specific, personal attributes of the spouse, such as being "nice" or "kind" or "strong-minded." A few men and women mentioned physical attributes, such as "smiling eyes," "a beautiful smile," "good-looking," "neat and clean."

Four of the men mentioned the woman's housekeeping or cooking ability as what first attracted them. Although none of the men mentioned having had difficulty with housework or cooking when living alone and said they had done "all right," their other comments indicated that many of them felt the lack of a person to do the housework and cooking for them.

Morris and Margaret Singer had an interesting exchange when he mentioned why he was first attracted to her. 'I liked her because she had a clean house. Very clean. And she cooks — I mean it wasn't what I was used to, but that doesn't mean much. I like a clean house."

"That's not the right answer," she said, with a hint of annoyance in her voice.

"She's very nice," he replied, laughing; "is that what I'm supposed to say?"

"You said you liked the house."

"Well, I say it was clean. That, to me is a great thing."

Courtship

Most of the couples did not have long courtships, even though they claimed they had not fallen in love at first sight. About two-thirds were married less than a year after they began the relationship as two single people, and seven couples were married after a courtship of one to two years.

The two couples that had long courtships — of two and a half-years and ten years, respectively — had to cope with religious restrictions on remarriage. The death of a previous spouse, in one case, and a special dispensation in the other made these marriages possible.

Most of the men took the initiative or sustained the relationship after meeting, as in the cases of the Whelans and the Paulsens. In a few cases, the man and woman contributed equally to initiating and sustaining the relationship. Only three women were dominant partners at the beginning of their relationships with their future spouses, including Mary Brooks, who invited Paul to a family party and gave him the encouragement he needed.

Three times more women than men had negative feelings about remarriage before meeting the spouse. Marion Nolan's account of her courtship typifies such feelings. After looking up his first wife's old friend, Harry Nolan suggested that they go to lunch: "I didn't want him to spend much money on me and go very far away," Marion said. "We went in to the Idlewild restaurant, and he wasn't satisfied with the dinner. 'So,' he said, 'can I come back again and take you to a decent place?' So that Saturday..."

"If we'd had a good dinner that time I wouldn't have come back," Harry interrupted, laughing.

"It was about a month or two I guess before we saw each other again," Marion recalled. "We began to write, and he called me up. Before I knew it, we decided to get married. I guess I didn't think I ever would get married. I didn't think I wanted to. But as he came to visit, I kind of missed him when he didn't come. The more we saw of each other, the better we liked each other. It just worked into something."

The statement, "it just worked into something," was made quite often, especially by the women who had had no professed intention of marrying again. The women were just "dating" — going out because they enjoyed it — whereas the men were seriously "courting" — directing their activity towards marriage with that specific woman.[1] Marion Nolan's feelings of gradual habituation and dependency were not unusual. They exemplify the stages in a love relationship: rapport, self-revelation, mutual dependency, and finally, personality need fulfillment, as described by one sociologist.[2]

When the future spouses lived some distance away, the pattern of writing and telephoning, followed by more frequent face-to-face contact was a typical one. When couples got together during courtship, the most frequent activity was dining out, especially among more affluent couples. People often mentioned the woman's having prepared meals for the future spouse and, less frequently, going out to a movie or concert. Several couples liked to go dancing. As the relationship became more serious, many couples spent time visiting family members and friends of one or the other. These visits served as an indication that the relationship was special to both people.

Most couples, in fact, did not mention formal "dating" experiences and did not reminisce about specific activities during courtship. Instead, they emphasized that they had just enjoyed being together and that the feeling of companionship and closeness had grown stronger as the relationship progressed.

Most couples were quite reticent about their physical relationship during courtship, with one exception. Mary and Paul Brooks described themselves as being "like two kids." "We petted," said Mary Brooks, "I didn't want him to go home. He'd say, 'They're waiting for me,' the relatives he was staying with."

"When I finally got back to my nephew's place," Paul said, "I'd usually find them up playing cards. I used to get embarrassed when they'd give me sly looks," he continued.

Not all courtships progressed smoothly. Nine women and two men admitted to some indecision about the relationship, either before or after they had made a definite commitment. "I had always thought I'd never get married again," stated Pauline Holmes, who had been a widow for nine years. "By this time, I was pretty used to being alone. But then I met Roger and liked him and finally agreed to marry him. After I agreed, though, I began to wonder if I'd made a mistake, if I'd be happy being married again." People wondered whether or not they would be happy in another marriage. Women who had nursed husbands through long terminal illnesses were especially hesitant about having to undergo a similar ordeal, as Greta Hayes mentioned in the previous chapter.

The Paulsen's ten-year courtship has all the elements of a romantic novel: feminine lack of interest followed by blossoming love, inability to marry because of religious restrictions, break up of the relationship due to alcoholism, serious illness of the man, a death-bed meeting, reconciliation, and finally a happy ending. Here is how Claire Paulsen related part of the story: "Earl was very sick. They didn't expect him to live. He asked if they could get ahold of me. I said no; I don't want to go up because I don't want to start this all over. They pleaded with me. 'He won't be here long.' So, I went up to see him. He was in bad shape, but so happy that I came. 'Claire,' he said, 'I'm really gonna change. I'll never take another drink as long as I live. I promise.' But he had promised so many times, you see. 'I really mean it this time. Just your comin' here, I've made up my mind I'm gonna get better. I'm not gonna die. Someday I'll make it all up to you.' And he recuperated. He couldn't do much, but he went to work for Mike's Cab. I still didn't go out with him.

"One day I was waitin' for a bus to go to work. He came along in his cab, pulled right around and said, 'C'mon, I'll take you to work.' He had passengers, too. I said no. He said, 'Please get in. I want to speak to you.' I didn't want to make a scene, so I got in. 'Claire, I'm gettin' better,' he said; 'Do you know what I'm doin'? I'll never spend a half dollar in my life again. A half dollar is a shot and a beer. Every half dollar I get, I save.' And, even if he didn't have enough money and he got a half dollar, he wouldn't spend it. He'd go without. And then after he was well enough he went to work for himself as a carpenter-painter. He did good. Very good. He came a long way, believe me. And he's never taken a drink since. So, we're very, very happy. God love him, he's come right up to this. He's done it all by himself. Bought the house and everything."

Despite some qualms, everyone eventually decided that the favorable factors outweighed the uncertainties. As they talked about what was uppermost in the decision to remarry, both men and women mentioned the desire for companionship most frequently. (See the figures in the graph on p. 185.) More men said that they had desired companionship, just as more men had said they were lonely before meeting their spouse.

The men's desire for care was second only to companionship as a reason for the decision to remarry. "She was a good cook" and "I needed somebody to wash my socks" were important factors in their decision. Had they not remarried, several of the older men would have needed some type of institutional care. None of the women mentioned a need to be cared for.

The Whelan's situation illustrates the importance of the care factor for the men in many remarriages. "It was an eatin' problem with him," Pearl stated. "I was doin' his cookin' and freezin' it for him so he didn't have to eat out so often. Then I started meetin' the lady that cleaned his apartment, worked for his wife for years and years. She got sick, and she couldn't do it. So, I went down, picked up the house for him on my day off or Sunday, you know."

"Then I got sick," Bill interjected.

"Yes, we had an appointment on Thursday night to go to the restaurant over here for dinner with my girlfriend. We were supposed to meet Bill and he didn't come. We called him on the telephone, and he didn't answer the phone. So we went down. I had a key to the apartment. We found him unconscious on the floor. So I called the doctor and rushed him up to the hospital. That time he was takin' a drink once in a while and takin' tranquilizers. The doctor didn't tell him you couldn't take both of them together. If we didn't find him, in two or three hours he would have died."

Reasons given by men and women for their decision to remarry. Only reasons that were given first or second in order of response are recorded here.

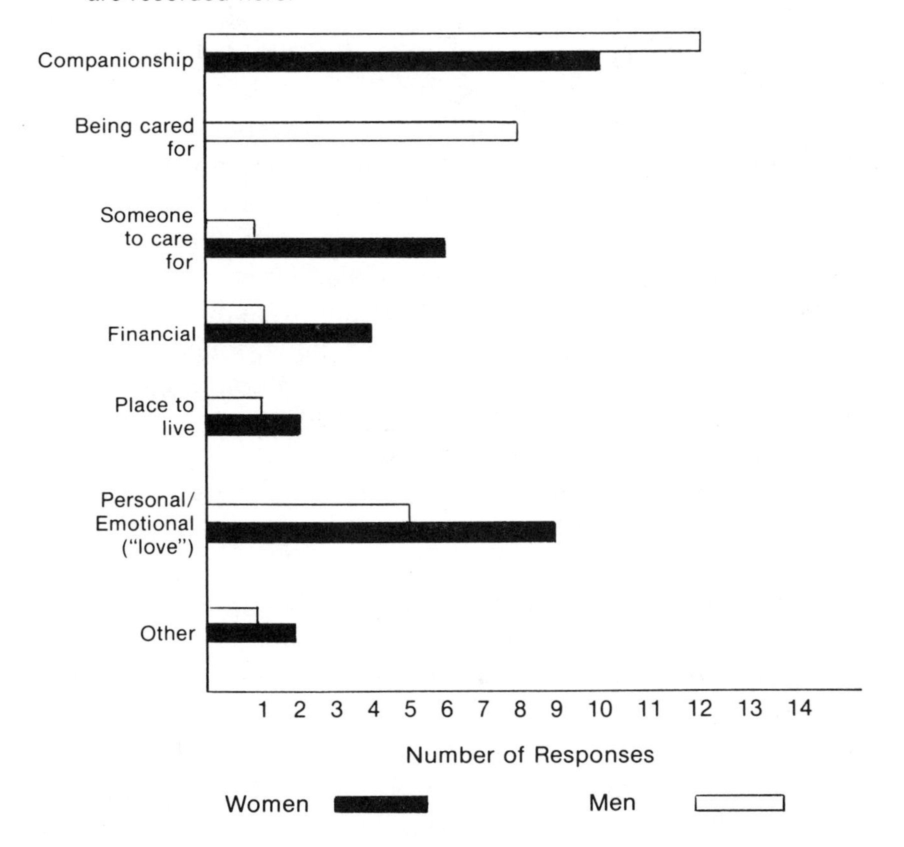

Women, on the other hand, mentioned personal aspects as frequently as companionship, citing the specific qualities of the mate and the fact that they had a deep emotional feeling for him. Some men also mentioned personal reasons, but women much more frequently than men stated that they were in love. This does not necessarily mean that men felt less love, but perhaps that women felt more free to talk about their emotions. Throughout the discussions, the men as a group were more reticent, especially in discussing "personal" matters.

One-fourth of the women wanted to care for the spouse, which, of course, meshed nicely with the men's desire for care. A few women mentioned the desire for a stable economic position. Marie King said, for example, "I didn't want to work any more." Three people mentioned that the spouse could provide a good place to live.

First Reactions of Family and Friends

Most people told their children and brothers and sisters that they were going to remarry; only four women and three men said that they had not informed any relative before the marriage.

"They thought it was wonderful," said Flora Williams; "Everyone was tickled pink." More than half of the people had received only positive reactions to their plans. Indeed, several people indicated that a sibling or child had recommended that they marry. "We hadn't really thought about getting married," said Bill Whelan, "until my brother came to visit from New Jersey. 'It's pretty stupid to pay two rents, two telephone bills and two utility bills,' he said to us, so we started to think about getting married."

"Both my children said it was dumb to get married to an old man who might get sick on me," murmured Theresa Parker. "Those were their exact words, and it hurt me to hear them talk that way." But only Theresa and two men received unfavorable reactions from their children.

The remaining three men and three women received a mixed reaction to their news. Usually one child was either unfavorable or unsure, but other children were pleased. There was no relationship between a child's closeness to the parent and his or her reaction to the impending marriage. Esther Rose, for example, said "My older son and his wife were very happy when I told them, but my other son, the younger one, wouldn't even talk to me when he heard. But my daughter-in-law, the one who was very pleased, later told me that she called my other son and talked to him. She finally persuaded him that I was doing the right thing because I was lonely and that it would be good for me to have a companion."

Most people, especially the men, informed children or other relatives only after they had made up their minds to remarry. Only a few women actively sought the advice of their children. The predominant sentiment was that even though children were consulted, it was up the people involved to decide. "It's *my* life, and my wife's, and we'll live as we choose!" one man had said to his children.

Eighty-year-old Will Hopkins recalled how he told his son: "Well, I went up to his house. When I got ready to leave, I said, 'Come out to the car with me.' I didn't want to say it in front of his wife, you know. I wanted to see what he'd say alone. I got out to the car and I says, 'I'm thinkin' a little about getting married. What do you think about it?' I don't know if he felt like fallin' over the car or not," Will said laughing; "but he said, 'It might be all right for you.' I suppose it was hard for him to face it. I imagine that he figured that if I intended to, I would anyway, regardless of what he said. No doubt I would've. 'Cause I'd just about made up my mind. It didn't take us long to decide."

Most of the children who reacted favorably were pleased to know of their parents' happiness. "My children both said they wanted me first to be happy," said Mary Brooks, "and when they saw how happy Paul and I were together, they were both very pleased." Many people also realized that now their children would not have to worry about their being alone, especially if they should become ill, and that the children would not have to provide quite as much companionship and care. Others commented that children reacted positively because they knew what a fine person the prospective mate was.

Children who did not express immediate happiness at the parents' decision usually said that they were shocked. On reflection, the children's amazement and shock usually were followed by approval.

A few children openly said that they thought their parent's remarriage showed disloyalty to the deceased parent. Interestingly, no one said that a child disapproved because his or her inheritance might be smaller. This is contrary to public opinion, which often attributes children's disapproval of a parent's remarriage to this fear. No parent, however, reported a child's having so selfish a motive, even though he or she may have thought it.

Negative reactions were more prevalent from friends than from relatives. Most men who told friends received some negative comments. John King said, "I used to be quite friendly with my neighbor across the street. He was retired, too. So, naturally, I told him that I was going to get married. Since then he hasn't spoken one word to me." John obviously was perplexed and hurt by his former friend's reaction to his remarriage.

Almost half of the women had received some negative or uncertain response from their friends. Dorothy Shore stated bluntly, "All my friends thought I was crazy." Several women said that their friends had asked them if they were sure they were doing the right thing and expressed concern about their future welfare.

Only one woman did not confide in any friends and, therefore, did not know friends' reactions. Eleven men, on the other hand, had no reaction from friends, either because they had no friends, or they chose not to tell them. "It was nobody's business"; "I didn't care what anybody thought," were typical responses of the men.

One study of remarriage conducted ten years before this one stated unequivocally that the elder newlywed's "friends, his children and the community at large rise up and condemn his remarriage. He is regarded as 'too old for that.'"[3] The idea is prevalent that society condemns remarriage for older people. But the comments of the people we interviewed suggest that this contention is an overstatement. Most men and women said that their children had been in favor of their remarriage. In addition, the majority of people whom we asked thought that, in general, younger people looked with favor on old-age marriage. Some people couched their remark in personal terms by saying, for instance, 'I don't know how other younger people feel, but *my* children thought it was wonderful.'

McKain's contention about hostility of friends toward old-age marriage fares somewhat better. But even then, only three men and five women with whom we spoke indicated that they received only unfavorable or uncertain reactions from friends. Most of the men and women who had ventured to discuss remarriage with friends received some encouragement, even if several friends disapproved.

Since old-age remarriage is still a somewhat rare though increasing occurrence, reservations among peers are not surprising. A man's friends may worry that he is making too hasty a change after the loss of his previous wife; a woman's friends may worry that having adjusted to life without a spouse, she will find it difficult to re-adjust. Margaret Singer said that her friend Sally "didn't have the courage to remarry" herself. "Every time I called her," Mrs. Singer reported, "Sally would ask, 'What's the matter?' as if expecting the worst." Some older widows and widowers may have felt threatened by the perceived desertion of a friend. One woman said that a friend, with whom she had eaten most of her meals, refused to have anything more to do with her when she learned of her plans to remarry.

Friends, like the children of the prospective brides and grooms, professed to "want the best" for them. But their identification with their friends' situations may have made the potential pitfalls more evident. Children may have downplayed any misgivings for the reasons mentioned previously — release from the burden of worrying about an aging single parent, or an unselfish desire for their happiness. Friends, who were not held back by strong family ties, more frequently expressed such reservations.

Significantly, not one of the older people either implied or openly said that society or "everyone" was against his or her desire to remarry. All of the people we interviewed for this study received some encouragement, and most people said that they had felt a great deal of support.

Notes

1. For a fuller description of the difference between 'dating' and 'courting,' see F. Ivan Nye and Felix M. Bernardo, *The Family: Its Structure and Interaction.* New York: The MacMillan Company, 1973, p. 111.
2. See the article by sociologist Ira L. Reiss, "Toward a Sociology of the Heterosexual Love Relationship," in *Marriage and Family Living,* vol. 22, May 1960, p. 143.
3. Walter C. McKain, *Retirement Marriage.* Monograph 3. Storrs, Conn.: Storrs Agricultural Experiment Station, University of Connecticut, 1969, p. 6.

Chapter Twelve

Phase III: The Transition to Marriage

"They're so happy he's finally happy."

The Beginning

Most couples wasted little time getting married. The average time between the first discussion of marriage and the ceremony was only five months. This short period obviously differs from the often lengthy engagement periods of younger people. Young prospective brides and grooms may have to finish school, save money, or complete military obligations. Because they were free from these constraining factors, most older couples did not want to prolong the courtship period. "We saw no reason to wait once we decided to get married," commented Joe Hayes. He and his wife, Greta, made their decision in October and were married in January, just three months later. They would have fewer years together than younger people, and most people looked forward to beginning those years together.

Men and women who had known each other for many years before courtship pointed out that a long courtship was unnecessary. "We already knew each other very well," said Ruth Somers, who married her former neighbor; "so once we decided, we just got married." Furthermore, in comparison with many first-time brides and grooms, they felt ready for marriage, and thus felt less hesitant than people who must make this important adjustment for the first time.

On the other hand, the older couples waited until they were absolutely certain that marriage was what they wanted.

Several women, including Reba Moran, said "my husband wanted to get married soon after we met, but I didn't want to rush into anything." With caution born of experience, they refused to make an impetuous rush to the altar.

One might assume that when two older people marry, they opt for very little festivity and "fuss." Many couples disproved this notion. Fourteen of eighteen couples were married in a church or synagogue, two in the homes of family members, and two by Justices of the Peace. Eight couples invited ten or more people to the ceremony. Several couples mentioned walking down the aisle and having relatives as attendants.

Pauline Holmes gave this account: "Oh, we had a very nice wedding, if I do say so. When we first started out, we said we'd have a very small wedding. We said we'd have just the immediate family. Then I said, 'What about all your brothers and let's invite all the children, too.' We were wondering how some of the active ones would sit still, but we had more comments on how quiet those children were! We finally had about 135 people, I think. We were married in the Lincoln Avenue Methodist Church — that's where I was going then.

"Our Women's Association at church does receptions. One of the ladies came out to the house and we planned what we wanted — the food, the centerpieces, the tableclothes, and everything. It was beautiful. Julie, my daughter-in-law, stood up for me. She was my matron of honor. And Keith, who is Roger's younger son, was his best man. My two boys were ushers and Chuck, his other son, was an usher. So, we really had quite a family affair. Somebody took pictures and gave us an album that all the kids, the grandchildren, love to look at." Other couples also display wedding pictures in their homes and like to show photo albums to visitors.

Many couples had parties after the ceremony, attended by relatives and friends. "Harold and I first though we'd have a small wedding, just a few relatives and close friends, in the church I'd been active in for so many years," said Flora Williams, a tiny woman of nearly eighty years. "But, when people heard about it, they wanted to come. They were all so happy for us. How could I refuse? So we ended up with, well, more than a hundred people at the reception after the ceremony."

Several couples who felt that large parties were not appropriate had small celebrations in local restaurants. Eight couples went home after the ceremony.

The decision about where to live after the marriage was based on pragmatic considerations. Most couples decided to live in the house or apartment previously occupied by one of the spouses. About as many women moved into their new husband's homes as husbands moved into their wife's home. If one spouse owned a single house and the other did not, the couple lived in the single home. If both owned homes, the decision was usually based on who had the "best" house to meet their needs.

"Fran and I each were living in our own homes when we got married," said Jim Cunningham. "But my house was in a really bad neighborhood. I mean property values were headed down, so I sold it and moved into her house [in a quieter, more suburban neighborhood]."

A woman who lived in a large two-story house moved to her husband's smaller ranch-style house. People who had lived in apartments as single people more often moved to a new apartment to begin married life; but if one spouse was satisfied with his or her arrangement, the other spouse often moved there.

One couple, the Paulsens, bought a new house. They had had a ten-year courtship because Earl Paulsen's wife, from whom he had been separated for many years, would not give him a divorce. They married soon after his wife died.

Earl said: "Claire and I, we were always savin', savin' for the future, not knowin' we would ever get a home. I dreamed about gettin' a piece of land and an old shanty. I didn't care, cause I would have made a palace out of a shanty. I said, 'as soon as we find a house we'll get married.' 'Cause I would *not* live in an apartment. I wanted to get our own place for her. I signed the papers for the house at 11:00 in the morning, went up to her apartment with some help, cleaned out her apartment, brought it all down here to the house, went over to my sister's where I lived, got changed, got all dressed up and, bingo, got married."

"I worked all my life," said Claire Paulsen. "This is the first time I've ever been able to sit and relax and enjoy my home. I love it, because it's the first one I've ever had. I always lived in small apartments. After his wife died, Earl said 'You've got this apartment here and I'm paying room and board to my sister.' He said I've got enough money for a little house if I can find one.' Now everyone is so happy we have such a lovely place. Earl's so happy now, too. He comes home and putters around. He's always working, doing something around the house."

For most people, deciding where to live was not difficult and ultimately presented few problems. In fact, as mentioned, three people cited the spouse's living arrangement as an important factor in their decision to marry.

A few couples, however, had difficulty adjusting to their new homes. For men, the problem most often was adjusting to living in what they considered their wife's property.

"Even after I moved into Mary's house," Paul Brooks said, "I wanted us to buy another house. A man has pride. The neighbors could think the wife is paying the bills."

"I had a hard time convincing him that this is *his* home," emphasized Mary. "He pays the mortgage. At first he didn't want to have anything to do with the house."

"Now," says Paul, "I feel a little more a part of the house." Mary likes to talk about the improvements her husband has made — "things that are *his* touches, like the kitchen that he did over. And now we've both just finished painting the ceilings upstairs," she added.

Theresa and Roy Parker were not able to reach as satisfactory an adjustment. Although Theresa had moved into her husband's comfortable suburban home, bringing many of her own furnishings, she could not bring herself to part with her former home.

"My house is filled with antiques from the business my previous husband and I had. I should sell it. The house has been broken into twice. After all, it's not the best neighborhood any more. And the taxes there are very high." She paused a moment, then added: "I suppose I'll have to sell it sometime soon, but I don't know what I'll do about my antiques; there's just no room for them here."

Later Reactions of Relatives and Friends

Most men and women reported that their relatives currently were pleased about the marriage. Only three women and two men felt some remnants of disapproval on the part of a child or sibling. and two men and two women said they had no idea how their children now felt.

Most people indicated that their children and/or siblings had approved of the marriage initially and now, of course, still approved. A few who had been "shocked" or inhospitable to the idea of a parent's remarriage now felt more kindly toward the arrangement when, as Morris Singer said, "my son saw it was working out."

The reactions of Paul and Mary Brooks's families illustrate the changes in attitudes of some family members. According to Mary, "Evelyn, Paul's daughter, was torn between loving me and not bein' able to stand it. She was resentful; everything I said bothered her. I hated myself, and I hated her. Soon after we got married, we took a trip down to Virginia. Evelyn called every day while we were there. She was oversolicitous. She once said to me, 'If anyone was mean to my father, I'd kill them.' She resented that I didn't cater to him. I didn't want him to be an old man, even if he is nine years older than me. It's all straightened out now. She now knows we love each other. *We* didn't know how well we'd get along at first," she laughed.

Paul then confided that his sister Jenny was "kind of lagging back when it first happened. Now Jenny and Mary are very close."

"I knew Jenny wasn't happy about the situation," Mary added. "She once said, 'You mean to say this was the grand passion for you?'" mimicking her new sister-in-law's sarcastic tone. "Recently, Jenny told me that Paul had a terrible life with Gladys, his first wife; she was mentally ill. They're so happy he's finally happy."

Conversely, relatives who had initially approved felt less enthusiastic when unhappy spouses confided in them. Sally Roberts, for example, had the complete support and approval of her two married sisters when she decided to remarry. Sally, who had no children, had always been close to her sisters, one of whom had herself remarried later in life.

"When I told them we were getting married," Sally said, "my sisters were very pleased that I'd be living in a fancy apartment complex with a swimming pool, and that I wouldn't have to work any more. But after we were married, Bud turned out to be a real miser and extremely immature. He openly resents my sisters. He acts rude to them and complains about our daily phone conversations." Sally recently confided her unhappiness to her sisters. For Sally, sibling approval has been replaced by disappointment and perhaps the wish that their sister had not made an unwise decision.

Almost half of the men claimed that either they did not know or care what friends currently thought of their marriage or that they had no friends. In contrast, all of the women knew their friends' reactions. This disparity obviously is a result of the closer relationships of women to their peers, as discussed in a previous chapter.

Most men and women who knew their friends' reactions claimed that they currently approved of the marriage. A few men and women felt some disapproval from a few friends. Only Dorothy Shore, whose friends thought she was "crazy" to remarry and who indeed is not happy in the marriage, said sadly, "all my friends still say I was a crazy person to marry him."

Although friends were more likely than relatives to express reservations initially, they also were likely to change their reactions in a positive direction when they found their apprehensions unfounded. Margaret Singer commented, "My friends were all kind of scared. I got the feeling that they always wondered because Morris and I are very different people, you know. Oh, afterwards they saw. They were glad it worked out. It's a matter of adjusting."

Relations with Relatives and Friends

After remarriage, as before, women continued to be more involved with their families than were the men. Women continued to see their children (or a sibling) much more often than did the men: most women saw a child once a week, or more, as compared with less than one-fourth of the men. In fact, most men saw a child only once a month or less. (See the following table.)

Table 15-1. Contact with Children after Remarriage*

	Percentage of Men	Percentage of Women
Everyday	---	14
2-6 times week	21	10
Once a week	---	38
Once every 2 weeks	26	5
Once a month	16	10
Six times a year	16	5
Less than 6 times a year	21	18
Totals	100%	100%

* People mentioned how often, on the average, they saw one child or another. (Childless people mentioned siblings.)

The difference in contact of men and women with their children or siblings occured in part because most women lived closer to their children. Women, however, also spent more time on the telephone with their children and siblings than did men. Almost all of the women talked to a child once a week or more, whereas only half of the men did.

On the whole, after marriage, both men and women saw children less frequently.There were fewer needs on both sides. Children presumably felt less need to "check up on" mother or father, or to provide companionship, entertainment, or a balanced meal. The older person, especially the men, now looked to the spouse for companionship and care. Since many children cooked and cleaned for their widowed fathers, it is not surprising that the men saw children less frequently now that their new wives could cook a good meal at home and clean the house.

"When I lived alone, my daugher used to come over about once a week or so to do some cooking and to clean up the place a bit," said Roy Parker. "But now she doesn't need to do that so I just don't see her that often. And I'm not one to pick up the phone and call, either."

Women's relationships to their children had been closer before marriage, and perhaps women made more effort to maintain them. "I feel just as close to my three children as I did before we got married," said one wife; "but I just don't need to see them quite so often. They all have their own busy lives to lead and now I have mine, too."

The people we met were not specifically asked about the financial assistance they gave to adult children and vice versa. Other researchers who have studied that pattern of mutual help between older people and their children[1] report that children tend to give financial aid to parents slightly more often than they receive it, but that many older people also give money to married children. Postnuptual changes in relationships between parent and child were quite obvious when the couples talked about financial help for their children. Several people discussed their reluctance to continue giving money to a child.

With sadness, Claire Paulsen related the story of her daughter's marriage to a man who "goes crazy when he drinks. Janie was a beautiful girl. You should see her now. She looks older than I do." Claire paused a moment then filled in the background of her daughter's story and her own involvement in it. "All the years that I was separated from Janie's father, I helped to support her and her five children with whatever I could manage. At that time, I was a saleslady in a dress shop. But after Earl and I got married, I realized that my daugher has to get along as best she can. My husband said to me, 'she's gotta learn to get along by herself; she's a big girl and she could get rid of her husband.' So I stopped giving her money. I've worked hard all my life and now we've got each other. Oh, don't get me wrong, Earl thinks the world of Janie. She still comes up all the time with her children. But when her husband comes with her, he stays outside."

Paul Brooks's marriage also led him to discontinue his financial help to his son. "One of my three sons is a gambler who's been kind of a burden to me if he's in trouble. He's taken money and never paid it back." Paul justified his past generosity to his son by appealing to family pride: "I felt I had to protect our name. But now it's a new life. I can't carry the burden any more." His wife Mary continued:

"We've had it understood that there'd be no more borrowing. Paul's son resents that I don't let him take advantage of Paul any more."

The Paulsens and the Brookses dramatically illustrate the prevailing attitude of older remarried people: the relationship with the spouse takes precedence over the parent-child relationship. Even if the individuals were not particularly happy in the marriage, the great amount of time they spent with the spouse, the proximity of the spouse, and the time spent in activities related to being a wife or husband usually insured that the spouse came first. When a conflict between spouse and child arose, the spouse was considered first either because of the power of emotional attachment ("I love her, and I want to please her") or because of the power inherent in the marital situation itself ("What can I do? I married him and since I want to stay married, I'll go along with him"). This latter comment was typical of a few people in less than satisfactory marriages, as we will see in the following chapter.

To one couple, however, this prevailing pattern was not applicable. One afternoon, the Shores were arguing bitterly. "After we got married," said Dorothy Shore, "we moved here, to the same apartment complex where my daughter lives. Since we moved in, Ben [her husband] has done nothing but bother my daughter and her husband. He calls them any time he needs to go any place and expects them to drop everything and drive him here or there. I keep telling Ben, he should leave them alone," she said angrily; "They need their privacy and relaxation and he could take a cab."

Even though Ben Shore's calls for assistance were seen by his wife as unreasonable, he refused to lessen his demands. Dorothy Shore, who lacked emotional attachment and commitment to the marriage (she was uncertain whether she would remain married, with certain justification) refused to give priority to her role as a wife above her role as a mother.

The Shore's situation is an excellent example of what sociologists refer to as 'role conflict.'[2] For Dorothy Shore, the important issue is not so much to whose set of expectations she will conform, but that she and her husband cannot establish a good working relationsip with another person who is important to them. The Paulsens and the Brookses forestalled any potential conflict by giving priority to the spouse, thus putting up a united front. The Shores, thus far, had been unable to do this.

Although many elderly newlyweds had the same amount of contact with friends before and after marriage, an almost equal number saw friends less often. (See the following table.)

Table 15-2. Changes in Contact with Children and Friends

	Percentage of Children		Percentage of Friends	
	Men	Women	Men	Women
More often	6	9	14	13
The same	22	41	43	33
Less often	72	50	43	54
Totals	100%	100%	100%	100%

Since the husbands were generally less involved with friends before marriage, they spoke very little about the changes in their friendships. The wives were more voluble concerning such changes because their friendships had been more meaningful before marriage. Some women openly regretted that they no longer saw their friends as often. This attitude often prevailed when the marriage was less than satisfactory. The majority of women, however, said that they preferred to be with their husbands. As Ruth Somers stated emphatically, "I don't want to go out with my friends as much. I want to be here when Dave is here."

Moreover, as Marion Nolan said, "I think my friends have a feeling I've got a husband and, you know, a lot of women go out together. Although they're all friendly just the same, we don't make it quite as often as we used to, when I was alone." As women become older — Marion was in her eighties — the married woman becomes the exception in a society of widows. This fact is further illustrated by one long-widowed and remarried woman's comments, not without some irony, about her two sisters.

"Within the past five years," said Marie King, "my oldest sister lost her husband and my other sister just lost hers. Here I was single all those years, and now it's just the opposite. Now they say, 'You've got a husband and we're without a man!'"

Remarried women who continued to see their friends as often as before marriage usually had discussed the continuation of their activities with their husbands before the wedding. A few husbands had urged their wives to continue their activities; they had not wanted to "tie them down." Flora Williams, a remarkably active seventy-eight-year-old club woman, who professed to be only "fairly satisfied" in her marriage, had forewarned her husband Harold:

"No, I didn't cut down on activities. I said, this is my life. I've driven the car since 1920. There are so many people that I take places and do things with, that I can't change now. I have meetings, things that are worthwhile. I work for scholarships and things like that. I guess I'm lucky. I have so many friends that I really can't count them all!"

The six men and women who saw friends more often had

socialized very little previously and had married socially active spouses. Paul Brooks, whose previous wife "went out of her head at the change of life," had seen people other than family members infrequently because "I had to be careful of her, what she'd do." As a widower he had no friends other than family members. "But now," he continued, "now that I married Mary, we have an awful lot of fun and friends."

Summary

For most remarried older people, the spouse became the most important person in their set of relationships. There often was a mutual withdrawal of contact and involvement by the older couple and by their children, siblings, and/or their friends. Children felt less obligation to provide aid or to offer companionship, and single friends sought other widows or widowers. The older person, on his or her part, felt less need for the companionship or services of friends and kin, since the new spouse now provided these supports.

For many parent-adult child relationships, the parent's remarriage provides the ideal solution to what sociologist Ralph Turner calls the "less-interest phenomenon."[3] When adult children marry and have children of their own, they transfer strong ties from the original family of their birth to their new family of spouse and children. Some elderly parents, however, cannot or will not loosen the ties to their children and the relationships between the children and their older parents become one-sided. The transfer of ties by the adult children has left no particular place for the older person in the core family. By remarrying, the older person most often achieves the "conjugal ideal not easily achieved in most families."[4] The elderly parent now can loosen the ties to married adult children as he or she strengthens the tie to the new spouse.

This chapter has emphasized remarried elders' relationships with friends and family because only a few studies have focused on the relations between older people and their relatives from the perspective of the older person.

Other factors also are important in the adjustment of older marriage partners. Some of the factors will be discussed in the next chapter in relation to marital satisfaction and the current domestic situation.

Notes

1. The flow of assistance between elderly parents and their grown children is reported in these publications: Marvin B. Sussman, "The Help Pattern in the Middle Class Family," *American Sociological Review,* 18 (February 1953): pp. 22-28. Marvin B. Sussman and Lee G. Burchinal, "Kin Family Networks: Unheralded Structure in Current Conceptualizations of Family Functioning," *Marriage and Family Living,* 24 (August 1962): pp. 231-240. Reuben Hill, et al. *Family Development in Three Generations,* Cambridge: Schenkman Publishing Co., 1970.
2. For a further definition and elaboration of the sociological concept of role conflict, see Ralph Turner, in Arnold M. Rose (ed.), *Human Behavior and Social Processes,* Boston: Houghton Mifflin Co., 1962, pp. 20-40.
3. In *Family Interaction,* New York: John Wiley and Sons, 1970, pp. 434-435.

Chapter Thirteen

Phase IV: Marital Satisfaction and The Current Domestic Situation

"Some of them are different — my ways and her ways. We meet halfway and they are fine."

Some older people changed their lives very little when they remarried; others had to make major changes. This chapter discusses some of the factors that can determine whether a late-in-life marriage will be successful or unsuccessful and some of the adjustments that all people must make when they marry. Finances, activities, relationships with family members, and problem solving are some of the factors discussed in light of the special circumstances of remarriage in old age.

Marital Satisfaction

Most elder brides and grooms were happy in their remarriages. Seventy-eight percent of the women and 86 percent of the men described themselves as being "very satisfied" or "satisfied" in their remarriages. Most of them said, "yes," they would marry the same spouse again if they had the choice again. One man and two women, however, said "probably yes," and one man and two women said "definitely not" or were uncertain.

Marital satisfaction for these couples was related to how

much their expectations before marriage agreed with the actual situation after marriage. The most satisfied people had accurately predicted what their lives would be like after remarriage. Men and women who had been unable to make correct assessments of the future — those to whom some aspect of life or the personality of the spouse came as an unpleasant surprise after marriage — were likely to be unhappy.

Flora Williams was one person who had not accurately predicted the conditions of her future remarriage. She had been uncertain about the desirability of remarriage: "I was happy without getting married, and, besides, I had so many physical ailments, including diabetes and a heart condition. But I finally agreed to marry Harold because I think I felt sorry for him — he seemed so lost and unhappy. And I tried to discourage him, but oh no, he wanted to take care of me. He didn't want me to do anything.

"Now," she says," More than a husband, I would have liked a man to live upstairs and take care of the garden, the yard, and do those things. I want Harold to take care of things. I want him to do things. He doesn't. I mean it isn't that I don't care for him. I do. But he doesn't cooperate, let's put it that way.

"He also has a quick temper and is picky and demanding about meals. He knows what he wants to eat and everything has to be 'just so.' I really hadn't thought that Harold would be this way; my first two husbands were easy-going and undemanding."

A person's ability to assess the future realistically often was related to the degree that he or she had to change after marriage. The older people to whom remarriage represented no drastic change were better able to predict what the situation would be like. They also had a better idea of their spouses' expectations and reactions than the people for whom remarriage meant a drastic change in how or where they lived.

The Women's Perspective

Often, the women who were satisfied with the marriage, for whom being a wife was a comfortable situation and to whom remarriage represented not much change, saw themselves primarily as wives and homemakers. These women had said that wanting someone to care for was an important factor in their decision to marry. Helen Johnson, for example, had married Bob, partly "to help him get along" after a serious operation, even though she had suffered a series of strokes and needed a walker to move around her apartment. These women, who have been called "reengaged nurturers,"[1] entered remarriage with relative ease. They defined themselves as primarily homemakers and nurturers, even though they may have held paying jobs and/or socialized in a group of other single women. Margaret Singer had been a nurse during her first marriage and had done some part-time nursing during widowhood. But she had found great fulfillment as a housewife during her brief childless first marriage. "I could never think to go through the rest of my life alone," she commented. Margaret is content in her remarriage and has no desire to return to her nursing career.

Several women whose remarriages had entailed great changes in their lifestyles also found satisfaction. They fortunately met and married men whom they now described as "thoughtful," "wonderful," and "kind." Mabel Larson, for example, had been orphaned at a young age and had worked all her life, with the exception of a few years during her second marriage. When her second husband died, leaving her without savings or insurance benefits, she opened a small needlecraft shop. After meeting Pete Larson, she was hesitant to remarry.

Mabel recalls, "I had been alone, and had my own way and everything. I could come and go and I didn't have to answer to anyone. But after he asked me a third time, I finally accepted the proposal. At times I felt as if something was missing from my life; and we were so congenial with one another. He was such a kind person. I was getting to the age where working was hard, and I wouldn't have to work if I married Pete."

The Larsons now live in a small apartment in a public housing project. Mabel says she is "very happy — honest to goodness. Even though I really liked meeting the public; you never knew who was gonna come in that shop, and I had some lovely customers. I'm not sorry that I retired. I had a heart attack the year before last and now must take it easy. I like collecting new recipes and cooking. Sometimes," she added with a smile, "after we've had dinner out, Pete comes home and rummages through the refrigerator. 'For goodness sakes, you just had dinner,' I tell him. 'It didn't taste like yours,' he says."

Remarriage had brought about a similar change in the life of Greta Hayes, who had taught high school. Greta was rarely lonely during widowhood; "I liked teaching and had a group of women friends whom I socialized and traveled with." Her marriage to Joe Hayes required moving to another part of the state, too far for frequent visits with former companions. Furthermore, she was reaching retirement age and terminated her teaching career when she remarried. "But I've made new friends and I still see my old friends every once in a while. Joe is always happy to see my old friends because he knows that they always meant a great deal to me, and he's become very fond of them. Our marriage," she continues, "is unusually good. I'm sure that second marriages could be very happy if everyone had the relationship that we have, the concern for one another. He's always thinking of something to please me. He is so thoughtful and kind."

Mabel and Greta, as well as several other women who had to change their lives in varying degrees, were fortunate in having been able to predict their own responses and their husbands' responses to the new marital situations. Most people, old and young, enter marriage with expectations of favorable outcomes — personal happiness, compatibility with the spouse, acceptable living arrangements. Most of these older women had had their expectations fulfilled and were happy.

A few women had not. The dissatisfied women generally had made drastic changes in their lives, too. But unlike the more satisfied women, they had felt "forced" into these changes by external circumstances. Their judgment may have been impaired, and they failed to find the compensations they had anticipated.

Dorothy Shore, like Greta Hayes, had emphasized the importance of her activities with other women. "I played cards and went to everything at the Golden Age Club," she said. After her son died, Dorothy could not bear to remain in her apartment, which overlooked a grocery store he had managed. When Ben Shore asked her to marry him, she accepted at age eighty because "I felt sorry for him." She could now move out of her apartment with a man who, she thought, was financially well off. They moved to a distant suburb, near Dorothy's daughter, and she now feels isolated. "Ben has no car and there are no buses or anything here. I've also lost all my friends. I used to go out every day in the week. And, it's awfully hard to plan the meals. I'm too busy. In fifteen years [of widowhood] you rest up just for yourself." Ben Shore is miserly with his money, which is a source of constant friction between them. "I try anything to save money. I try to skimp in the kitchen as much as I can. That's why I stay in the kitchen — to save a dollar. To buy in the store costs a lot of money. He doesn't know these things and he doesn't appreciate them," Dorothy says.

After the interview, which was a protracted series of accusations and counteraccusations, the Shores agreed to look for housing in a more fully developed area of the city, closer to public transportation. Such a move would help to relieve their isolation, but would probably not help to reconcile their different monetary values.

Marie King also is less than satisfied in her remarriage. She had worked at a variety of domestic and factory jobs since girlhood. At age sixty-five, she met and married John King, her second husband. "I was tired of working and looked forward to staying home with John," who was a retired optician fourteen years her senior. "But now," she says, "I would like to go back to work. My nerves bother me and honestly, how much time can I spend doing housework?" She describes her husband as overly possessive and resentful of her relationships with members of her family. "John absolutely does not want me to go back to work," says Marie. "His first wife had been a nurse who had retired after marriage, even though they had no children, so that's what he expects." Marie shrugged resignedly; "I guess I'll stay home," she sighed.

Sally Roberts also had married as an escape from a too demanding secretarial job and an uncertain financial future: "I had a responsible job; it was taking a great deal out of me. I was beginning not to feel well. What was I going to do when I wasn't able to work? I wasn't left a rich widow. What was I going to do? I had something to give him — kindness, attention, love. How could kindness not be reciprocated? The only factor I couldn't foresee was the man's character. It undoes me. I'm shaken to the core."

Sally hopes that an anticipated move to Florida will improve her husband's disposition. "We're moving into a retirement community, so there should be a lot for me to do there by myself. Things may work out better if we don't have to spend every waking hour together," she notes perceptively.

The Men's Perspective

More men than women described themselves as "very satisfied" or "satisfied" with the marriage. Although the difference between the men and women was small, it is important. Men were more satisfied in part because they had changed their lifestyles to a lesser extent. For one thing, marriage had not brought about a change in employment, as it often did for women. Nearly all or the men had retired while married to the previous spouse, or had continued the same employment pattern after remarriage. Only two men had retired after remarriage.

In addition, most men had been widowers for only a short time and thus probably found it easier to re-accustom themselves to being a spouse. Men were more highly motivated to marry; they had more to gain from the marriage. They usually lacked the close family and friendship ties of the women and the women's homemaking skills. Because of the greater availability of eligible women, men were less likely to feel pressured into a particular marriage.

The one man who described himself as very dissatisfied was Ben Shore, who, as a widower, was mired in depression, isolation, and need. "When my first wife died, I was lost. I couldn't cook anything. I couldn't make my supper. Three weeks I lost fourteen pounds. I used to keep away from people." In this unhappy state, he misjudged his current wife. "The way Dorothy spoke to me, I thought she acted to me like my first wife. But has my first wife come to me? No! I thought, what have you got to live? Another few years. What's the use. Let's get married." Ben's jaundiced view of remarriage apparently contributed little to his and Dorothy's chances for marital happiness.

Men and Women: Differing Needs

Although men often had greater need than women for a spouse, remarriage often was more important psychologically to women, who seemed to have a greater need for the intimate, sharing, caring aspects of the marital relationship. Just as the women had developed more fully these aspects of their relationships with relatives and friends, they now had a greater need for these deeper emotional aspects in their marital relationship. Both men and women said that companionship was the best aspect of remarriage by a wide margin. For men, however, companionship usually meant having someone to "go places with," whereas women usually mentioned emotional companionship — having someone to talk to, or share with.

A conversation with Frank Lane, the exalcoholic mentioned in chapter nine, who had since happily remarried, points up the lesser emphasis of men on sharing and communication. "My wife and I, we're as different as chalk and cheese. I have a little education. She don't have any. She can't read a comic book. We can't talk about literature, can't talk about psychology, things I'm interested in. But I'm very satisfied and glad that Wilma doesn't argue back. I'm argumentive [sic] and she isn't. I'm not goin' to argue with myself. I do like the companionship of having someone around the house. We're not lonely any more. Like, I play cards here. And when we get through playing cards, the others will go home. And I used to be here all alone. Since we've been married we play cards here, and when they go home, I'm not alone."

Men's marital satisfaction is at least partially related to their physical and mental well-being. The men who were younger at the time of marriage were more satisfied, as were the men (but not women) who were more vigorous and who were free of any mental abnormality. Perhaps men in failing health felt forced into the marriage, as had some of the women. Like Ben Shore, their need for care may have impaired either their judgment in deciding whom to marry or their capacity for satisfaction in marriage. Men whose health was impaired and who felt dependent on their wives may have felt inadequate, and therefore less satisfied with life. The inequality of the relationship may have been threatening to them.

Men who had close relationships with children or siblings before the remarriage, who saw or spoke with a child more frequently during widowerhood, and who visited family members more frequently at present also were more satisfied. It appears that some aspects of men's individual personalities are responsible for their ability to maintain good relationships with other family members and also with the spouse. Conversely, men who found it more difficult to get along with their children also found it more difficult to get along with their spouses.

A couple's financial situation and living arrangements were important aspects of marital satisfaction for women. Women who had some savings and lived in more affluent surroundings were more likely to be satisfied. The relationship between finances and marital satisfaction was not as important for men. Other aspects of the marriage, such as being well cared for, overshadowed financial considerations as a reason for being satisfied or dissatisfied with the marriage.

Some Social Characteristics of the Couples

The average age of the men was seventy-three years at the time of the marriage; the average age of the women was sixty-seven years. Husbands were older than their wives in all but four marriages, and the average age difference was five years, eight months. The spread of more than five years between husband and wife is greater than the three-year average age difference among married couples of the general population. Because couples were excluded in which the wife was under sixty, even though the man was sixty-five or older, the age difference between elderly remarried men and their wives is, in reality, even greater.

As we have stressed, statistics point up the odds faced by a woman in her seventies or eighties who wishes to remarry: not only is there a dearth of eligible men due to the longevity factor, but eligible older men also can choose from a much larger field of eligible women. A woman who marries a younger man, as did four of the women in this study, is relatively rare; a man who marries a younger woman — sometimes considerably younger — conforms to the normal marriage pattern in our society.

In three of the four least successful marriages, the age difference between the husband and wife was the greatest.[2] Of the four couples with the wife older than the husband, only one marriage (the Shores) was unsuccessful according to the participants. Three couples were satisfied: Helen and Bob Johnson, and Claire and Earl Paulsen, whom we have met, and Reba and Charlie Moran.

In comparison with the general population of elders, the newlyweds in this group were more highly educated. The average number of years of education was 10.2 for men and 12.9 for women. Four women and three men had a professional degree and/or had graduated from college.

Thirteen wives had more education than their husbands. Only seven husbands had had more years of schooling than their wives. This difference in education agrees with national figures, which show slightly higher educational achievement of women in comparison with men in the same age group and higher educational attainment of people in their sixties compared with those in their seventies and older. The relative educational attainment of husband and wife was not an important factor in marital satisfaction or dissatisfaction. Some spouses had the same level of education and were dissatisfied in the marriage.

From these figures, we can tentatively conclude that similarity of education is less important for older-age marriage than for younger marriage. Considering the period when the older people were high-school and college age (several years before World War I to the middle-to-late 1920s), their educational achievement probably depended more on what money was available for schooling than on intellectual ability. Boys often had to leave school to help support their families, as did several men we interviewed. In addition, these elderly brides had married men who many years ago had attained their highest level of financial and status achievement. There could be no disappointment or disillusionment, as in young marriages.

Forty percent of the remarried elders classified themselves as Protestants, 30 percent as Catholics, and 30 percent as Jews. Within most couples, both partners shared the same religion. There was only one mixed marriage between a Catholic and a Protestant. For them, the difference in religion presented no special problem and both partners considered the marriage very satisfactory. In another case, a man who described himself as a "Christian" often went to church with his Catholic wife, and in a third case a self-professed "atheist" had married a Protestant who was not a church goer.

There was a somewhat lower rate of marital satisfaction among the Jewish respondents. More than one-third described themselves as "fairly satisfied" or "not satisfied." Because family life has been so central to the Jewish experience, perhaps the expectations of the Jewish remarrieds were higher and, consequently, their disappointment was greater. Or perhaps the Jewish respondents were more prone to airing their complaints and discussing their negative feelings.

The individual ethnic backgrounds of the older couples was much more mixed than their religious affiliations. The spouses in half of the couples each brought a different ethnic background to their marriage.

American-born elders tended to marry other native-born Americans; foreign-born elders also married each other. In only two cases did a foreign-born marry an American-born. The foreign-born in each "mixed" couple came from Eastern Canada, an area from which there had been a large migration to the Eastern United States where the couples lived.

Employment and Finances

Except for four people, all of the older remarrieds, both men and women, had retired and were not currently doing paid work. The exceptions included two full-time and two part-time employees. Pauline Holmes, who was in her early sixties, had worked during her first marriage and subsequent widowhood and now had a full-time secretarial job; Earl Paulsen, who was approaching retirement age (his wife Claire was the partner over sixty-five), was employed full time as a truck driver. Dave Somers worked part time in his family's business and George Field worked part time as a janitor.

One-third of the men had worked after the death of the former spouse, either in their original jobs or as re-employed part-time workers after retirement. Charlie Moran was re-employed as a school crossing guard and George Field, just mentioned, still worked as a janitor. None of the men had retired during the time they were widowers. This fact probably reflects the brevity of the widowed situation for most men as well as their reluctance to forfeit work after the loss of a wife.

As widows, half of the women had worked, either to help fill the time or, more often, because of financial necessity. Many women had worked during their entire adulthoods, including the previous one or two marriages. Only one-third of the women could be classified as "housewives," — that is, they had worked for such a short time that they could be classified in no other work categories.

Nearly half of both the women and the men had had "white collar" jobs before retirement, including professional positions, such as teachers, accountants, and engineers, and jobs such as managers and proprietors, salespeople, clerical workers, and secretaries. The other men and women had been "blue collar" workers, holding such jobs as factory foremen or craftsmen, factory workers, and service workers such as cook and lady's companion. Nearly two-thirds of the women had been in the white collar occupational group, as opposed to less than half of the men; but more women than men were in the lowest occupational category of service workers.[3]

The current economic situation of each couple roughly paralleled the range of their occupations during work years. Some couples, mainly those in which the husband had been employed as a "professional, technical or kindred worker" or as a "manager, official and proprietor" were quite affluent; a few couples, in which the husband had been employed as a blue collar worker, appeared to be just making ends meet.

According to their sources of income and the appearance of the house or apartment, only a few of the couples could be classified as needy. Although every couple was receiving Social Security, only one, Mabel and Pete Larson, had no other source of income. The Larsons lived in a public housing project and professed to be very happy in their small apartment. "We were lucky to get this apartment," said Mabel, "because there's a long waiting list. If we didn't live here, all our money would go for rent."

Almost half of the couples lived on their Social Security and the husband's and/or wife's pension, which in three cases was combined with salary from employment. An equal number of couples had assets in the form of savings from the sale of real estate, shares in family businesses, stocks and bonds, or other securities. These assets were combined in five cases with pensions and/or salaries from employment of a spouse. Only one couple, the Paulsens, lived on his wages from his full-time employment as a truck driver and on her Social Security.

Very few people complained that they had inadequate income. Only two men and three women admitted that they "could use more money" or bemoaned the "high prices of everything." These complaints were not necessarily voiced by the people with the lowest standard of living by objective appearance. A person's own assessment of how adequate his or her income is often differs sharply from the external appearance of the situation. The Larsons, for example, the only couple entirely dependent on Social Security benefits, commented, "We have enough to get along. We don't have to ask anyone for anything. Our needs aren't tremendous." Another couple, the Morans, lived in a small apartment in a housing project for the elderly. Charlie Moran had been a factory worker, and Reba Moran had worked for many years as a domestic. Their modest standard of living had enabled them to save for several trips to visit relatives in Florida before ill-health precluded any more extensive traveling. Similarly, the Fields, while living modeslty on George Field's pension and part-time janitorial earnings, were excitedly planning for a month-long trip to a European resort on a special Senior Citizens' "package."

One-fourth of the couples lived in an obviously affluent manner, as evidenced by charming homes, talk of trips abroad, charitable contributions, and sizeable legacies from the previous spouses. Most couples, however, were able to manage the expenses of daily living without want, but with few frills. They met daily expenses from current income, and, by cutting corners on some expenses, saved for something special, like a trip. More than half of the couples had substantial savings, usually from the sale of a house.

Most individuals who came into the marriage with some assets kept those in their own names. Current needs were met by pooling income resources, such as pensions and Social Security benefits. Anything left over was saved jointly. Depending on inclination, temperament, or ability, either the man or woman handled the finances.

Before getting married, most couples had discussed the dispersement of their income and had arrived at a satisfactory understanding. Only a few couples differed philosophically concerning the spending of money. Dorothy Shore and Sally Roberts, as we have noted, complained that their husbands were misers.

The Brooks's candid comments on their financial arrangements were typical. Mary Brooks had worked in a bakery before her remarriage, and Paul was a retired machinist.

"I can see where money could be a problem for some people like us who remarry," Mary commented. "After all, at this age we're all pretty well set in our ways of handling everyday things. Besides, both Paul and I had been used to handling the money before. So one day we sat down and figured out everything together. You can have trouble if you don't figure out things like that," she emphasized. "We were both about the same as for money. The small savings we each had before marriage will go to our own children. The money Paul got when he sold his house is in the bank for his children, and, this house that we're living in will go to my children. We live on Paul's pension and Social Security and on my Social Security, which was reduced sixty dollars when I got married. But I get sixty dollars worth of pleasure," she beamed. "Anything that's left after our household expenses goes into our savings account for good times. We've managed to save enough to go South several times and now we're planning a trip to Hawaii."

"She really knows how to stretch a dollar. There's no skimping on food, but she makes all her own clothes and some of mine. Besides, we don't like restaurants so we save money by not eating out."

Aside from a few couples who could afford to own a car but did not because of physical infirmities, car ownership was closely related to income. The six couples who did not own a car used public transportation and walked a great deal more than those couples who could afford a car. People who did not own a car were less mobile; they did their grocery shopping at small local stores, for example.

Attendance at spectator activities also was closely related to income. Only couples with more than adequate incomes went to movies, plays, concerts, or sporting events. About half of both the men and women said that they never attended such events.

Health and Morale

Most elderly newlyweds were in good to excellent health, according to their own evaluations. In addition, an evaluation of the health of each individual was based on his or her responses to an "index of incapacity." Each person was asked to rate the relative ease or difficulty with which he or she could perform six common activities: going out of doors, walking up and down stairs, getting around the house, washing and bathing oneself, dressing and putting on shoes, and cutting toenails.[4]

Only one man and one woman rated themselves in "fair or poor" health. The correlation between a person's self-rating of health and his or her actual, observable physical and medical condition was not perfect. It was our impression that most of these elderly people downplayed their illnesses and rated themselves more highly than an objective assessment would warrant. This contention is supported by the health statistics of the remarrieds: fully one-third of both the men and women suffered from a serious, chronic illness, such as a heart condition, hypertension, diabetes, or arthritis.

Flora Williams, in her late seventies, rated her health as "good," then went on to say: "I have a bad heart and diabetes and thyroid problems, and I've recently recuperated from an ear operation." A good friend of Flora's in her sixties, who was visiting, talked about her own health: "Instead of doing something with Flora, I'll say I have a commitment tomorrow, and I don't tell her what it is. Then I stay home in bed all day. I can't keep up with her."

Even people with many physical ailments rated their health as "good," frequently mentioning that in comparison with other people their age, they were in fine shape, or that at their age one has to expect some little ache or pain.

The score of incapacity became higher as age took its toll. Several people who felt they were "slowing down" and unable to do as much as before displayed some anxiety. Marion Nolan, who was eighty-three, commented, "Thank heavens I still drive and do everything like I always did. You never know how long that's going to last when you're my age." Jim Cunningham had had a heart attack and had arrived home from the hospital a week before the interview. A long period of interview time was spent discussing his health. He was depressed and uncertain about the future.

"I always had the feeling since I retired — 'Another day is coming. I don't have to do any more today. I'll save something so I'll have something to do tomorrow.' That's the way I figured it, until I landed in the hospital and now I'm just lazy. That's disturbed me, because I figured I had a dozen years yet to mow, paint, rake leaves, like my father."

Although health is a key factor in the morale of both men and women[5] in this group of remarried people, the health variable was especially important to the men. More men than women rated their health as excellent or very good and more men than women said they had no difficulty and needed no assitance in performing the six activities mentioned. The men who were in better health had higher morale.[6] In fact, their comments reveal that health was much more important than marital satisfaction to their morale. Analysis showed that for men there was little relationship between morale and unsolved marital problems; for women, however, the relationship between morale and marital satisfaction was much more important.

The psychological importance of good health to men is further supported by our impressions of the "vigor" and "intactness" of the remarried people we met.[7] More than four-fifths of the women appeared to be vigorous and intact, as compared with just slightly more than half of the men. Moreover, one-fourth of the men seemed to be mentally abnormal in some respect; none of the women, however, were so judged. These impressions, when contrasted to the peoples' responses, suggest that men were less willing than women to admit to infirmities. The men, in general, felt more threatened psychologically by illness. This conclusion is supported by other studies showing that although their life span is shorter, men visit doctors less frequently and are hospitalized less frequently.[8]

Health care and maintenance are important factors in late-life marriage. Despite the fact that men rated their health more highly than women, five men were judged to be quite feeble, two were less than vigorous, and six had some form of mental abnormality, such as forgetfulness, incoherence of thought, or what appeared to be mild paranoia. In addition, nine men also were hard of hearing; four were so deaf that communication was difficult. Although three women had mild hearing problems, they did not interfere with communication.

Most people claimed that their health was the same now as before marriage; but as Paul Brooks said, "My health is about the same, I guess. But since I've gotten married, I feel better; I have a healthier outlook on life."

Twice as many women as men said that their health had gotten worse since marriage, although more men than women had been hospitalized for serious illness or accidents. Reasons for hospitalization included heart attacks, mastectomy, and the loss of the use of an arm in an accident.

Even though the women said they found it more difficult to go about daily activities, they appeared to function more often as the caretakers for their husbands than the reverse. As Sally Roberts said about her husband's children's approval of the marriage, "Of course they were happy. If he hadn't gotten married he would have had to go to a nursing home." Although the Roberts were an extreme case, a few of the oldest men probably would not have been able to continue to care for themselves had they lived alone. Women with the same degree of infirmity probably could have functioned better by themselves because of their many years experience as housekeepers and cooks.

Harry Nolan was eighty-two and had no particular health problems when he married eighty-year-old Marion Nolan four years ago. Now, a little exertion leaves him out of breath, and, although he is still lucid and coherent in some of his thoughts, he cannot remember how many children he has and other important personal facts.

"I'm older now and I haven't been as normal either physically or mentally. I had a very severe illness about three years ago. They told me afterwards my lungs seemed to be the principal trouble. I wasn't deathly sick, and I'm a good deal better, and for my age I've been pretty good since." He tries to go for a walk every day in good weather "depending on how I feel." The morning before, Marion said, "I was all in when I got up, so Harry made breakfast." She was quick to point out that this was an unusual occurence. "I get all the meals, don't I, Harry?"

Like Marion Nolan, most other women considered themselves as the caretakers of their husbands. They took responsibility for running the household — the daily cooking and light housekeeping. If a wife were incapacitated or not feeling well, a husband would "help out." Sometimes the help would become part of the couple's routine. "After my heart attack the year before last," Mabel Larson said, "I couldn't do any heavy work. So now Pete always washes and waxes the floors."

In general, each spouse did what he or she could to make the other comfortable and to insure the smooth running of the household. One of the most incapacitated women was eighty-three year old Reba Moran, who rated her health as "poor." She apologized for her apartment's not being as tidy as it should be. "I do a little work — make the beds or something — then I get dizzy and have to rest. I have high blood pressure and a heart condition. Charlie does all the housework that requires bending down. When we got married, we decided it was his home as well as mine and he's been helpin' me ever since. But sometimes he's not well himself. He has epileptic seizures and his nerves bother him. To help him relax, I rub his back and neck before we go to sleep."

To summarize, most of the elderly newlyweds were in good mental and physical health when they married and remained in good health. A few people, especially men who were older than the women, had become less vigorous after marriage. Spouses helped to care for each other, with the major responsibility usually taken by the wife for the care of the husband.

It is interesting to note that elderly men and women react differently to illness. Men seem to have a greater tendency to deny poor health. High morale for men depends, in large measure, on a self-concept that incorporates good health.

Marital Problems

Most marriages undergo a "period of adjustment — that stage between the bliss of the honeymoon and the mellow years of pure conjugal love."[9] Couples usually undergo a process of forming "interlocking habit systems"[10] by modifying old habits and forming new ones. Most elders admitted to some difficulties after marriage, from simple matters of adjusting to each other's habits to real problems that had not been solved or were in the process of being solved.

About one-fourth of the men and one-fifth of the women claimed to have no problems after marriage, even minor ones of adjustment. "We just moved in together, and we're happy as can be," said Gil Norton. The people who had no problems either were denying reality or, as is more likely, had made small adjustments that they had forgotten or thought too trivial to mention.

"Well, we had a different background, and we had to get used to each other's little differences, ideas, and habits. It's just perfectly natural," stated Harry Nolan.

Some of the small matters of adjustment for a few couples included Roger Holmes's slovenly habits in putting away his clothes and Dave Somers's poor taste in his choice of apparel. These "problems" had been solved, in the former case by reminders from Pauline Holmes and in the latter, by Ruth Somers's selecting her husband's clothing.

A more weighty matter was discussed by Mabel Larson. "I was ready to jump out of my skin the first year we were married. Everything I did, Pete's first wife would do better. Almost every day — 'She did it this way, she did it that way.' So finally one day, I blew my top, and I said, 'Listen, I am not that person. That person's been dead many years, and there's no way to bring her back. You can't make me into her.' I said, 'I do things my way and that's the way it's going to be done. I've adjusted to your ways, but I'm not adjusting to somebody dead.'"

Now Mabel says: "I should have brought it up at the very first, instead of letting it go on and on. When I came out with it, everything adjusted itself and now he likes my way. There's never any mention of who does this and who does that."

Mabel's comments about the competition with her husband's first wife illustrate clearly what could be a potential problem in late-life marriage. In fact, however, rivalry was rarely mentioned. Most people were open and sensitive to their spouse's feelings toward the previous spouse. Mabel's comments on how she solved her problem by blowing up were unusual, too. Most couples put a premium on calmness and holding back angry feelings. It was more typical that Mabel had restrained herself for a year before she let her anger show.

About half of the people mentioned their temperament or that of their spouse as the biggest problem in the marriage. They usually did not mention substantive issues, but remarked that they or their spouse had or used to have a bad temper; anger over "little things" as the problem.

The first year they were married, Mildred Gold got upset when her husband, Sam, would get angry "over nothing." Now, Mildred reports, "Sam finds it easier to smile and things get better."

Half of the couples managed to solve their temperament problems. The volatile partner was able to control himself or herself to the benefit of the marriage. For the other couples, however, the loss of temper by one spouse was still a problem and was symptomatic of other unsolved problems in the marriage.

Serious problems usually had their roots in a spouse's inability to predict accurately the conditions of marriage. This failure was, in turn, related to the motivation to marry — whether or not the individual had felt coerced. About one-fourth of the men and women reported some unresolved issue that was important to one or both partners. These other troubles, which have been discussed in previous chapters, included differences in interests, differences concerning finances, difference in friends, relations with other family members, difficulty adjusting to new living arrangements, desire of a spouse to work, plus some uncategorized minor adjustments.

Most couples who had adjusted well or were in the process of solving their problems strongly believed that a spirit of compromise and understanding was in the best interest of a happy marriage. Margaret Singer expressed the sentiments of many other people when she said, "You have to give and take, you know. I'm not too interested in the local Senior Citizens' group, but I go to activities with Morris because he needs people. I don't feel so much at home there, but he does. This I started for him. We also had a very nice music appreciation course which I like so he came, too. And he got to like it, too." As for Morris Singer, his problem was "to adjust a little bit to her ways, her friends. Some of them are different. My ways, and her ways, we meet half way and they are fine."

Current Domestic Relations and Activities

"Live and let live."

The comments of the couples, including remarks about losing one's temper, point to an ideal, often realized, of calmness and serenity in remarriage. Young marriages have been characterized as a "crisis of ambition for men and a stultifying role prescribed for women within the family."[11] Old-age marriages are free from many strains that beset early marriage, such as child rearing, ambition for higher status, and conflict with in-laws. Comments by Helen and Bob Johnson, who were related before their marriage, bring home these points.

"He never gets mad," said Helen. "Since he got older, he has a different disposition."

"Ain't nuthin' to get mad about now," Bob replied. "Just livin' and let live now."

This "live and let live" attitude was typical of the interaction between remarried people. Many men and women emphasized that "it doesn't pay to get angry," "it takes two to make an agrument" and that one should contain his or her feelings. The attitudes of these elderly newlyweds, and the obvious satisfaction with their marriages, belie the value of "communication" between marriage mates, a notion often emphasized in the popular literature. Inhibition, rather than free expression of negative feelings, was considered conducive to marital happiness. This is not to say that the elders did not value the ability of the spouse for discussion of everyday events or helping with problems. Women, especially, often mentioned these aspects as "the best thing" about their marriage.

Sex

Although no specific questions were asked about sex in marriage, several people offered some information. Three women and one man mentioned or implied cessation of sexual interest or activity. Pearl Whelan, who was divorced, had married in the Catholic Church only because of a special dispensation. As she said, "Bill and I married only for companionship; no sex anyway because of his prostate operation.[12] But that didn't bother me because I'd been a widow for eleven years, anyway. And that poor soul, he was no good from sixty-nine until he died at seventy-three. Bill wanted me to know about his operation 'cause I was nine years younger and I said, 'That don't bother me. Don't worry about that.'"

Charlie and Reba Moran, both in their eighties, had had a double bed until just the month before, when they had switched to twin beds. Said Reba, "He kept twistin' and turnin' and pullin' the covers away." "You didn't mind that five years ago!" Charlie laughed.

Four men and two women mentioned or implied continued sexual interest and activity. They were among the people who also stressed the "love" aspect of remarriage — the fact that they married because they loved their partner. The important aspect of sex was not necessarily the physical act, but the warmth of another body, the holding, the intimacy.

"Sex is the least of our worries," said Mary Brooks, "but we have had it. Generally he gets into bed first and watches television. I come up a little later. We have twin beds, but I get in with him and we snuggle together. It's so nice to be close. It's beautiful."

Dave Somers, who is seventy-three years old, expressed himself fully on the subject of sex:

"I don't know if I'm oversexed, but I'm a lover. I like to pet, kiss, hug. I have more fun out of loving somebody I love than the ultimate end. You know, some people — and this is the failure of sex, too — some people want sex and forget the rest of it — the hugging and the petting, and I think that's wrong. People say, 'What will happen to me when I get older? Well, I'm still alive! There's no thrill like that today. People try dope, they try smoking, they try drinking. This is the one thing that's good for the body."

In a separate interview, his wife Ruth said, "It's turned out beautifully. There's nothing he wouldn't do for me, and me for him. How can I say no to anything? He's so grateful, and he kisses me. The affection and love is worth everything."

Activites

As we have noted throughout Part II, these elders were mobile and active, with wives tending to be more home-centered than their husbands. Every man but one and more than half of the women said that during the summer they left the house "every day." In the winter, elders are more house-bound. But despite the cold, snow, and wind, almost half of the men and one-fourth of the women made it a habit to get out of the house more than once a week.

Cooking and housekeeping activities were usually the wife's responsibility. A few husbands, including Jim Cunningham, who enjoyed cooking and washing dishes, routinely performed these tasks. Many husbands did minor repairs around the house and some, including Sam Gold, had basement workshops. Several men had accomplished jobs of major renovation, including Paul Brooks, who installed a new kitchen in his and Mary's house. Couples were proud to show off their home and point out the improvements made by the husband. These improvements represented a better home environment at a great economic saving.

About three-fourths of the men and women belonged to formal organizations. Some men and women were "organization people," belonging to four or more groups. For men, the most popular type of organizational affiliation was social, such as the Masons; for women, the most popular affiliation had a church or religious orientation. Except for Senior Citizens' groups, men and women belonged individually, not as couples.

About half of the people had curtailed such activity after marriage, citing loss of interest, desire to stay at home with the spouse, changes in membership, loss of energy, disinclination to go out in the evening, or impossibility of attendance due to change of residence.

"I used to go out every Wednesday night to my Mason's meeting, regular like clockwork I went," said Will Hopkins. "But since Kay and I have been married, I just don't go as much. I like to stay home more now that I got someone here."

People who were members of informal organizations,

such as bridge or poker clubs, also tended to become less active, as we noted in discussing changes in relationships with friends.

More than half of the men and women were involved in some enjoyable individual activity in which they participated either outside or within the home. For men, activity often involved fixing and renovation. Ray Parker sang in three different choirs and was out several evenings a week; Bill Whelan went fishing almost every day in season; Pete Larson, a retired mariner, helped friends with boat maintenance. Paul Brooks, who had been a pianist in a dance band as a young man, had started to play the piano again after a twenty-year hiatus. Several women enjoyed sewing: Mary Brooks commented, "Every morning when I wake up, I say, 'What am I going to sew today?" Other women enjoyed gardening and playing Bingo. Wilma Lane was a Bingo expert who played three times a week. Another woman drove weekly for the Red Cross. One woman proudly displayed the costume jewelry she made; another, the trays she painted.

Joint activities included traveling, going for walks, dancing — "We enjoy a couple of steps at the Elks," said Gil Norton — going to Senior Citizens' club activities, and family parties. The Paulsens went camping frequently in the summer, and the Holmes' chaperoned a group of teenage band members. Many couples had friends in for dinner or cards. The more affluent couples occasionally went to the movies, plays, or concerts.

For both men and women, the most popular activity was watching television; only two people said they did *not* watch daily. The television watchers preferred programs that were news oriented. Many couples watched a local early evening bowling show. A few women were addicted to soap operas, and a few men were so interested in a football or hockey game that they often left the television set on as they talked with company. Almost everyone read a newspaper daily. Only two men and one woman said that they did not read something every day.

Half of the women and almost half of the men visited with

family members at least once a week; many people saw friends and relatives more often, women more than men, as we have observed.

Eighty-three-year-old Marion Nolan described a typical day in her and Harry's married life:

"We get up about eight o'clock. I generally get breakfast. I get all the meals, although we go out occasionally. We're going out today. It's too hot to stay here and cook, so we're going out and having our lunch somewhere. I do everything in the morning, as far as housework. In the afternoon I read, or go out for a ride or go to a show or something like that. I go to my clubs, different things. You know, that takes a couple of days a week. I don't know where the evening goes. I get dinner, and I love to watch the bowling and we hustle in here, and lots of times we bring it in and eat on a card table. And then the news comes on. You read your paper and it's pretty near time to go to bed — 10:00 or 10:30. We don't go out at night any more. We haven't for two or three years. I don't like to drive at night, and I don't like all these things you hear going on around town."

Amount of Activity

What were the changes in the activity levels of elders before and after remarriage? One-fourth of the men and about one-fifth of the women claimed that their level of activity had remained the same. But one-third of both the men and women had become more socially active after remarriage, many because they now had someone to accompany them.

Ruth Somers said, "People treat you differently when you're married. You're treated as a whole person. You're invited to parties. A lot of men and their wives don't like an extra person around. I know loads of widows. If anyone has to go any place and they ask to come with us, I always say yes."

Some people attributed their increase in activity to the peppiness of the new spouse, who had introduced them to new activites and new friends.

"I had never danced before I married Morris; not even at weddings. But Morris loves to dance and he helped teach me and now I really like it," said Margaret Singer.

Nearly half of the men, however, and more than half of the women felt that they were now less active, partly because they now saw their children and friends less often. Much of the decrease in activity also was undoubtedly due to the natural decrease in energy that comes with advancing age. Several people remarked that they were "slowing down" as the years passed. Many of these less active people, however, still maintained a high level of activity by objective standards. Nearly all of the people, men and women alike, said that they definitely had "plenty to do most days."

Some people wanted to do more, or wished that they could. Men in impaired health seemed to be most emphatic in wishing that they could be more active; Bob Johnson, remember, desperately wanted to go back to work, and John King wanted to undertake some major household repairs.

The finding that several people wanted to be more active is, perhaps, not surprising. These remarried people had not accepted the loss of a central role — that of the husband or wife. Instead, in their old age, they had chosen to re-engage in a valued role. They had not "adjusted" to old age, if adjustment means passive acceptance of loss and a decrease in activity.

Most people, however, held the view articulated by Frank Lane:

"The fourteenth of every month since we've been married, I always take her to dinner. It's our anniversary. The first couple of years we were married, we'd go to the Senior Citizens' drop-in center. We got sort of tired of that. Now we play cards with other couples, and she goes to Beano. You don't have the same urge to go. You sort of calm down. One of the ancient Greek philosophers said, 'When I was a youth, I looked forward to my old age as a relief from youthful passions.' That's something like it is with me. It's good when you can be content and settle down."

In this chapter, we have tried to put into perspective most of the elements of the current marital situation. The assessments were based, for the most part, on subjective criteria, on what people told us. Other types of information also were used, including our own impressions, results of scales and tests, information from public records, and results of statistical procedures. Elements of the current situation ranged from the most "subjective" topics — marital satisfaction and marital problems — to objective social characteristics such as education, age, employment, religion, and ethnic group. Between these two groups of topics were those amenable to both subjective assessment by the people we interviewed and more objective criteria — health, morale, finances, and activities. Our goal has been to present as complete a picture as possible of the elderly remarried couple.

Notes

1. For a full definition and discussion of the concept of the 're-engaged nurturer,' see Ruth Harriet Jacobs, "A Typology of Older American Women," *Social Policy 7,* No. 3 (November/December 1976).
2. Because of the small number of couples interviewed for this study (24), it is difficult to generalize accurately about the relationship of age or age difference to success of the marriage. The findings of this study do, however, agree to some degree with previous research. McKain, in *Retirement Marriage,* says: "If . . . the man was more than fourteen years older than his wife, the ratio of success was lower" (p. 48). The age differences of unsuccessfully married people we met — from ten to nineteen years — support McKain's point.
3. These occupational category designations are taken from Albert J. Reiss, Jr., *Occupations and Social Status,* New York: Free Press of Glencoe, Inc., 1961, pp. 264-75. The socioeconomic ranking of occupations, plus the number of older remarried husbands and wives in this study who held each of the various types of jobs, appear in the following table.

Major Occupations of Remarried Elders During Working Years [a]

Socioeconomic Rank	Occupational Category	Number	
		Men	Women
1	Professional, technical and kindred workers	2	3

Socioeconomic Rank	Occupational Category	Number Men	Number Women
2	Managers, officials, and proprietors (except farm)	7	1
3	Sales workers	2	2
4	Clerical and kindred workers	0	4
5	Craftsmen, foremen, and kindred workers	10	1
6	Operatives and kindred workers	2	1
7	Service workers (except household)	0	3
8	Farmers	0	0
9	Farm laborers and foremen	0	0
10	Private household workers	0	1
11	Laborers (except farm)	1	0
	Totals	24	16[a] =40

[a] Eight women were classified as 'housewives' and thus were not included in this occupational scale.

4. This "score of incapacity" can be found in Ethel Shanas et al., *Old People in Three Industrial Societies,* New York: Atherton Press, 1968, pp. 26-30.

   A person's index of incapacity is determined by assigning a number to his or her responses to each of the six index items mentioned in the text.

   0—with difficulty and without any help
   1—with some difficulty but without any help from another person
   3—with extreme difficulty and only with the help of another person

   Most of the older remarried people here scored very low on the index, thus indicating that they were quity physically healthy and independent.

5. For an interesting, up-to-date discussion of health and morale among older women, see the study by Leslie A. Morgan, "A Reexamination of Widowhood and Morale," *Journal of Gerontology* 31, No. 6 (1976) pp. 687-695. She reports that health is a key

factor in the morale of both married and widowed women, but that for widows the relationship between health and morale is much stronger — that is, that a widow's health is more important to her general morale than is married women's health.

Glenn reports basically the same finding, but from a somewhat different angle: "Marital happiness is more highly associated with global happiness (morale) among women than among men." That is, the morale of a married woman relates more to marital satisfaction than it does for men. For additional comments on the difference between older men and women, see Norval D. Glenn, "The Contribution of Marriage to the Psychological Well-Being of Males and Females," *Journal of Marriage and the Family,* August 1975, p. 598.

6. The morale of the elderly remarried people was determined by the Philadelphia Geriatric Center Morale Scale, a list of twenty-two Yes-No questions. For each "correct" answer, the respondent scores two points, and for each "incorrect" answer, scores one point. The higher the score, the higher the person's morale. The morale scale includes a variety of both negative- and positive-sounding questions. Some questions and "correct" answers include:
   1. Things keep getting worse as I get older.
      (Correct answer: No)
   6. As you get older, you are less useful.
      (Correct answer: No)
   12. Most days I have plenty to do.
      (Correct answer: Yes)
   22. I get upset easily.
      (Correct answer: No)

7. As the most convenient way of determining and categorizing our impressions of the vigor and intactness of the elderly remarried people we met, we used th VIRO Scale. See Robert Kastenbaum and Sylvia Sherwood. "VIRO: A Scale for Assessing the Interview Behavior of Elderly People" *Research, Planning, and Action for the Elderly,* D. Kent, R. Kastenbaum, and S. Sherwood, eds., New York: Behavioral Publications, 1972. After conversing with each person, the interviewer rates him or her on thirteen different and detailed characteristics. The person is assigned 0 to 3 points for each characteristic, depending on his or her facility and ability in each area. Sample areas and points include:
   1. (3) Vigorous — to — (1) Feeble
   3. (3) Keen Attention — to — (0) Poor attention
   8. (3) Controlled thought — to — (0) Tangential, Fragmented.

8. Women, as we have noted earlier in this book, tend to live longer than men. As Robert C. Atchley succinctly states: "Older women predominate among the sick, and older men predominate among the dead." For an elaboration of this point, see Atchley's *Social Forces in Later Life,* Belmont, California: Wadsworth Publishing Co., 1972, p. 130.
9. Sociologist Arlene Skolnick offers this definition in *The Intemate Environment: Exploring Marriage and the Family,* Boston: Little, Brown and Col, 1973, p. 208. Other literature on marriage and the family supports this idea.
10. Willard Waller and Reuben Hill, "Habit Systems in Married Life," in *Marriage, Family, and Society,* Hyman Rodman (ed.), New York: Random House, 1965, p. 87.
11. These characteristics were applied to young marrieds by the noted sociologist C. Wright Mills, as quoted by Arlene Skolnick in *The Intimate Environment: Exploring Marriage and the Family,* p. 127.
12. Impotence following prostate operations usually is psychological rather than physiological in origin. Men do, in fact, sometimes become impotent if they think that impotence is a "natural" result of the operation; their attitude becomes a self-fulfilling prophecy. Actually, the ability to achieve erection rarely is impaired by prostatectomy.

Chapter Fourteen

Conclusion

"We're not lonely any more."

Summary

Phases of Remarriage

In Part II of this book, remarriage in later life has been discussed in relation to four time periods or phases: the time alone before meeting the spouse, the meeting and courtship, the transition to marriage, and the present situation. In this final chapter, we will review and coalesce the findings detailed in the discussion of each phase and then comment on the implications of these findings.

- In many ways, the time before remarriage was easier for women than for men. Even though women had suffered more financially, they had received more social support. Their closer ties to children and friends somewhat assuaged the loneliness reported by such a large percentage of men. Women could ease loneliness by activity; men found it more difficult. Moreover, women had been used to cooking and housekeeping, whereas most men were not. Both men and women generally lived alone and valued their independence.

- Because of these social circumstances, men were more motivated to remarry. They remarried after being alone for a much shorter time than women, on the average, and had fewer qualms during courtship. Couples met most often via an introduction by a third party, or had known each other while married. For women, especially, the growth of an emotional attachment towards the mate was gradual.

• Relatives usually approved of the marriage, often because they were relieved of some responsibilities and happy that their relative was happy. Friends were apt to be more hesitant in their approval. Because they were better able to identify with a peer, they recognized potential pitfalls. Some friends probably had felt deserted, and others, who had not had the courage or opportunity to remarry may have felt threatened. Later, after the marriage, friends became more enthusiastic.

• After remarriage, couples saw children and friends less frequently; they relied on the spouse for fulfillment of many social needs. The wishes of the spouse usually took precedence over those of other people, including children, siblings, and friends.

• Most people were satisfied with their remarriages and quite often mentioned the several desireable aspects of compansionship. Men valued the services provided by the wife, and women emphasized the emotional aspects of togetherness and often valued the opportunity to nurture another person they cared for. The people who had been realistic in their expectations of a late marriage and had felt free in their choice of a mate were the most satisfied. The ideal marriage, to which many corresponded, was calm and free of conflict. Most couples had had to make some adjustments to life with another person, often concerning "little things." In general, remarriage was more a social necessity for men, for whom coping alone had been more difficult, but was psychologically more important for women.

• The health of men and women was generally good. Women took care of their ill husband more often than vice versa, although women more often cited health problems themselves. Couples were, by their own evaluation, adequately situated financially, but few lived lavishly. Activity level lessened somewhat as couples became more home-centered after remarriage, although the level of activity for many couples remained generally high.

Activities and Adjustments

Much of our discussion of remarriage has concerned older peoples' activities as parents, friends, and workers, in addition to their relationships with their spouses. We were interested in the importance of these various activities to older people as well as in the changes brought about by the remarriage as summarized here.

- During widowhood, most men and women reported a close relationship with at least one child. A greater proportion of women spoke about strong family ties, and the women tended to see their children more often than did the men. Women also were more deeply committed to their friendships; they saw friends more often, had a greater number of friends, and more often confided in them. Women, more often than men, had retained or regained employment during widowhood.

- During courtship, women were open to the opinions of relatives and friends. After remarriage, just as before, women were more involved than men as friends and with friends.

- During courtship and after remarriage, older people interacted less frequently with friends and relatives. Activities associated with being a husband or wife became paramount. In some cases, couples put up a united front against the expectations or sanctions of a child.

- The emotional aspect of the relationship between the mates developed gradually after meeting. This emotional growth was especially true of women, who talked more openly about their feelings. Most couples had some problems getting used to living together. In most cases, the problems had been solved or were being solved to the satisfaction of both partners. The extent of this marital adjustment was related to agreement between prior expectations and the current reality. In turn, people could be more correct in their expectations when the marriage did not necessitate a great amount of change. Men, in general, had made fewer or less drastic changes, partly because they had weaker ties to family and friends before remarriage. Moreover, men were usually already retired when they remarried, whereas many women stopped working when they remarried.

- One of our major findings is that remarriage is a good alternative to living alone in old age, inasmuch as 78 percent of the women and 86 percent of the men categorized themselves as "very satisfied" or "satisfied" in their remarriages. Other information from the interviews as well as the sense of comfort and calm in the domestic atmosphere support the conclusion that remarriage is good for older people. Several people, for example, would have needed community or institutional aid, if not for the care provided by the spouse. In addition, an intangible something had been "missing" in these peoples' lives that only a spouse could provide.

Implications

Remarriage in old age is an important topic. As noted in the introductory chapter, more older people are marrying than in years past, and the number will increase. In fact, most of the men and women we met knew other older people who had remarried.

As the numbers of later-life marriages increase, so will the number of elderly people who must make decisions about remarriage and also the number of relatives and friends who will be in contact with these remarried elders.

People of every age should be made aware of remarriage as a viable alternative. Awareness of this alternative is especially important for older people who, as Alex Comfort postulates in *A Good Age*, "have been imprinted with the negative attitudes to themselves and to their age which fear of aging generates.... [Old people] consider themselves open-minded, bright, active, adaptable and sexually active, but 'old folks' generally are not — 'I'm fine, but then, I'm an exception.' "[1]

A negative response of this kind to our findings occurred among a group of elders in an audience addressed by one of the authors. Several elderly people doubted that such a large percentage of older people could have been happy in remarriage; these critics thought that most older people married only for financial gain. In general, as we have seen here, elders in the sample received more support from younger relatives than from their peers.

Old-age marriage deserves encouragement as well as attention in order to combat such attitudes. There are indications that the needs and desires of old people for interaction with the opposite sex are being recognized and even, in some cases, being incorporated into social planning and policy making. For example, among federal standards incorporated into a "Bill of Rights" for nursing home patients are: 1) provision for privacy when a spouse visits a patient, and 2) permission for couples in nursing homes to share a room, unless medically contra-indicated.[2]

Financial ramifications often are mentioned in connection with old-age marriage. A few of the women we met mentioned friends who would not marry because marriage would have entailed loss of a pension or a portion of Social Security benefits. Monetary considerations are usually of primary importance in the decision of two elders to live together, rather than to marry.[3] If older couples could marry without any financial loss to either one, old age marriages would, no doubt, increase.

As mentioned in the Introduction, the Social Security Administration has changed its policy in regard to old age remarriage. Previously, when a woman sixty years or older remarried, she retained either half of the benefits she had been receiving on her former husband's work record or gave up the full amount and received the dependency allowance on her new husband's record, whichever was greater.[4] As of January, 1979, remarried men and women age sixty and over were albe to retain whatever Social Security benefits they had been receiving as two single people. Widows sixty and over who have remarried before January, 1979, receive increased benefits; they regain the amount they lost when they remarried.

A woman who has been receiving a pension from her former husband's company confronts a more rigid system; in almost every case, she loses all of his pension when she remarries. If this loss should entail a change in lifestyle, as it would if the man she married were receiving no pension, it is easy to understand the dilemma that could result. Pension plans that provided some benefits to remarried widows would ease such financial problems.

Although remarriage is a desirable option for an increasing number of elders, it cannot be the answer for all older people. Single older women will continue to outnumber single men by a wide margin, despite changes in longevity figures. Remarriage will be available only to a minority of women over sixty years old. Other arrangements therefore must be considered and implemented for older people who cannot or desire not to live alone.

One arrangement that has met with considerable success is congregate living, in which men and women who are not married have meals together, are responsible for the upkeep of common living areas, and give each other mutual aid and support.[5]

We broached the subject of people living together without marrying to about one-fourth of the couples we interviewed. Only one woman professed to know a couple with this living arrangement. No one else knew anyone personally; they knew that such things went on, but not among *their* friends, even among those friends who were "going with" people. Various comments of these older remarried people lead to the conclusion that living together would not have been acceptable to them.

For people who were brought up in an era when living together meant "living in sin," a partnership without benefit of clergy can be guilt-provoking and difficult, even among people who have chosen this course.[6] Such living arrangements would be especially difficult for people who live close to kin and premarriage friends, as did almost everyone in our group. Marriage, on the other hand, provided these men and women with an acceptable self-image and a positive identity among their relatives and friends. Claire and Earl Paulsen, remember, went together for ten years before they married. During this time, Claire lived alone in an apartment and Earl lived with his sister and her family. Rather than live together, they waited until Earl was free to marry.

Although, as Comfort points out, "Living in sin is a highly satisfactory solution. . .to loneliness and is in favor of sexuality and mutual support" in the face of financial penalties that follow remarriage, he also mentions that not all states have laws entitling the surviving spouse to any assets after the death of the other.[7]

Success in remarriage was most likely if men and women had realistically assessed what the marriage would entail — how their lives would change and how they themselves would react. Elders thus should be counselled not to "rush into" anything, but should be encouraged to take a chance if the indications are positive. The primary indications are, perhaps, warmth of feeling between the two people and an enjoyment of each other's company. Secondary areas that should be discussed before the wedding are finances, relationships with family members and friends, activities, and the sexual relationship.

We have received many letters from women who have heard about our study and are requesting advice. Most of the women who write are in their sixties; they would like to remarry but are disappointed and discouraged at the lack of eligible mates. (We have not heard from men, who apparently do not have the same difficulty.) Some of these women have joined organizations in the hope of meeting a man with whom to have a relationship, but have met few single men. We sympathize with the situation of these lonely widows. Their not unusual plight is the result of the lopsided ratio of women to men in the older age groups.

We have counselled these women first, not to give up hope: The majority of the women with whom we spoke did not remarry until many years after becoming widows. On the average, women have to wait much longer to remarry than do men.

We suggest that women speak up about their desire to

meet men. Many women in our group met their husbands through introductions by relatives or mutual friends. Acquaintances may hesitate to bring two people together unless they have some assurance that an introduction is welcome to the two parties involved. So, don't be silent about wanting to socialize with the opposite sex.

A few people we met had looked up old friends from younger days. At the least, such an inquiry about an old friend could lead to an interesting and entertaining visit; at the most, it could lead to matrimony.

We also have advised people to be as active as possible outside their homes. People who have networks of friends and relatives with whom they socialize have a better chance of meeting a spouse than do people who isolate themselves. Most of the women in our study who remarried had been involved in other activities that were important to them before remarriage. Most had close relationships with family and friends, had worked, and/or belonged to formal organizations.

People who are involved in life and who are interested in the world around them, who have retained their zest for living, probably have a better chance of finding a spouse. They will be in a better position to meet one, and after the meeting probably will be more interesting and attractive as a potential mate. Anyway, the effort to make contact with a greater number of people or to strengthen existing relationships, even if it does not result in remarriage, is worthwhile in itself as a way to make life more satisfying. This effort is especially important because not all women who want to remarry will be able to do so. Although the loneliness never dissipates entirely, women can and should try to compensate for a missing element by making other aspects of life as fulfilling as possible. Indeed, most of the women in our remarried group had done so.

With the increase in the number of Senior Citizens' groups around the country, including subsidized meal programs, mobile elders have more opportunity to socialize with the opposite sex. This should be encouraged, not only as a means to facilitate relationships leading to marriage, but also because friendships with the opposite sex can make life more interesting, more exciting, and more varied for older people.

Remarriage is a viable alternative to loneliness for men and women in their later years, an alternative that should be and increasingly *is* being supported by professionals, average citizens, and older people themselves.

Notes

1. Alex Comfort, *A Good Age,* New York: Crown Publishers, Inc., 1976, p. 27.
2. For a complete transcript of the "Bill of Rights" for nursing home patients, see the Office of Nursing Home Administration, Department of Health, Education and Welfare, *Patients' Rights: Standdards and Interpretive Guidelines,* 20-CFR, 405. 1121 (k) Rockville Center, Md.: Office of Nursing Home Administration, 1974, Section 14.
3. For comments from a psychiatrist who has treated older people living together, see the article by Stanley R. Dean, "'Sin' and the Senior Citizen — Revisited and Re-examined," *Medical Tribune*, 7 April 1976.
4. These facts are based on the author's interviews with the District Manager and a staff counselor of the town of Sumner's Social Security office (May, 1975).
5. Judith Wax, "'It's Like Your Own Home Here,'" *New York Times Magazine,* 21 November 1976, p. 38. In this article, Ms. Wax portrays the daily activities of eleven older people in the Weinfeld group living residence in Illinois. For people with "an instinct for sociability," a trait necessary for adjustment to such a living situation, life is good. Residents have support from each other and staff members, and privacy when they want it in their own rooms among cherished possessions. When the article was written, only one man was a resident; two others had died.
6. Dean, op. cit.
7. Comfort, op. cit., p. 126.

Index